RHYTHM AND ROMANCE

An Oral History of
Popular Music in York
Volume 1

Van Wilson

York Oral History Society
2002

Published 2002 by York Oral History Society
c/o 15 Priory Street, York. YO1 6ET.

ISBN No. 0 9513652 1 5

Printed by J. W. Bullivant and Son, York. Tel: 01904 623241

Cover designed by Mike Oakenfull

Front cover, main picture: Johnny Sutton's Modernaires Dance Band at the Co-op Ballroom c1948. L to R - Malcolm Tindall, Ron Backhouse, Ken Wray, Alf Thomson, Alan Stillborn, Geoff Towse, Bill Ibbotson, unknown, Leo Burrows, Duncan Cooper, Johnny Sutton. *(Courtesy Alan Sutton)*

CONTENTS

ACKNOWLEDGEMENTS

The Oral History of Popular Music in York project, has resulted in this publication (in two volumes), the accompanying exhibition and the collection of interviews, photographs and memorabilia housed in our archives. The following people have generously added their story to our collection, and in most cases have also allowed us to copy photographs:

Charlie Abel, Paul Acton, Tony Adams, Murray and Avril Addison, Carol and John Addy, Gerry Allen, Robert Atkinson, Colin Baines, Sue Baker and Liz Calpin, Nick Banks, Wilf Bannister, John Barry, Johnny Bell, Hilda Bennett, Colin Berriman, Brian Bousfield, Trevor Bousfield, Ray and Tony Broadhead, Dave Brough, Bob and Elsie Brown, Mick Brown, Arthur Burcombe, Ron Burnett, Dave and Sue Byworth, Liz Calpin, Phil Calvert, Colin Carr, Joan Carr, John Cartwright, Steve Cassidy, James Cave, Frank and Lyn Chelin, Rosemary Clegg, John Coleman, Olive Connell, Ray Cooper, Gordon Cottom, Mike Dann, Doreen Davis, Walter Davy, Percy Dinsdale, Charlie and Doreen Druggitt, Glyn Edwards, Neville England, Steve Flint, Gill Fox, Dave Garlick, Joan Gaunt, Arnie Gomersall, Ron Goodall, Gerald Goodwin, Mary Goss, Freddie Graysmark, John Greenwell, Neal Guppy, Audrey Halder, Dave Halford, Jean Halford, Bettine Hall-Jackson, Graham Harris, Prue and Neil Hartley, Norman Henderson, Christine Hepton, Terry Herbert, Adrian Holmes, David Horner, Nore Hull, Charles Hutchinson, Steve Jackson, Dave Johnson, Eddie Johnson, Arthur Jones, Dave Kendall, Graham and Val Kennedy, Gloria King, Trevor King, Eddie Lamb, Keith Laycock, June Lloyd-Jones, Malcolm Luker, Trudy Luker, Godfrey Machen, Adrian Macintosh, Brenda and Derek Mackfall, Tiddy Mead, Wilfrid Mellers, Graham Metcalfe, Mick Miller, Pete Morgan, Valerie Mountain, Brian Murphy, Father John Murphy, Harry Murray, Ken Newbould, Johnny Newcombe, John Olive, Brian Parker, May Passmore, Barrie Pawson, Ken Pickering, David Plues, Chris Poole, Noel Porter, Mike Race, Molly Robinson, Ricky Royle, Graham Sanderson, Bob Scott, Phil Scott, Alfie Shepherd, Lew Skords, Peter Stanhope, Barry Starkey, Brian Sutcliffe, Alan Sutton, Violet Taylor, John Terry, Clarice and Dawn Tudor, Pete Varley, Wal Walsh, Sheila White, Joan Whitehead, John Whittle, Pete Williams, Pete Willow, Alwyn Wilson, Brian Wilson, Linda Wood, Denis Wright, Sheila Yeates. Since speaking to us we are sorry to say that James Cave, Doreen Davis, May Passmore, Trudy Luker and Clarice Tudor have died.

I would like to thank the following who helped with research and conducted interviews : David Armstrong, Glyn and Ruth Edwards, Richard Foster, Caroline Stockdale, James Wigby; and the following who helped with transcribing interviews : Joyce Pinder, Philippa Wilson and especially Gill Fox.

For their financial support for this project, we are indebted to :

Supported by the
Heritage Lottery Fund

R M Burton Trust, City of York Council, Joseph Rowntree Foundation, Sheldon
Memorial Trust, Patricia and Donald Shepherd Charitable Trust, York Branch of
the Musicians' Union, York Common Good Trust. We would like to thank Frank
Johnson of TDK for the generous donation of tapes, and Jessops for support
with the cost of copying photographs.

We would like to thank the following, who have provided information and
allowed us to copy photographs : Tim Addyman, Martin Boyd, Mary Cundall,
Sheila Barrie, Judith Carr, Catherine Cole, Michael Cole, Frank and Muriel Day,
Angela Dunning, Angela Hill, Ben Jowett, Edith Keech, Christine Lancaster, John
McClay, Fred Mills, Richard Monfort, Bryan Pearson, Janet Pigott, Terry
Pritchard, Bill Serby, Stuart Thomson, Ken Turner, Greg Wadman, Margaret
Weston, Gill Wignall, of the Evening Press, Staff of York City Archives, Sue Rigby
and Staff of City of York Library.

I wish to thank Mike Oakenfull for designing the covers of the two volumes,
Richard Foster for kindly proof-reading the manuscript and making useful
suggestions, and the York Oral History management committee over the last
two years, in particular our treasurer Nigel Taggart who managed the funds so
brilliantly.

**Most of all, I am greatly indebted to Mike Race, Chair of York Oral
History Society, who generously devoted so much time to all aspects
of the project: interviewing, transcribing, copying photographs, and
much of the research (particularly for the first volume), as well as
reading and commenting on the final manuscript.**

If you are interested in accessing the collection or in becoming involved in
oral history, please contact committee member Philip Johnson at York City
Archives or on 01904-644381.

INTRODUCTION

At the beginning of the year 2000, York Oral History Society embarked on a three year project investigating the history of popular music in York from 1930 to 1970 and I was appointed as co-ordinator.

Our remit was to find people who had been involved in popular music in York and to look at the relationship between music and social life in the city. The definition of 'popular' means 'whatever the people like', but in the case of music it tends to mean music which is not classical, (though much classical music was the popular music of its day)! Some types of music are in a class of their own, such as choral and church music, light opera and brass bands, and have been subjects of other publications, so we have not included them in our project. Some music defies categorisation and we may have used labels which are open to question, (one man's swing is another man's jazz), but we decided to keep fairly rigid boundaries to make for easier reading.

In two and a half years, we have conducted more then 130 interviews. Extracts from their memories, together with background research from the local press and other primary sources, form an oral history collection which will soon be available at the York City Archives for public access. A selection of the material will also be deposited with the city library. The interview tapes, together with more than 1,500 photographs and some memorabilia, provide a resource which is a crucial part of York's social history of the 20th century.

It became clear, as the project got under way, that there were two very different periods within our 1930-1970 time scale, and that both played a significant part in York's culture. Instead of writing one book embracing music from four decades, I decided to split it into two volumes which cover the two separate areas of music in this period. There is obviously some overlap in terms of the time-span, but most musicians fit into one or the other of the volumes. The period of 1930 to 1970 is obviously artificial because music did not start in 1930 and did not end in 1970, but two quite distinct types of music do fit comfortably into these 40 years. The first period, that of dance band music, began in earnest in the 1920s with the arrival of jazz from America. The difficult years of the 1930s meant that ordinary people were in need of escape from their drab and sometimes depressing lives and 'going dancing' to a live band or small orchestra became the most popular form of entertainment in the city, and probably in the country as a whole. It might have 'had its day' in the 1940s, were it not for the Second World War breaking out, and the need for dance band music becoming even greater, as a means of linking people together and lifting their spirits through dark days. It was clear that after the war, the new generation coming up would no longer have those same needs, and the young people born in the late 1930s and 1940s were ready for a change. They were born into a country battling with rationing, blackouts, hardships and little money and they longed for something better. The new music of the 1950s was a reflection of this need and it came fast and furious. The dance band musicians and their older audiences were horrified when rock 'n' roll entered the picture, but they believed it was only a passing fad and their own tastes would prevail as time went on. What they didn't realise was that the change was permanent, and that rock 'n' roll opened the door to ever new forms of music which gave the younger generation ownership of music for the first time. The 1950s and 1960s heralded a social revolution in all aspects of life, and music was a large part of it. Songs about nostalgia and lovers who had to part until war was over, were gone. The new music was upbeat and lively, and it made its presence felt!

I was born in the 1950s and brought up on a diet of Glenn Miller, Tommy Dorsey, Frank Sinatra, Vaughn Monroe and all the 78s my parents played regularly. Even now when I hear Moonlight Serenade and In The Mood, I am taken back to childhood days. There was an enchantment and a romance about that music which still exists but when I saw the first appearance on television of the Beatles, I knew this was something new and exciting, and although I was only a child, it was the beginning of a love of 1960s music for me. At school we talked constantly about pop music. We went to WH Smiths on Saturdays to listen in the record booths to the latest releases and soon knew the lyrics of almost every song that came out. I had a giant poster of the Beatles on my bedroom ceiling and soon came to adore the Small Faces, the Rolling Stones, Simon and Garfunkel, and Bob Dylan. Yet, and this was the unusual thing, I still loved big bands and the songs of Cole Porter, George Gershwin, Jerome Kern and Irving Berlin, but I could not admit this to most of my contemporaries! I only had one friend at the time, Jan, who shared my love of dance bands, 1960s pop, and later classical music.

I recall my mother taking me to see Tommy Steele at the Rialto on my birthday and how the event stood out in my life as being quite mind-blowing, (though I would not have used that phrase at the time!) I couldn't remember the year but assumed I must have been nine or ten. When I recently looked at some old Rialto programmes, I discovered that we actually saw Tommy on my sixth birthday! The Evening Press review of this concert described it as a 'screaming success' when 'nearly everybody from Tommy down to the just-more-than-toddlers (and there were a few) joined in the fun'!

Volume one of this publication covers the music of the dance band era and jazz in the 1940s and 1950s, whereas volume two covers the beat explosion, and the minority interests of folk music and jazz in the later period. The two volumes explore what music was available and where, and try to show why people decided to become musicians and what music meant to them. Many people cannot explain exactly what it is about music that speaks to our emotions like nothing else can, that has such power to transform our mood. What is it about a few notes played in a certain order and at a certain tempo, which can communicate with us somewhere deep inside? It was William Congreve who wrote, 'Music has charms to soothe the savage breast'. I saw evidence of this when walking through York city centre recently. A pair of musicians were playing a selection of Irish ballads in St Helen's Square, a sweet and gentle sound. Beside them sat a man who can often be seen fighting and shouting abuse at the public from a park bench near the City Art Gallery, but his face was that of an angel as he listened in raptures to the music. He was positively beaming.

Music is the only universal language which people of all nations and races have in common. Our tastes in music may vary but we must agree that music in itself stands out as a prime feature of our lives, and that all people, from babies in the womb, to teenagers and adults in all walks of life, are affected and touched by music. There are instances of people who have been in a coma, and when their favourite music is played to them again and again, they are restored and come back to life.

Although bigger cities like London, Liverpool, Manchester and Leeds are known for their popular music, York does not always spring to mind as a centre for music. But throughout the 20th century it has had a strong and vibrant music scene, with countless musicians living and performing in the city, entertaining audiences large and small. In fact York is still a vibrant and busy place, and even in the present days of discos and karaoke, live music has not died. In the last year I have joined with many others in seeing and enjoying musicians at the Barbican, Grand Opera House, Theatre Royal, City Screen, Black Swan Folk Club, Olde White Swan, National Centre For Early Music, Three Legged Mare and other places in the city.

The aim of this book is to give a taste of the popular music scene from the 1920s to the 1970s, letting the musicians tell their own stories. The subject is such a large one that it is impossible to cover everything and everyone, and though we spoke to more than 130 people, there were many others who also have their story. The time limit for the project has meant that we have had to omit some of the people we wanted to interview, but the publications and exhibition will give the reader a flavour of what it was like to play and listen to popular music through those decades, and for those who want to look at our collection, it will be available in the city archives when it has been fully catalogued in 2003.

Throughout York's history, things have progressed because of the belief and determination of individuals with a vision. This is certainly the case with music. John Xaviour (Jack) Prendergast, who ran the Rialto cinema and ballroom from 1927 to 1961, was an entrepreneur and a pioneer with numerous friends in the world of showbusiness. He was instrumental in bringing many famous national and international artists to the city and encouraged his own son, York's most famous musician John Barry, to make music his career. In the 1940s Bert Keech had the concession at the De Grey Rooms and provided music for dancing night after night through the war years, not only for locals but also the many airmen and women stationed in the area. From 1950, Johnny Sutton ran his big band there, and was known for giving young budding musicians the opportunity to play and to learn their craft in his band. In the 1960s Neal Guppy with his Enterprise Club took a lot of young beat groups under his wing by opening a live music venue specifically aimed at young people.

Mention music to anyone who has lived in York during the last 50 years and these names crop up again and again, along with the Bousfield Twins, Len Cundall, Derek Dunning, Neville England, Bob Halford, Bobby Hirst, Hugh Robertson, and later Steve Cassidy, Johnny Newcombe and the Goodall Brothers. But there are many more well-known and well-loved musicians who have spent years entertaining the people of York, who provided music as a boost to morale in wartime, who lifted the spirits in the grey austerity of post-war Britain, and who took advantage of the new music of the 1960s and made music less elitist and open to everyone.

Nearly everyone we spoke to in this project testified to the importance of music in their lives, some even said that their lives centred around it and others that it was their way of expressing what they wanted to say. They would probably echo the rock musician Sting, who recently said, 'If I had my way I'd never speak to anyone, I'd just sing. To sing is to soar, to be like a bird with total freedom to go where you want'. The American writer Robin Meyers put it like this, 'The best way to listen to music is to go where human beings are making it, to see the faces attached to its creation for the ear is close to the heart'. Arthur Mason, in an article in 1931, wrote that music has the power to 'soothe and restore the sick and suffering', giving the Biblical example of King Saul being healed of his nervous sickness by David's skill on the harp. He quoted Shakespeare's description of music, 'a medicine, a sweet and oblivious antidote', explained that even Pythagoras played the harp night and morning to keep his mind active and went on to say that, 'Our pleasure in music's beauty, the sense of restfulness, or of exhilaration, we get, our consciousness that there is that in music which inspires thoughts outside the pressing thoughts of every day, these things prove music to be a mental and emotional restorative'.

Music can also, perhaps more than anything else, evoke memories of an important time, place or person. Just to hear a few bars of a particular song can take you back to those special moments when you first fell in love, when you first discovered the joy of living, when, in the face of despair, you found hope. And music, as well as speaking to our emotions, can help develop the senses. Educationalists have acknowledged that calm classical music in the background can help children concentrate more on their studies. Perhaps loud hip-hop music has the opposite effect? In a recent speech, Neil Hoyle, of the Incorporated Society of Musicians, said that the society wanted music to be 'a spiritual focus, a mutual bond of real meaning, a shared medium for daily hopes and fears and a means of giving people their identity in a world of globalised pap', for, 'we believe music and the arts exist to nourish the soul'.

This book is dedicated to all York musicians past and present,
who have given so much pleasure to their audiences

May your heart always be joyful
May your song always be sung
May you stay forever young

Bob Dylan

CHAPTER ONE. I GOT RHYTHM
Music Before 1930

1900, the dawn of a new century and one which would see more changes than any other in history. The end of an era was approaching, Victorian values were soon to be questioned, even overturned, cracks would appear in the old order with its defining class system, and in less than two decades would come the 'war to end all wars'. Meanwhile the Boer war was still in progress and on the home-front, patriotric fervour was high, leading to huge sales of sheet music of war songs.

In 1900 roller skating, cycling clubs, whist drives, amateur dramatics and church socials were all popular leisure pursuits. But in York, as in most English cities, music was a favourite form of home entertainment, with families gathering round the piano and singing in the evenings. There were also brass bands and glee clubs which had a repertoire of popular songs. At this time there was a lot of crossover between different types of music, and the categories of 'classical' and 'popular' were not as defined as they are today. Thomas Holt, for example, who died in January 1910, was a well-known York musician who played cornet in a brass band but also performed at circuses, in the music hall and each Sunday morning at Layerthorpe Adult School. In his obituary it stated that he was 'an original member of the band which formerly played daily in the streets of the city, but whose members have now passed over to the great majority'.

There were many choral societies and groups attached to churches, and various companies, including Rowntree and the London and North Eastern Railway, had their own choirs and chamber music groups. The York Musical Society itself was the oldest in the country, dating from the 1780s, and in the 19th century had regular meetings with supper at the King's Arms in Fossgate and the White Swan Hotel in Pavement. The Corn Exchange, now the Grand Opera House, provided Saturday night penny concerts (of brass band music) mostly over the winter months and these not only offered music to the public but also encouraged many young musicians to play. The Yorkshire choral competitions were held every year in York with competitors totalling more than 2,000.

There were many small music halls in the city and a lot of pubs had concert and singing rooms. Lamb's Varieties, held in the singing room of the Lamb public house in Tanner Row, provided regular acts such as the coster singer and male impersonator Madge Denmar.   The Elephant and Castle in Skeldergate offered singers like Holbery Hagyard, comedians like Bead

Alfmore and Beta Franklyn, and the Wellington Music Hall in Goodramgate entertained its customers with May Trigg, 'serio' and dancer.

In the first month of the new century there was a Great Musical Festival held at the Exhibition Buildings behind the City Art Gallery, featuring various military bands as well as Mr H Bartley's Special Saloon Orchestra. In 1904, Burton Lane Adult School held social evenings with songs and selections on the gramophone, the Primrose League held monthly dances at the De Grey Rooms, and the Co-op Employees Athletic Club and Amalgamated Society of Railway Employees held their annual dances in the city. Working men's clubs, such as South Bank and the Phoenix Club, began to advertise in the early 1900s. By 1914 there were 38 clubs in York with 7,000 members, and many singers, comedians and variety acts were finding work in them. This was an age when ordinary people could and would perform, seemingly with no stage fright! Annual club dinners, smoking concerts and other gatherings would see members indulging in songs and recitations, each person 'giving a turn'.

The annual St Patrick's Ball in the Assembly Rooms was the scene of energetic dances such as the lancers, which was done in sets of eight, the cotillon, shottiche and gavotte, which must have been hard work for the ladies in their long and tight-fitting gowns! There were many dances where a variety of partners was usual, but the 'couples' dances were becoming more and more popular, though the waltz and the polka had scandalised decent society when they were first introduced in the middle of the 19th century. The cinematograph had also arrived, and this was the place where people saw the new American dances such as the cakewalk. The Cowper Academy of Dance in Stonegate offered tuition in the lancers, minuets and gavottes as well as 'refined and artistic skirt dances'.

For the upper classes, there would be grand balls such as the York Civic Ball of November 1900 which was held in the Assembly Rooms with music by Bartley's Band, including the Blue Danube waltz, Flitter Flutter for the polka, and Runaway Girl for the lancers, as well as Gnimble Gnomes for the barn dance. The Yorkshire Evening Press reported that, 'The Assembly Rooms looked beautiful, its walls hung with fluted muslin of rose pink and apple green. The ends of the ballroom were luxuriously furnished with comfortable seats for tired dancers, and Kentin palms and other foliage from the nurseries of Mr Key of Clifton. Supper was laid out in the Festival Concert Hall and there were a number of beautiful palms and bamboos drooped gracefully over the front of the gallery, with the orchestra filled in with foliage, their sombre green relieved by dazzling blooms of splendid chrysanthemums. In the centre were a number of supper tables adorned with fruit and flowers and illuminated by candelabra with yellow shades'.

The Bartley Orchestra was very popular at this time and issued a booklet of testimonials in the early 1900s for its band. These included, from Richmond Badminton Club in 1903, 'I beg to say that all agreed, including Lord and Lady Zetland, that it was the best band anyone heard in Richmond at a ball, good music, perfect time'. From the Hon. Mrs R Parker, of Clifton Lodge in 1905, 'On the occasions of the Balls and Dances in York of which I have undertaken the arrangements and requested the attendance of your Band, it has given universal satisfaction'. In the same year from H Cape, Captain of the 18th Hussars, 'The music supplied by Mr Bartley's Band at the Ball given by the Officers was quite excellent and all that could be desired'. And from Carlton Towers in 1906, 'Lady Beaumont was very much pleased with Messrs Bartley's Band'. Albert Bartley was the principal of Bartley's orchestra until his death in 1924 at the age of 43. He ran a music shop in Stonegate from 1900 to 1920. Walter Bartley was a pianist in his father's orchestra until the First World War came and he died in 1917. Jack Bartley, Albert's other son, continued to run the band and also taught piano.

James Arthur, music publisher in Davygate from 1891 to 1916, played banjo and violin in the city, and sold sheet music as Arthur's Sixpenny Edition. He composed and arranged a lot of his music, including Military Sunday for the piano in 1918, a piece describing a grand military church parade, from the dawn of the day and the bells of York Minster, to the final God Save the King

Jack Bartley's Royal Crescent Hotel Dance Band, Filey. 1930s, with Harold Arthur on drums, Harry Wheeler, bass and Billy Mendez, sax.   *(Courtesy Christine Lancaster)*

played by massed bands. His son Harold was born in 1909 and by 1931 was running his own dance band in York. Later that decade he played drums for Jack Bartley's Royal Crescent Band from Filey. Others in the band included York musicians Billy Mendez and Harry Wheeler. Harold went on to play in the late 1940s with the Norman Holmes Orchestra, and in the 1950s took over the running of the band, which became the County Players, playing at many fashionable functions in the 1950s and 1960s.

In 1902, the Grand Opera House was built on the site of the Corn Exchange (of 1868) in Clifford Street at a cost of £23,000. The legendary music hall star Florrie Forde appeared on opening night. Over the next two decades many national and international stars would appear there including the Russian ballerina Anna Pavlova, Flanagan and Allen, Laurel and Hardy, Gracie Fields, Marie Lloyd, Harry Lauder, Vesta Tilley, and both George Formby Senior and Junior. As it became more popular and successful, so the smaller music halls gradually closed, unable to compete with family entertainment offered twice nightly and featuring such top acts.

In 1908 the Palace of Varieties (which later became the Tower Cinema in 1920) opened in New Street. The first night featured some new films, and performing in person Harry Cranley, the world's champion clog dancer. In 1909 the venue was renamed the Hippodrome, and continued to offer films and live music. In 1910 the first European demonstration of the tango, a dance which had originated in the slums of Buenos Aires, took place in Paris and 'tangomania' quickly swept through England, with Mr Cowper of Stonegate beginning to offer classes in this new craze. In March 1911 the first municipal concert which combined classical pieces with popular songs was held in the Exhibition Buildings. This was initiated by Alderman Forster-Todd who felt that there should be music available during the winter months to complement the band performances which took place in open spaces during the summer.

In January 1913 there were 'new dances' on offer at the Albany Ballroom, with Bostons, singles, doubles and nine-steps. There were ragtime dancing competitions at the Empire in June, with a first prize of £5 and in August the De Grey Rooms advertised a Merry Meeting Dance with Lumley's City Band from 8pm to 2am.

The First World War brought more military bands and patriotic songs. In 1914 the Archbishop of York, Dr Cosmo Lang, dedicated the new organ in St Saviour's church and in his sermon spoke of the importance of music and how 'the voice of music is specially helpful at the present time for it rises above the discord' of war. He mentioned the memorial service that had been held for those who died in the German naval bombardment of Scarborough where 'the music of the Frenchman Chopin so wonderfully interpreted the rising voice of love and hope above the conflict'. He believed that 'music, almost more than any other power brings us to the deep common heart of man' and urged the congregation to 'cherish music in the midst of these divisions'.

The war did not put a stop to entertainment and as it continued, concert parties were formed to entertain in hospitals and other venues providing music and variety shows. For example, a concert took place at York Military Hospital in 1916 where wounded troops were treated to the music of Miss Guy's Ladies Orchestra.

For those who enjoyed dancing, this was available every Monday night at Layerthorpe Adult School, at the Coffee House, Walmgate or occasionally at the Co-operative Large Hall, Acomb Adult School, and Foster's Gymnasium in Spen Lane. The Ebor Hall behind Leak and Thorp, Coney Street, charged ninepence for dances which lasted three hours, but was also available for private dances and parties. Dances at Bishophill Adult School cost sixpence but only threepence for soldiers. For those who desired to improve their dance skills, private lessons were available from Cecil Taylor, president of the Imperial Society of Dance Teachers and member of the Academies des Danse de Paris, who ran his school for tuition in society dancing and operatic dancing at 17 St Mary's, to complement his branches in Leeds, Bradford and London, or Arthur Cowper's Academy where he and his two daughters taught elementary and advanced classes, with lessons on violin and mandolin. One man who went to the Cowper Academy described it as having a dancehall on the first floor and a supper room on the ground floor. There was a big mirror at each end of the dancehall, which ran from the ground to the ceiling. The Misses Cowper looked rather like Hinge and Brackett, and invariably wore long silk scarves, one red and one green. The principal of the Albany Ballroom, Mr H Boyes Cooper, the past president of the British Association of Teachers of Dancing, also offered 'advanced assemblies' every Thursday and Saturday in the Davy Hall. The Albany had 'rooms fitted with gas and electric light and a polished maple floor on springs'. When Mr Cooper died in the 1920s, it was taken over by his brother Mr A Cooper, and later sold to Charles Atkinson. Classes also took place at the Feasegate Restaurant, with 'all the latest dances including the cazaret and hesitation waltz'. Some might desire to dance in the comfort of their own homes, and in October 1914, Wright's, of Market Street, advertised 'all the latest records in stock, with popular patriotic airs', and Bradbury's Sewing Machine and Cycle Depot, of Davygate, boasted that, 'We supply any make of gramophone from 21/-, and large selection of Cinch, Phoenix and other records. Double sided from 1/1'. They added that, 'Time need never drag if you have a gramophone in your home'.

The American influence on popular music which had begun in the latter part of the 19th century as communications improved, rapidly grew after American troops arrived in Britain in 1917 and after the war, the public's appetite for music and dancing increased. In fact there was a lot of employment for musicians from 1919 onwards, with most cinemas having their own little orchestras. The Tower Cinema had its own symphony orchestra, St George's had Alfred Wilde as its musical director offering musical interludes from the famous York Quintette and the Grand cinema in Clarence Street had its 'talented Grand Orchestra' under the direction of Herbert Cooper. The Tramways Employees Dance Orchestra was formed to entertain the staff and the Crescent Café had the Crescent Orchestra playing 'all the latest music as played at the Savoy'. In November 1924, the Evening Press ran the following advert, 'Fascisti, Fascisti! To members and others, whist drive and dance at the Crescent Café'. (Come and learn the latest dance craze, the goose step?). The Picture House in Coney Street with its Wedgwood tearoom, oak lounge café, Rendezvous and American bar, became the place to go, with the Picture House café orchestra providing music.

Victoria Hall, the cinema in Goodramgate, had been granted a music and dancing licence in 1902, and its Victoria Orchestra played between films. In 1924 it was closed for alterations and re-opened as the Palais de Dance. Daily tea dances from 3.30 to 6pm were offered for 2/- including tea which was 'daintily served in the balcony café'. There were also dances each evening except Tuesdays, with tickets at 2/6d, and supper dances on Tuesdays from 8pm to 12am, which cost 5/-, where evening dress 'must be worn'. The dance hostess was Miss Norah Bevan, late organiser of the Cambridge University Dance Club, and music provided by Alex Sylvester (of Jack Hylton's Olympic Band) and his London Five, described as 'a revelation in modern dance music'.

Life after the First World War was very different with enormous changes in the very fabric of society. The class distinctions were no longer so absolute. Modernism in all art forms took hold and people became more open to new influences. In York, as in every other city in the country, there had been great losses due to the war. Families were affected deeply and people began to question what the ruling classes told them, rather than blindly accepting it. James Joyce and Virginia Woolf with their stream of consciousness writing, the Surrealist movement in art, and Stravinsky's Rite Of Spring were innovative ways of showing that artists did not have to bow down to what their predecessors had done, but instead could push back the boundaries and present new ideas.

In popular music, the 1920s heralded a new era. Jazz had arrived in Britain in 1919 with the visit from America of the Original Dixieland Jazz Band, who caused a sensation at their concerts. They claimed to be the originators of jazz but were in reality a vigorous but undistinguished Louisiana band with an innovative line-up. The origins of jazz really lay in the Creole and Negro heart of New Orleans.

In York, little jazz combos began to spring up everywhere, although when St George's Hall in Castlegate advertised select Tuesday dances in January 1920, they warned 'no jazzing!' But the war had changed the lives of those who had fought in it and for the ones who returned physically unscathed, there was a new restlessness. They were ready for change. Many of them embraced the new music though others were scandalised by this 'hot wild music'. This shock and dismay would be repeated when the dance bands found their music being overtaken in the 1950s by rock 'n' roll.

The social dances of the 1920s like the Charleston and Black Bottom are primarily thought of as jazz dances but the sophisticated style of Fred Astaire also came from jazz dancing as have many dances in more recent times, such as break-dancing. With the advent of ragtime music after 1910, song lyrics graphically described the movements for particular dances, such as the bunny hug, monkey glide and chicken scratch. The famous American couple, Vernon and Irene Castle, gave respectability to some of these crazes, and made the 'turkey trot' popular with the upper classes.

The York Mayfair Dance Band.   *(Courtesy York Oral History Society)*

14

At Christmas 1920 the Grand Ballroom in Clarence Street held a Confetti Carnival with dancing, streamers and novelties, plus coloured and limelight effects. The following year the George William Baines Orchestra was an attraction at the Grand. George Baines, who became director of music for the Electric Cinema in 1920, was the father of William Baines, York's most famous classical music composer. Mr J P Thompson's Band of 1904 had become Mr J P Thompson's Famous Jazz Band by 1921 and was appearing in various venues including the Grand and the same year, Mabel Wilson, was 18 and recalls:

You had a little pencil and would write in who's having which dance with you. There wasn't any liquor. Whoever took you for the interval dance, took you for your supper which was a cup of coffee or tea, and then you would have the next dance with him after that and then you were free. The person you had the last dance with automatically took you home.

Billy Pritchard and his Blue Chevrons were well-known in the city during the 1920s. Billy had served in the First World War running a concert party called the Detonators, playing piano and singing, sometimes in drag. After leaving the army in 1919, he was employed to play the piano in a Penny Arcade in Scarborough. His sister, Violet Taylor, remembers:

Blue Chevrons Concert Party in 1919. Back row - Fred Gofton, unknown, unknown. Front row - Billy Pritchard (in dress), Freddie Cleveland, Dick Culley, Frank Langstaff, Joe Ramsden. *(Courtesy Angela Hill)*

15

At Scarborough along the front, there were places open and a music counter with all sheet music. He played the piano and somebody was engaged to sing the songs and people then bought them.

The Yorkshire Evening Press of November 10, 1919, had run a small ad amongst advertisements for lectures, boxing bouts and boots for sale, which simply read, 'Who are these 'Blue Chevrons'?' A few days later the answer was given with the report of an Armistice Anniversary Celebration Concert at the YMCA from the Blue Chevrons Troupe, 'the official concert party of the York branch of the Comrades of the Great War'. All the members were discharged soldiers - Frank Cleveland, Fred Gofton (who had enlisted at the age of 15), Richard (Dick) Culley, F Hurst, H Marston, and Billy Pritchard. The Blue Chevrons entertained a large audience at the Festival Concert Rooms soon after, with renditions of serious and comic songs as well as an exhibition of ragtime dancing.

Two of the members, Dick Culley and Fred Gofton hosted Bohemian Balls at the Assembly Rooms and the Palais de Danse. They went on to broadcast as a comedy team from Savoy Hill with Jack Payne and were believed to be, the first two men from York to broadcast on radio. Their double act 'Broad grins in broad Yorkshire' was a popular feature in the 1930s and by the time they dissolved their partnership in the early part of the Second World War, to join ENSA, they had broadcast 68 times. After the war, Gofton went into the licensing trade, running the Rose and Crown in Lawrence Street and Culley went to be a wine waiter on the RMS Orion, visiting Australlia 20 times, and voyaging to the Pacific Islands and Canada. The two met up again in York in 1954 in what was an emotional reunion.

From 1920 to 1930 Billy had a travelling dance band Billy Pritchard's Roadio, as well as playing with the Blue Chevrons and the Premier Jazz Band. He also played at Masonic Lodges and provided accompaniment in cinemas. His son Terry remembers how his parents would go to dances with evening dress pockets and beaded handbags always full of confetti and streamers. The Yorkshire Evening Press of March 28, 1924 was advertising 'The last night at Ebor Hall of W Pritchard's streamer dances. 7.30-11.30'. This was where streamers of coloured crepe paper were thrown over couples as they danced. At ordinary Saturday night dances, each one was announced by an MC but at private dances organised by firms and societies at places like the Drill Hall, cards would be put up at the side of the stage showing the name of the next dance.

In 1926 Billy went to work in the music section at Marks & Spencer's for about 18 months, where his work included playing and singing songs for customers

Billy Pritchard's Roadio Band with Billy on piano. 1924.   *(Courtesy Terry Pritchard)*

buying sheet music. Later he ran the Queries concert party. His sister, Violet Taylor recalls:

When our Billy came back after the war was over, he decided to get a concert party up. There was Freddie Cleveland, Fred Gofton, a lovely baritone singer, and Joe Ramsden had a banjo. Billy started playing the piano, but then he'd do a turn where he'd get dressed up. They used to go all over, Duncombe Park, to Lord Feversham's, out to Escrick and Helmsley. And then Ebor Hall. You went down the side of what was then Leak and Thorpe's, and it was beautiful.

Violet and Billy lived in their parents' pub, the Leeds Arms, next door to the Black Swan in Peasholme Green. Although Violet helped in the pub, she was still eager to go to the dance at the Ebor Hall:

A chap would come and give me a hand, he was one of the customers and I'd encourage him, and say, 'As soon as it's ten o'clock, will you take over for me, and help me mother to get all t'glasses. I'm going just for an hour', and I'd run like mad up Spen Lane and Coney Street to have an hour's dancing.

After the war Billy went to Mr Connell, music teacher and organist. He played popular songs then learnt to play classical music like Rachmaninov. Our Billy used to play the piano Friday, Saturday and Sunday nights and for family occasions in the Leeds Arms with 24 people at once dancing the lancers. Billy bought me mother a gramophone, His Master's Voice, and he'd say, 'Would you like to have a record? I'll buy you a record'. And he'd go into Banks and up into the recording room where they did records and then afterwards Woolworths started selling these sixpenny little records, and I'd go in there with me pocket money and often buy these'.

In 1924 the Terrace Jazz Social Club in Garden Street in the Groves was advertising functions in the local paper with music by 'an augmented orchestra'. For sixpence you could learn to 'toddle'. Billy Pritchard began to run dances at the Premier Ballroom, above F R Stubbs store on Foss Bridge, which was advertised as the 'coolest dance hall in York', but warned, 'New maple floor, light boots are essential'! The ballroom held a 'jockey night' in October, a form of excuse-me dance where everybody, men as well as women, could tap people on the back and 'jockey' for position to dance with various partners. The other new dance steps which became popular in York were the tapper, Java foxtrot, Yale blues, Charleston and charlestep. Dancing was probably the favourite entertainment in the city, and in March 1923 two couples from York, Nellie Flynn and Jackie Rawling, and Ivy Collins and Joseph Simpson, had broken a world dancing record, dancing continuously for 17 hours and 20 minutes.

But not everyone approved of the new jazz age. In 1926 a case in a London court concerned two women saxophonists. One of them, a dance band leader, was suing the other, claiming that she had entered into an exclusive agreement for her band. When the case began, the presiding judge Mr Justice Eve asked counsel, 'What is a saxophone?' and counsel replied, 'I am told that it is an instrument that resembles a cornet and is used in what I understand are called jazz bands'!!

Tower Cinema advertising jazz film.
Yorkshire Evening Press April 1924.
(Courtesy City of York Library)

In York there was some opposition. Alderman Birch, chairman of York Musical Society, who was attending a concert of the York Male Voice Choir, claimed that concert listeners were disturbed by a dance band in the adjoining room. He wrote 'The only time I feel like murdering someone is when I hear jazz music, for of all the inventions of modern time, this, like poison gas, is one we could well do without. Strange contraptions are brought into play like the tapping of wood across iron railings, curious instruments produce sounds like long-eared quadrupeds in pain, and sounds like the wail of the lost in the desert mixed with various squealings. These force themselves on the ear of the unwilling listener with a deadly monotony, the concerted result of which defies description. I think there must be something wrong with the musical and mental make-up of those who spend their time shuffling along a polished floor to the accompaniment of such infernal trash'!

But jazz was becoming more popular than ever. In 1927 York Theatre Royal offered cabaret evenings presenting a selection of classical music with dancing and a comedian, but in amongst the waltzes and piano concertos, there was a jazz band who played five songs, the Black Bottom (a Charleston), Jazz Babies, Yes Sir That's My Baby, Jazz Wild, and All In. The band comprised Kathleen Gerrard, Leon Kellaway, Vivienne Mal, Juliette Phillimore, Dorothy Jackson and the Johnson Sisters and was one of the first occasions where women played jazz.

There were several music shops in York at this time. John Gray & Sons, of Coney Street, had opened in 1883 and were known for specialising in pianos. Waddington's, of Stonegate, made and sold pianos.

Banks, of Stonegate, was the oldest music shop, having opened in 1756, and claiming to have the largest stock of music in England. It was advertising the 'new Columbia Grafonola, the gramophone advance of the century'. J Sharpe & Sons, of Fossgate and Goodramgate, offered 'hundreds of phonograph and gramophone records from 1/- to

800 PIANO BARGAINS

This week in the Waddington organization there are 800 real piano bargains. For that matter every piano we sell is a bargain. These 800 pianos are the bargains you meet only once in a lifetime. Naturally we do not keep these all in one shop.

We have only the best for your inspection. Then of course we have the best radio, complete sheet music stocks, piano repair depots and everything that matters in music. Whatever it is, it's a bargain, if you get it at

WADDINGTON'S
Waddington (of York) Ltd.

YORK : 43-44 Stonegate.
SCARBOROUGH : 22 Huntriss Row.

Waddington's Piano Shop. Yorkshire Evening Press November 1933.

(Courtesy City of York Library)

19

21/-s' to play on 'our wonderful new disc machine splendidly made with new tone arm and large brass horn'. By 1931 J Noyes & Son, of St Helen's Square, was billed as 'York's most modern music shop' offering His Master's Voice gramophones and Columbia Viva-Tonal Grafonolas. As well as pianos, music and records, it also offered tuning and repairs. Reg Smith's store at Micklegate Bar was selling records by HMV, Columbia and Zonophone for prices between 3/- and 4/6d, and other lesser-known names such as Broadcast, Piccadilly and Perfect for less than 2/-. Turnpenny's, of Colliergate, offered Radio Broadcast and Imperial records and Robertson's, of Davygate, were selling 'all the leading makes of gramophones - Gilbert, Academy, Apollo, Karna, Maxitone, and records to suit all'.

Bettine Hall-Jackson recalls her father-in-law, Arthur Jackson, who ran a piano store:

It was in Union Terrace. He'd send for all the parts for the piano and build them. He'd tune them as well, he was very clever. His shop sold gramophones and he built his own wirelesses. All his brothers played some sort of an instrument. There was a big family and he left home and joined the circus, and that's how he got playing, this circus came to York Empire. He also played the bass, it was as big as him. He had a taxi to come and pick him up. Then he went to Lord Mayor's Walk [with his music shop] and they were there quite a while then he had a heart attack, so he retired, but I think he went still to the Empire.

May Passmore was the third generation to work in the music world. The tradition continued with her daughter Trudy Luker who became a jazz singer and pianist, her grandson Malcolm Luker, a 1960s beat group singer, and now record producer in Los Angeles, and her great-grandson, Ben, a record producer in Germany. May died in the autumn of 2001 only weeks before her 100th birthday. Within a few months, Trudy also died, and after her funeral, Malcolm (whose story is told in volume two of this publication) asked family and friends to raise a glass 'to the girls'. They were toasting two very talented ladies whose lives had been spent in entertaining others. May was born in York in 1901 and first went on the stage at the age of four. Her mother, who had come from London, was called May McCabe and played for silent films. But the family's connections with showbusiness began even earlier, with May's grandfather and his brother, who were very famous, the Two Macs:

They were Irish comedians and acrobats and featured in a book by Conan Doyle. [The magazine The Entr'acte showed a cartoon of the Two Macs in their edition of October 9, 1836]. And my mother was always known as May Mac so when I started professionally, I took that name. The 'Stage' was called the

'Era' at first and in that paper I read that when my grandfather died, there were 40 cabs at his funeral. They used to work about five halls a night and there'd be a cab waiting at the stage door to take them to the next theatre, and they were earning about £100 per week between them! That was a lot of money.

When I was four I was taught to sing and dance. There's a room at the side of the 'Mucky Duck' [the White Swan in Goodramgate] as you go in, that's where we used to rehearse, Tootsie and Margaret Race and I, and my mother played the piano for us. Father was earning 5/- a week but my mother, when she played at the picture houses, got 18/-, and we never went short of food, never.

I was at the Empire when I was four and I remember a song, I Wouldn't Leave My Little Wooden Hut For You. Teddy Race and I sang that, he used to kneel down, and I'd sit on his knee. And when we were at the Empire, my grandmother promised me a penny if I did well, and I went up to my mother at the piano and said, 'Is grandma going to give me that penny?' And she said, 'Go and sit down, you little monkey', and there were 12 white stools round, and Harold Hemmings was playing the violin, and when I got back to my stool, I missed it, and then I put it on my head. And the audience howled with laughter.

I left school when I was 12, and went to join a concert party when the war started, and I was taken to the hall above a piano shop called Noyes. In the First World War, we'd go around hospitals, entertaining wounded soldiers and I'd sing and dance. After the war I joined a juvenile troupe. I was 17. I saw this advert, and I wrote after it. I never told my mother, and I got a letter back asking me to go to Newcastle for an audition. And I went up there and they kept me. The group was the Eight Sunny Brooks. Four of the girls were still at school.

They wouldn't let you work under 12, unless you had a licence. And I can remember it, we were in Scotland, and this man burst into the dressing room and we only had bras on and little briefs, and he wouldn't believe I was 18, he thought I was younger. However we got over that, then when the kids that went to school got a bit fed up, we four went in their places in their names. And kids at the schools used to bring us bars of chocolates and all sorts, because we were looked up to. We went to Glasgow, to a theatre in the Gorbals and on the Friday night they had 'trial turns', and people from the gallery started throwing rotten eggs and tomatoes on to the stage - they didn't give the poor devils a chance! We thought, 'I hope they don't do it to us'. But they didn't do it to the professionals, only to the trial turns.

We worked in the troupe for four years. We had a week out now and again, but I ran away once. I put my case in the garden and when everything was clear I went to the station in Newcastle, and I was tuppence short of the fare and I was just on the point of going to ask somebody to give me tuppence, when her and her husband walked into the waiting room and they yanked me back again. Eventually we had a week out and there was Topsy Garret and Olive Bell and me, from York, and we didn't go back. And that was the end of that. I got fed up, you know, the way we were treated. I was very stage struck and it wasn't very long before Olive, Topsy and I, and Dot Diamond ran a quartet. And I answered an advert for a show called Fun Larks, so the four of us went in this revue. There were 12 chorus girls as well and sometimes we joined them but the leading lady was always getting drunk and one night she didn't turn up, and it was a flower song, and all the chorus girls came on dressed as different flowers. And they got me into her dress and I went on and I sang and eventually they gave her the sack and I took over. And my husband, he was the leading man.

We used to do a 'pony trot' in the troupe. Six girls were ponies with a pony's head on their head and there were two of us drivers in red coats and we dance-stepped the pony trot. We opened at the beginning of the show dressed in Welsh costumes, with high hats and I had to strip everything off and underneath I was dressed as a boy. And they got us to go to have our photographs taken, and

May Passmore in 1923.
(Courtesy May Passmore)

they paid for them. Oh, and I've signed hundreds of autographs, hundreds and hundreds of them.

I only knew my husband Jimmy six months when I married him. He and his brother and father did an act together, and the mother played the part of Jemima in the revue. So the four of us joined and we called it the May Mac Ebor Girls. Then the girls left and Jimmy and I did quite a few acts in a concert party in Morecambe for three years, and then Southport for three years; Jack Audley's Varieties. We played at the top of the pier, there was a theatre there, and half of it was under cover for the audience, and the other half was in the open. They took over from the pierrots.

We went straight from pantomime into revue and after the concert

Jack Audley's Varieties at Morecambe 1929. May aged 28 at very front in centre, husband
Jimmy Crasey on her right. *(Courtesy May Passmore)*

party in the pantomime. We were classed as music hall artists but as the
'illegitimate'. The legitimate side was the actors. We were touring till 1932. I
had Trudy in 1925. I was in pantomime, and it was called Bluebeard, and we
were in Liverpool for seven weeks and when the pantomime finished I came to
York and she was born a month after I got back. So I was only out of work
seven weeks through having her, because they brought the show to York to
rehearse in Bishophill church hall, and they did that for my benefit, because I'd
only just had the baby. And I took Trudy away to Sheffield when she was a
fortnight old, and I travelled her 'til she was four years and ten months. Most
of the pros used to farm their kids on to their mothers, and their kids didn't
know their own mothers, and I said, 'If ever I have a baby I'm going to keep it
with me', and I did. I breast fed her as well, and my mother-in-law had a
Pekinese dog, and I had an awful lot of milk and I squeezed it in to a saucer,
and gave this dog some, and every night after that, that dog came to my
dressing room for milk.

I think we played nearly every club that was in York. We'd do a cockney act, and
a schoolboy and girl act. My mother played for us. I suppose there were plenty
of pros that were in the position we were in, and they would do the clubs as
well. Once when we were living in Rougier Street my father said the artiste at
the Angler's Club had let them down, and so we went, just in our ordinary

Trudy, May and Lillian. 1939.   *(Courtesy Trudy Luker)*

clothes. We had no stage clothes with us and no music or anything, but my mother knew everything we did and played the piano for us.

Trudy, May's daughter, was part of the Winstanley Troupe of Children. She remembers:

I went to dancing school, the Three Graces that was near the Empire. I was very happy about it. I loved showing off. I loved to sing and I loved to dance. My first theatrical engagement was when I was 11, I was one of 20 Winstanley Babes in pantomime. The pantomime was Cinderella, I can still sing all the songs, Tally Ho, Tally Ho A Hunting We Will Go. That was the opening scene. We toured all around with the pantomime then I came back to York and went into a show with my mother and a girl called Lillian, I was 13 then. May, Lillian And May we called ourselves, and we toured different towns, and I had to go to different schools every week. We were about a 20-minute act, which is normal in variety. When I was 14 I joined Danny Malone, the Irish tenor, as his accompanist, and I was with him for nearly two years. We played York Empire, and all the big theatres in London because he was very famous.

There was an outcry in 1928 when the chancellor suggested taxing gramophone records, and dancing schools claimed this 'would deal them a severe blow' as 'thousands of records are used every year'. Statistics showed

Rialto Ballroom. Yorkshire Evening Press November 1933.

(Courtesy City of York Library)

25

that 60 million records were sold every year in this country, 50 million for home use and ten million for export. Yet live music was still the favourite. In September 1928 the Rialto Cinema and Ballroom hosted Charleston competitions and was billed as the 'home of the famous Rialto Revels Dance Band, eight rhythm kings' and offered dancing on Monday, Wednesday, Friday and Saturday on 'York's biggest dance floor with velvet-like surface'. The band was described as 'the brightest dance band in the district - the boys who are making a name'. In Wigginton, the Metronomes Dance Band had 'Reg Skinner, York's hot drummer' and the Golden Serenaders performed at the Casino Picture Hall, billed as the 'princes of pep'.

The Rialto Orchestra also played between films. But January 1929 saw the advent of a new feature in cinemas, when St George's Cinema advertised 'Frank Olsen at the mighty Jardine orchestral organ'. The organist played incidental effects to the film as well as solo music. The organ had come from the Tivoli in London and at the opening ceremony Olsen played Evensong, In A Monastery Garden, Flapperette, two foxtrots and a selection from The Girlfriend.

Cyril White's Dance Band c1928. Dick Cambage 4th from left. Born in Walmgate in 1903, Dick Cambage played trumpet and saxophone. He performed with a circus band and dance bands, and during the Second World War with the York Home Guard Band. After the war he played at St Clement's Club and the New Central Working Men's Club. *(Courtesy Sheila Barrie)*

1929 was a big year for dances, from Mr Blenkarn's Harmony Dance Band at the New Earswick Association Football Club, Noel Stubbs' Dance Band playing for W P Brown's Hockey Club Dance, Bert Keech's Synco Band for York Rugby League, and Eddie Worthington's Band at the York Retail Dairymen's Association dance at the Crescent Café, the thirst for up-tempo music continued. Everyone jumped on the bandwagon from parish hall dance promoters to cinema magnates and at the cinema you could see Jazzmania, Children Of Jazz and Nice People (billed as a 'sensational jazz drama'). Young people had charlestoned their way through the decade and as it came to a close, the more sedate dances and concerts which were available at the turn of the century, were now gone. One writer to the press asked 'Are the young people of today going to the dogs on a wave of jazz and cocktails?' Popular music would never be the same again.

CHAPTER TWO. PUTTIN' ON THE RITZ
The 1930s

In the 1930s, York was alive with popular music. Dance orchestras flourished and smaller bands played at village halls in rural areas surrounding the city. The Depression meant that more people than ever needed to escape from reality, if only for a while.

In January 1930, for example, the Treasurer's House Quartet played at a Scout dance at St Lawrence's Club, the Royal British Legion dance orchestra for a dance at the City Art Gallery and the Rialto Revels band entertained at the Assembly Rooms. The Pavilion in Flaxman Avenue hosted a dance with the Radiance Dance Band, and Paul Edwards And His Music for a dance at the Co-op Hall. In February 1931, the LNER police dance at the Railway Institute had engaged the York Popular Dance Band, York Mayfair Band were at the Drill Hall and Lew Simons's Revels Eight at the Grand Ballroom. In December Gus Nolan, the jazz drummer, spoonist and step dancer, made the semi-final in the York Amateur Variety Final.

One of the most popular 1930s bands was the Bobby Ward orchestra, who advertised as 'String or Dance, for all and any occasion'. Bobby Ward and his wife Muriel ran the 43 Club for a number of years from 1928, at both the De Grey Rooms and Assembly Rooms. His orchestra played and Mrs Ward was the hostess. Before forming his bands, Bobby had played piano at the Tower cinema for silent movies. After the Second World War, he played with the Doug Green Dance Orchestra right up until his death in 1960.

Stanley Brough
& his Orchestra

13 ST. JOHN STREET, YORK

- - - - - - - -

All Comms : S. BROUGH
13 St. John Street, York
Tel. 56244

Stan Brough Dance Band in 1930s.   *(Courtesy Dave Brough)*

Arthur Burcombe came to York in the 1930s and was immediately part of the music scene, playing several different instruments. He recalls the Bobby Ward Band:

Bobby played piano and he was a classical pianist. He was very very good. There was another good player, he played tenor sax as well as fiddle but he liked whisky. When you was beside him playing tenor, you got fumes!

Regular dances in the Tang Hall area continued in 1932 with the Pavilion in Flaxman Avenue, the Social Hall in Fifth Avenue and Parochial Hall as venues, with the Blues Dance Orchestra, the Follies Dance Band and Tutill's Modern Dance Band helping to amuse the population on the newly-built estates. It seems that any church or social halls that were available would present dances. As the year continued, Miss Andrew's Orchestra played for a Royal British Legion dance at Newburgh Priory (though the legion had its own dance orchestra which played at the Albany), the Imps Dance Band provided music at the Rialto and Bobby Ward's Band Of Seven played with the Sisters Gawthorne. Cora and Lillian Gawthorne were daughters of Samuel Gawthorne, owner of a big furniture shop in Petergate. From childhood they were given music lessons, Cora playing the piano accordion and Lillian the piano, and throughout their youth, they performed at many concerts for charity. Many years later, Cora was quoted in the Evening Press saying, 'We were booked up for three years in advance. Father was always buying musical instruments for us and once we had the smallest concertina in the world'. The girls also took part in a number of radio programmes for the BBC. In 1957, when record-buying was an even bigger industry, Mr Gawthorne opened a record bar in his shop.

The Rialto cinema and concert hall in Fishergate, which had been bought by Jack Prendergast in 1927, was to become the most popular venue in York over the next four decades. In 1925 it was still the City Picture Palace, and was granted a dancing licence for its ballroom and skating rink. A year later it had become the Casino and, in January 1927, hosted a Fun Carnival Dance with a 'free packet of Sarony cigarettes for all dancers'. By 1928, Mr Prendergast had changed the name to the Rialto. The house band, the Rialto Revels, had a new billing on October 5, 1932, as Wynn Derr And The Rialtonians, (a play on the name of band member Oliver Winder, whose father supported the band). Mr Prendergast had the Rialto refurbished and the New Rialto Ballroom opened on September 8, 1933, and featured the famous London bandleader Lew Stone And His Complete Monseigneur Band on only their second provincial appearance. Others on the bill included Lew Davis, Nat Gonella and 'the one and only' Al Bowlly.

Friday, Sept. 8th.   Opening of
THE NEW
RIALTO BALLROOM
YORK
Entirely Reconstructed, Decorated to the Latest Modern Ideas.
New Cafe and Cloak-room Appointments, &c.

The 2nd Provincial Appearance of the Famous London Band Leader
LEW STONE
AND HIS COMPLETE
MONSEIGNEUR BAND

JOE GROSSMAN   BILL HARTY   LEW DAVIS
EDDIE CARROLL   TINY WINTERS   NAT GONELLA

Al Bowlly *(the one & only)* Vocalist & Guitarist

GET YOUR TICKETS NOW
TICKETS **5/-** EACH

LEW STONE and his BAND arrive in York, 1.30 p.m.,
Friday. JOIN THE CROWD TO MEET HIM.

THE MODERN ELECTRICAL EQUIPMENT in the
NEW RIALTO BALLROOM, including:—
KELVINATOR REFRIGERATOR and ICE CREAM
MANUFACTURING PLANT
SPOT LIGHTING, GENERAL ILLUMINATION and
COLOUR EFFECTS
SPEECH and MUSIC AMPLIFIERS and MICROPHONES
Supplied and Installed by

John Stubbs & Company
ELECTRICAL, RADIO AND
REFRIGERATING ENGINEERS,
BOOTHAM, YORK
Phone 1246.

Opening of New Rialto Ballroom. Yorkshire Evening Press September 1933. *(Courtesy City of York Library)*

Unfortunately the Rialto burnt down two years later in 1935, causing £30,000 worth of damage. Only a few hours before the blaze a dance had been in progress but by 5.45am the fire brigade was on the scene. Firefighters were unable to save the building, and all the instruments belonging to the Rialtonians, were destroyed. Mr Prendergast was devastated and said, 'I had worked hard to make the hall one of the best in the country. Now it has all gone and it is hard to believe. But even this big disaster will not mean the conclusion of my activities in York.' He was certainly not defeated and the place was soon rebuilt, with a new ballroom to hold 1,800 people.

Jack Prendergast was a man with a passion. He wanted the Rialto to offer world famous artists and he got them, from Jack Buchanan, (a personal friend), the Halle Orchestra, (whose conductor Sir John Barbirolli was also a good friend), Louis Armstrong, Gracie Fields, Stan Kenton and many more. He went out on a limb as some of the acts he engaged were perhaps too big, or too expensive for this provincial town, and the theatre was half empty on some occasions. But he was determined to get the best and over the next 30 years he would provide York with an enormous wealth of entertainment.

In August 1932 an advertisement in the Yorkshire Evening Press announced that 'The world's greatest trumpet player, Louis Armstrong and his New Rhythm Band' would play at the York and District Dance Band Contest run by the Melody Maker at the Rialto. Banks record store announced that it had all Louis Armstrong's records in stock and offered readers the chance to 'call and hear them' on the telephone. The Evening Press reported that 'the noted Selmer trumpet player, popular in rhythm style and a versatile musician, is declared to have an uncanny mastery over the trumpet which he calls the satchmo, a contraction of satchelmouth. He plays the instrument with wonderful skill, his presence at the contest will be attractive to those interested in modern dance music and Mr Prendergast has done well to secure his visit to York'.

Wynn Derr and the Rialtonians at the Rialto 1930s. L to R - Jack Prendergast, George Barnes, George Robson, Len Cundall on bass, Oliver Winder, Les Cowell, Jack Potter on drums, Hugh Robertson on trombone. *(Courtesy June Lloyd-Jones)*

The Rialtonians playing in the ballroom. *(Courtesy June Lloyd-Jones)*

Louis Armstrong in the Rialto with Jack Prendergast third from left, and Louis's manager Johnny Collins second from right. 1932. *(Courtesy June Lloyd-Jones)*

James Cave played saxophone with the Benny Connell Band who were normally resident at the Station Hotel, and who took part in the contest. Eleven Yorkshire bands entered and the Connell band. Mr Cave recalls:

Louis Armstrong wished us all good luck as we were the last band on stage. We also had the pleasure of his company for refreshments later on.

Len 'Ginger' Cundall founded the band resident at the Rialto, the Rialtonians, in 1931 and led the band until it disbanded in 1939. He actually began playing banjo when he was 14 in 1925, at a dance at St Maurice's School, later part of the County Hospital. He went on to play double bass, clarinet and saxophone. Harry Murray remembers the band:

They were without doubt, pre war, the best dance band in York. They had dances every Friday and Saturday and the MC there was a man called Tony Lister who was a ballroom dancer. The Rialto was beautiful. The auditorium was lit in a very spectacular fashion because the lighting was all hidden along where the picture rail is, and it changed colour, the walls were plain and the colour swathed the walls with blues and yellows and pinks and it would appear as though bulbs were going that way and this, because colours blended. I played with the Rialtonians on one big occasion when the society that was sponsoring wanted a ten-piece dance band. Ginger Cundall who was leader, manager and organiser of the Rialtonians didn't normally have a ten-piece, he probably had eight. So I was roped in as tenor sax. The drummer was Jack Potter, trombone player and vocalist was Hughie Robertson. He worked for Noyes and Co, who had a music shop in Davygate which rivalled Banks but was more on the popular music side. Later Hughie took his own shop in Pavement. The pianist was Eric Betts and George Robson, the violinist.

Although Mr Murray filled in with the Rialtonians, he actually played with the Astorians. One night the two bands played at opposite ends of the Assembly Rooms:

It was non-stop dancing, can you imagine it, 8pm until 2am on a Friday. The Rialtonians kicked off at their end and they were a super band, and we were at the other end and not so super. They did their bit with a quickstep no doubt and a 'chssh' finish. We had a big fellow called Trevor Baines who was our leader and he had big feet and he went '1, 2, 3, 4' and nobody came in, not one. We were all sort of nervous playing against this. He gave us a black look and said, 'Next time' and off we went. When we stopped they started and that's the only dance I ever knew which was non-stop. The dancers must have been pretty worn out. For a fortnight's special intermission, our band played at the Tower Picture House. We were second band to the Rialtonians. They were so popular and so much in demand that they could pick their venues and naturally they played at the Rialto weekly and had a band room. They had more work than they wanted and Ginger used to shove us all the rustic dance halls and church halls with stages that rocked and rolled when you played, and folks swang round with their dresses and knocked your music stand down. The

Wynn Derr and the Rialtonians 1930s at the Rialto. L to R - Jack Prendergast, George Barnes, George Robson, Len Cundall, Oliver Winder, Les Cowell, Hugh Robertson, Jack Potter.   *(Courtesy Mary Cundall)*

headquarters of the Astorians was English Martyrs' schoolroom off Blossom Street and we rehearsed every Friday night and had a Saturday night dance. There was Alf Allcock on piano, Jack Dunkley double bass, Ted Daniels on drums, two brothers trained by the Salvation Army on trombone and trumpet, who were very good indeed. Trevor Baines was first sax, and I was next to him. It was a very balanced band with four solo voices at the front and the pianist was able to keep the thing going. If anybody failed, which might have been me, he bashed louder on the piano and brought the melody out and kept the rhythm going. I had a solo in Liebestraum, a slow waltz, and had to do it all in one breath blowing through a saxophone, getting the note out. That was phasing. You can imagine your lungs shipping that out on a low register to fill a ballroom. We usually started with Sweet Sue, and then Alexander's Ragtime Band and Tiger Rag, quicksteps. They were the sort of tunes when the place got hotted up, when it was really jumping. Foxtrots were a different kettle of fish, slower and more moderate, like Souvenirs and I'll See You In My Dreams. There were slow foxtrots like Deep Purple, Mood Indigo and Lovely To Look At, then the modern waltz like Glamorous Nights. There'd be a valeta, the two step was Blaze Away, tango was Jealousy, of course, and the rumba Lady In Red.

The Astorians at the Tower Cinema 1930s. L to R - Trevor Baines (leader, alto sax, clarinet), Ted Daniel (drums), Williamson brothers (trombone and trumpet), unknown, unknown, Len 'Ginger' Cundall (alto sax), Bob Ashton (alto sax), Harry Murray (piano, tenor sax), Jack Dunkley (bass, guitar), Alf Allcock (piano, accordion).

(Courtesy Harry Murray)

For the band to be properly laid out, you'd have the drummer, made a hard, loud sound, and in front which was softer - the saxophones, and then in the middle, in front of the drums would be a quiet violin who had to really cuddle the microphone. When I was doing Liebestraum, the bloke grabbed the mike, and ran over and put it near my bell to get me out into the auditorium, for them to do the soft shoe shuffle. Sometimes there was an old time waltz, barn dance or Boston Twostep or St Bernard's Waltz, those sort of things. Occasionally you'd get at Christmas what they called party dances - conga, Lambeth Walk, Balling The Jack.

I learned to play the piano when I was a boy. My uncle taught me, Mr Porteous, who was editor for Banks. I'd be about 12, 13, and he taught me for about five years. Len Cundall knew I could play. I didn't play the piano in the band but he wanted a tenor sax so he approached me, and Trevor Baines and I went to Leeds and bought one, not a Selmer, not the posh top one. I think it was a Cavalier and looked a bit like silver plating. Lovely instrument, and I had to keep it clean. I didn't have any tuition, I could read music, so I was shoved into the band more-or-less straightaway. A couple of weeks at Rialto band room and a couple of weeks at Ginger's home, post office in Bishopthorpe Road, and you're in, chum, so I was a bit nervous about it.

Funny things used to happen at English Martyrs, somebody would switch all the lights off, when we were having supper. As you know, when you blow in a cold instrument with your hot breath, it goes into moisture, saliva at the bottom of the bell. They thought they'd put some potted meat sandwiches down there while I was at intermission and when we all started I couldn't make a blessed sound, blew my guts out and couldn't make any sound, and I up-tipped it and you know what cows do, clap!

We were registered with four music publishers, Chappell and Keith Prowse, about four, and every month they brought out their issues of popular dance music and there was an A side and a B side like records. And on Friday nights after we got these, we rehearsed them at the hall. Some we took into our repertoire and some we discarded, some were too difficult probably, some weren't necessarily for dance, most of them were good tunes but what were in short supply were quicksteps. The sheet music was for each instrument so I should imagine I only got my own copy, but it was a long sheet of music and you folded it. We had music stands. They looked rather gorgeous but they were as cheap as you can make.

One or two in the band had cars. The drums fell off the back of the car going through Malton once and we had a little catastrophe there. You piled into a car and you didn't bother about seating four in those days. Two cars would at least get seven and the drums and the saxophones, trumpet and trombone and whatever, in. I remember one night, we'd go to these country places and they used to keep us on a bit longer 'cos we were so popular, so we said, another two quid. Anyway we were walking through this little village and we thought we'd liven the village up so we started doing it down the main street and we got told off through the windows. They'd had enough.

Men were always in dark suits, your Sunday best, blue serge.   Collar and tie always and you never took your jacket off. And girls were in evening dress. I remember I danced with somebody and she'd gone to town with all this taffeta or whatever it was, swinging round there, and it was a weight, it got under her heels and one or other of us had had to yank it up. I didn't bother to ask her anymore, I had enough of that. Then another one had steel corsets on, I didn't like her much either. For the summer dances we were in grey flannels and red open-necked shirts.

His Master's Voice National Show Train' was dispatched from Paddington by the Prime Minister, Ramsay Macdonald, on April 27, 1934, carrying a complete range of HMV and Columbia products. It visited York on July 10. The Prime Minister described it as 'an outstanding example of British industrial enterprise'.   Its 3,000-mile tour meant that it visited more than 60 towns in England, Wales and Scotland, showing the very latest developments in radio and gramophone research.   Aerials were built into the roof and the construction provided acoustic conditions similar to that of an ordinary living room. The train had all types of instruments from the self-contained battery receiver to a luxurious ten valve automatic record changing radio-gramophone. About 10,000 workers were kept in employment at HMV throughout the year because of public interest in the train and its equipment.   Free tickets of admission were available at J Gray & Sons, the music shop in Coney Street.

The same month as the train's visit, Con Lamprecht, the noted saxophonist and member of Jack Payne's band, came to York. As well as performing alone, he also helped the Rialtonians who were a player short due to illness. Percy Bedford played solo violin and directed the Rialtonians. In 1932 he had come to York from Huddersfield to conduct the orchestra which played at café concerts at the Rialto. He was brought to the city by Mr Prendergast. After the fire at the Rialto he went to manage Mr Prendergast's new cinema, the Clifton, and later joined the orchestra at the Empire and began to teach music as well as repair instruments.   He joined the trio which played during the interval at York Theatre Royal and helped to build up York Youth Orchestra.   Percy spent the early part of his life with orchestras on ships of the Cunard White Star Line. It was even rumoured that he had been on board the Titanic, though the list of passengers does not include his name.

But the big event for music fans that month was the appearance of Coleman Hawkins, 'the world's greatest saxophonist' at the Rialto Ballroom, with dancing from 9pm to 2am. Another coup by Mr Prendergast! 'The Hawk' was originally due to play on July 8, but the gig was put forward to the previous night, the 7th, as he was due to play on Jack Hylton's broadcast from Manchester on the 8th. The report in the Melody Maker stated that 'the Rialto Club Hot Rhythm members yelled for more'.

The writer in the Melody Maker also mentioned Mr Prendergast, 'I have never yet come in contact with a manager in the provinces with as much thought for his band, ballroom and patrons as Jack, and his efforts in the Rialto have been well merited'.

There were young musicians in York who saw this concert who would never be the same again, so influenced were they by this giant of jazz. One of them was Bob Brown:

I had a word with Coleman Hawkins and got his autograph. He played a tenor sax from Banks and it was advertised after he was gone that he'd played this tenor sax.

Bob was born in 1915 and got his first guitar when he was 16.

I started on a Hawaiian guitar. I heard it on the radio, and I thought 'I'd like to play that'. So we got one, second hand, from Merriman's Pawn Shop, and I got a book from Hughie Robbo [Hugh Robertson's music shop] and started to learn myself from the book. I was getting on pretty well with it and a bit later I was listening to Henry Hall and it said, 'Saxophone solo by Bert Gillis'. When me father came in I said, 'I want to play a saxophone'. 'Where are we going to get the money for a saxophone?' Anyway, eventually, he signed for me one, we went to Ackroyd's in Leeds and I got an alto, and I got an old chap named Albert Dale to teach me for half a crown an hour. I was getting on pretty well with it and we had a record of Nat Gonella with, 'Tenor Sax solo by Pat Smuts'. Well I said to me dad, 'I'd like a tenor sax'. Up in the air he went! And it took me ages, but I persuaded him, and eventually we took the alto back and I got a tenor, and I've been on tenor ever since.

Alf Foster used to play with Bob Mason on guitar. Now Alf Foster worked nights sometimes, so he asked me if I would go and play with Bob, I had me sax - but I couldn't play it! I thought he said, 'Go down to practise'. Well I went down and took me sax, he piled us into this car, took us out somewhere to a dance. I said 'Where are we goin'?' He says, 'We're playing at this dance.' I said, 'I can't play the damn thing'. I'd just got it! So I had to change Alf's guitar to a Hawaiian and play Hawaiian guitar all night. Oh I've had some right goings on!

The Blue Aces in Walpole Street. 1934. Sid Watson on accordion, Bob Brown on baritone sax, Ron Backhouse on bass, Les Backhouse, drums.
(Courtesy Bob Brown)

My two cousins, Les and Ron Backhouse, I got them interested and then Les said, 'I'd like to play the drums'. And Ron said he'd like to play the trumpet, but he wasn't much good on it, so we decided we'd have him on string bass. Sid Watson, he was later me brother-in-law, we got him on accordion and finally switched over to piano. And that's how we started, the Blue Aces. We played all over the place, jazz, old time with quadrilles and schottiche, and 50/50 dances [part old time dancing and part modern]. We used to go all over the place for nothing, just for the sheer love of playing. We played with the police concert party for a long while. Bob Halford and all them were in it. We bought the orchestrations from Banks. And we'd practise in me auntie's room, and when we'd had enough of it we'd go and put records on. Coleman Hawkins, my idol, playing Chicago and Honeysuckle Rose.

I was sat listening to the radio and it said about George Scott Wood and his Six Swingers. Well I'd never heard owt like it, Freddie Gardner and his alto sax. I went straight down to Banks's as soon as I could and I bought every [record] he had, and they were all there.

That first guitar I bought, I got more-or-less an old do-it-yourself book, and it told you how to electrify it. There was a chap at the railway, he was pretty good at that, and he did it for me. He took magnets out of telephones and put them underneath each string, and an electro-magnet under it, and he plugged it into t'radio - it worked! Electric guitar, yes. That was before all these come out.

The sax I bought was a Selmer. In fact I've had all the saxes barring a C Melody. Alto, soprano, tenor, baritone, bass. I had this bass sax, it was just like a coffin. I had too much to lug about so I took it back to Ackroyd's and I swapped it for an electric guitar, and I used to play it for waltzes then.

One time I went to Leeds, I had a sax I wanted to exchange. Sid went with me, and I believe our Les went. We went to Ackroyd's and they showed us these saxes, a Selmer, a Beuscher and this Con. The Con was all wrapped in cellophane, never been touched. So I tried the Selmer and I tried the Beucher and he unwrapped this Con, and I got on that, and I said, 'That's the one I want'. And he said, 'Yes, you know what you're doing.' Well with that Sid picked a great big accordion up and he started, and I started on tenor with him, and this bloke, he picks the clarinet up and there were three of us! We had a right go in there!

Jimmy Thompson. He used to sing with us, So Deep Is The Night and all stuff like that. But I've played with some fellas, years back. There was Jimmy Thread on trumpet, Gordon Waller, trumpet and Percy Yeoman on alto and violin. And Benny Connell, when he got on those drums, he didn't half give you a lift!

I played up at the Oasis on Tadcaster Road with Benny Connell, Binny Mann on alto sax and tenor, and Georgie Long on piano. Benny used to play like Buddy Rich, he was smashing. Oh I've had some real good times, but they'll never come again.

Bob's wife Elsie met him at a dance:

I think music was lovely compared to what it is today. Dancing was so important to people. I met him in 1939, when he was playing at Rowntree's. I used to go out about four nights a week, to the De Grey Rooms, Assembly Rooms, New Earswick and Co-op Hall. I'd be about 16. I walked home on my own to Dodsworth Avenue, mind you dances finished about half past 11. But on winter nights, dark nights, you could walk, there were never any problem that way at all. When you think back, how lovely it used to be. People could go round without being molested.

In the Blue Aces, Bob played all over the area. Most of the band not having cars, they had to often cycle, as he explains:

We used to play at Bell Farm, Earswick, Kelfield. We built a trailer, just like a miniature horse box, dropped the back, shoved all the lot in and pulled 'em on t'back of the bike. At one time I ran my own dances at Heworth Hall. We had Dickie Bailey with us (a multi musician, he played saxes, trombone, euphonium), on baritone sax, Brian Mullinger on alto and me on tenor. It was great. Dickie also played the piano. We used to get Sid and him, two of 'em playin' on one piano. Big Noise from Winnetka, Ron on bass and our Les on sticks. Then Whispering and Tropical Moonlight. Me mother liked that, she bought me the orchestration for it.

We had a young trumpet player with us, they called him Joe Casselli. We were going to play at the De Grey Rooms and we were short of a trumpet player and we asked him if he would come with us, he was smashing and at finish he joined us. At one time we'd go over to Leeds on our day off, and he went with us, and they were demonstrating King Instruments. Well Joe picked this trumpet, he hits C, top C, and C above that! Well the man who was there was Lew Davies from Ambrose's Band, and he came over. He said, 'Would you do that again?' Well he picks a trumpet up and he started. He said, 'I never knew you could get that note in that position'. Professional player but he said, 'It just shows, you can always learn'.

Harry Strain was a smashing alto sax player, and he played at the Coach and Horses at the corner of Nessgate. He'd let us get on t'stage. Les on drums, Sid on t'piano and I used to get on Harry's alto, and he'd get on clarinet. And all t'beer comin' in! After he'd played there he'd go to the police station and play

The Embassy Players 1930s. L to R - MC Wilf Smith, Ron Backhouse, bass, Bernard 'Bunny' Hall, trumpet, Les Backhouse, drums, Bob Brown, tenor sax, Sid Watson, accordion, Brian Mullinger, alto sax.

with a police band with Bob Halford. Well after we'd played at the Co-op Hall one time we went there. Bob Halford says, 'Hey Bob, I've got a tenor here, away'. And I picked this tenor up and it was a Clydesdale effort. I said, 'Well I don't think much to this Bob' and I walked from the police station to Walpole Street on Haxby Road, collected me own tenor and walked all the way back again to play.

After the Blue Aces, Bob formed the Embassy Players in 1936 and they soon became the resident band at the popular Rowntree dances in the dining hall of the factory. The band split up when its members joined the armed forces during the Second World War. They reformed in the early 1950s and regularly played at the Co-op Hall dances, under the name of Len Cundall and the Embassy Players. Bob recalls:

When I played at the Co-op Hall, I always went early, got me sax and had a blow, then I'd go in t'Corner Pin and have a couple of pints, and then go back again. It steadies your nerves. I mean when you're sat on that stage and it was absolutely choc-o-bloc with people. The best compliment I ever had was from Derek Dunning. We used to go to the Corner Pin and Derek was there, and he said to me, 'I've been listening to Coleman Hawkins tonight, and I said to my friend, I've got a mate who plays like that - you'.

At one time at New Year's Eve, we were playing just this side of Hull with Len Cundall's band. Len had this big Humber. It had bald tyres and anyway we got a puncture. Got out of the car, one getting t'spare wheel out, the other jacking it up. We were blathered up to t'eyeballs by t'time we got there. We were nearly an hour late but we got there in t'finish.

Then that competition at Hull. We'd rehearsed for it, and that night, oh terrible fog. We finally got there, but they shoved us straight on t'stage. Well that was it, we never won it or anything. But me uncle was taking Elsie and his wife in his car as well. Coming back Len had the old Humber sailing on, in the fog, me uncle at the back watching the tail light. And I was watchin' as well and I could just see his head lights. I said, 'Hey Len, I can't see me uncle's headlights, I think something's happened'. We went back, me uncle's car in the ditch! Luckily there were beams right across the ditch. We pulled up and looked at him and Len said, 'I've got a rope at the back, we'll try and pull him out'. Well me Uncle Ted went to fix the rope to his car, up to here in mud! What a state! Anyway, there was a house with lights on, and we went across and they were smashin', they lent him clothes and everything. He got real pally with them eventually.

Bob particularly enjoyed his time with the Embassy Players:

We went all over the place with Len. Selby Baths, Assembly Rooms, De Grey Rooms, Bettys. When we had that band at the Co-op Hall it was a terrific band. We used to rehearse at Len's post office and he was very strict. 'Play this thing, no good, no good! Call me what you like, we'll get it right, play it again'. At the finish, of course, we would get it right, and it was a smashing band. We played Glenn Miller stuff - String Of Pearls, In The Mood, all that. In the finish the bands finished for dancing and started in t'clubs. I played at Holgate Club for years; there was Nora Mack on piano, Les on drums, Alan Whitely on guitar and me on tenor. We played for ages up there. As soon as this rock 'n' roll stuff came in, that was it, finished.

Sid Watson went on to play piano and organ with various York bands and when he died in 1989, his wife said that he was 'a marvellous pianist who gave a lot of people a lot of pleasure'. What better thing to say about someone? Les Backhouse also went on to play in working men's clubs in later life, and when he died in 1996, he had been resident at the Holgate Club more than 40 years, right through the 'beat boom'.

Bob's sister Mary sometimes sang with his band:

I used to go round with them wherever they were playing. We had a good laugh, we'd travel in cattle trucks. All poshed up, hired from farmers, where animals had been transported backwards and forwards. Because some of these

Bob Brown and Kathy Flint with the Embassy Players at the Co-op Hall in the 1950s.
(Courtesy Bob Brown)

places were way out in the country. Maybe once or twice if they were playing a number that I knew, I would go and give a rendering.

Then I got singing with Neville England, my cousin, and he had a very nice voice. We both worked at Cooke, Troughton and Simms, which was a munitions factory, and we'd do concerts for employees during the dinner hour. We'd sing the Indian Love Call together, and Rose Marie. Our Nev and I sang at the De Grey Rooms at one time and he'd rig all this sort of stuff up, the microphones, and you had to sing right into it. I remember singing in a competition in Blossom Street, somewhere over the Odeon. I went to sing with the band, and when we got there they were having a competition, people were dancing and I sang, Love Walked In And Drove The Shadows Away and got the prize. Instead of a clapometer, they put their hands on top of their heads, clap for who they wanted to win.

James Cave started out when he was very young:

I played saxophone, clarinet and violin. I started lessons in about 1930, sixpence a week. Used to walk from St Saviourgate to Haxby Road. There was no cars and there was a tram, but it would probably cost you tuppence and you hadn't got tuppence to spend on that. So I'd walk right to Fountayne Street once a week. Then one day a gentleman knocked on our door and asked my father, 'Does Jim Cave live here?' 'Yes, that's my son'. And this was Bert Keech, his mother and father had a public house in Marygate. Now Bert Keech got to be one of the councillors round here, and I'd only be about 15 or 16. He said, 'We've a little parish do in Marygate at the church hall. They want me to play the piano but I want someone else to play the violin. Would you come along?' 'Oh yes, yes'. I think I played from 7 till 10 o'clock. We finished and he put his hand in his pocket and give me three half-crowns. Well you know I nearly collapsed. I nearly fainted. Three half-crowns! 7/6d. I started work for 6/- a week as an apprentice!

Well after that I thought, 'Right, I'm going to get stuck in here' and I started practising seriously, an hour a day every day. And of course I got better and I improved and I went to Leeds and paid 4/- a week on hire purchase for a tenor saxophone. And, of course, I was earning a few bob. Fantastic. Then I took up the clarinet. I've played in pubs, I've played in clubs, I've played in youth orchestras, I've played in pit orchestras, I've done concerts. Been all over in my lifetime with music. Believe me.

Benny Connell's sister-in-law, Olive Connell, recalls first meeting Benny in the Black Swan, which was run by her Aunt Elsie. She remembers Benny doing a terrific impersonation of Louis Armstrong singing Georgia. Olive later married Benny's brother Raymond. Olive's own brother was Geoff Towse, who became a dance band leader in the late 1940s.

Wedding of Raymond Connell and Olive Towse, St Maurice's Church, Monkgate, May 1945.
L to R - Benny Connell, Raymond Connell, Olive Towse, Doreen Towse, Mr and Mrs Towse.
(Courtesy Olive Connell)

There had been some earlier music in the family as Olive explains:

My grandfather was the bandmaster at Nafferton, just outside Driffield. It was a silver band, 'cos when I was a little girl, we always went to Driffield for a fortnight's holiday, and we'd go on Sunday morning, and listen to the band. Mr Kell at the Empire, he taught our Geoff the violin, well tried to do, but Geoff didn't want to play the violin, he went on to saxophone. Our Auntie Elsie was a singer as well, who was stopped going on the stage because her father said, 'No daughter of mine's going on the stage.' That's what happened years ago. And she had a lovely voice. She used to play all the old musical comedy things, and I remember when I was little, Chocolate Soldier, Desert Song, Rose-Marie and all those. Lovely.

My mother paid a guinea a term for me to have music lessons at Noyes' music shop, where Bettys is now, in an upstairs room. Then I went to a Miss Hague in Burton Stone Lane who taught singing, mandolin and piano, but I didn't like the music she gave me. She was very strict and would put her finger under my chin so I didn't look down at my fingers. Grand marches! I've never seen so many black dots in my life. I'd go home and play Red Sails In The Sunset and mother was very cross with me. 'You stay there until you practise what you're supposed to be practising'. They were good days really, I loved music, and I love piano music now, but I just didn't like what I was being taught.

I listened to the radio, Jack Payne, Henry Hall and Roy Fox, all the old music. Well it wasn't old then was it? Geoff started playing the sax, and just went from there, and he worked at Cookes during the war and knew Nev England and some of the lads there. He would be 18 when war broke out. He wanted to go in the air force but he couldn't because he had a perforated eardrum.

Auntie Elsie would go to whist drives, and they always had a whist drive before a dance in those days. I'd go and meet her, and she was my chaperone. I was about 14. The grocers would have a dance, the butchers would have a dance, the Conservative Party had a dance, all biggish dances. I used to love it, and when young men would come up and ask if they may have the next dance, oh when I think about it now it makes me laugh. I had a pink dress, it was more like a nightdress, straight, with a little frill round the bottom. That was my first dance dress. And we had evening shoes, silver or black, and evening handbags to match. There was a man, he had a pub in Pavement, and he was the MC. White gloves and evening dress, and by jove you couldn't swing each other round the floor, because when they were doing the Lancers, you'd got to do it properly or he could order you off the floor.

I went to the Grand Ballroom once, as a Charleston baby, it was fancy dress and I won a prize and it was a gent's shaving stick! And I had a little black pill box hat edged with blue ribbon and a suit, and little trousers and a blue garter, and some Charleston shoes.

During the war, a crew of Canadians used to come in Auntie Elsie's, [she ran the Black Swan in Peasholme Green], they were grand fellas and a crowd of us would go dancing. It was in the De Grey Rooms when this happened. You know, the jitterbug when they used to throw you. Oh I played pop, 'don't you dare do that again'. I wondered where I was going, he threw me off me feet he did, jitterbugging. They were good pals, they really were, and those Canadian lads, they all got killed. They were on Wellingtons and I think they'd done about 30 ops, and then they got transferred, and it's when the Halifax came, and I remember one saying, 'They're death traps'. First operation they were on, they'd gone.

All the musicians would come in the Swan. We had some great times. I think it was because of the musical evenings, the chat and the banter and the fun we had, it was packed. Benny Connell, he was lovely. He'd come in and have a couple of whiskies. He played in Knaresborough every week at one time, Ray would take him in the car. Take all the kit and what have you. He was well known was Benny, a real comedian as well. In the pub, the piano was on one side, and Elsie would be in there playing all night sometimes. There was a lad called Stan Agar, a lovely pianist, and during the war there was Geoff Love, and Ernie Pontecelli and anybody else that wanted to come and play the piano. And I sang with Geoff Love, I'll Never Smile Again.

As the 1930s continued so did the craze for dancing, with all kinds of novelty dances on offer as venues competed with each other. In May 1932, for example, there were flannel dances each Wednesday at St George's Ballroom and in 1933 Ted Brown And His Eight Maniacs provided the music for a Brighter York tea dance at St George's Hall. The Rialto advertised its 'general practice class' on Tuesday nights at a cost of 1/6d, for which you could 'learn to dance and be popular'. An Eat More Fruit dance promoted by Mrs Etherington, the 'well known Heworth Conservative worker' at the De Grey Rooms offered old-time dances to Ted Neal's band.

The introduction of gramophone records at dances came in February 1930, at the Pavilion, Tang Hall. The advertisement said 'come and dance free to gramophone pick up and wireless demonstrations of dance music given by Messrs Stevens at the Pavilion', but it does not seem to have lessened live dances. However there was correspondence in November 1930 in the Yorkshire Evening Press concerning the 'unemployed cinema musicians' forced out of work by the Talkies. One letter writer (an anonymous pianist) contrasted proper music (such as the waltzes of Strauss) with modern music. He said that cinema musicians 'sound quite good from a melody standpoint but have no rhythm and that is as important as the melody in the making of a good dance band'. 'A drummer' answered by saying that there is no work for bands 'unless they possess rhythm, syncopation, personality and good time keeping'. If that is true, then many bands must have shared those qualities.

There were fewer dances in the summer months but by October 1932 among the bands offering entertainment, were Reg Skinner's Rhythm Boys at Huntington Memorial Hall, the Nursery Orchestra at a dance at Seaton Ross, and the Nightbirds at a dance at Burton Lane Adult School. The Rialto was offering demonstrations of 'the latest dance success, the Charlestep, by Toni and Mabel', as well as yo-yo dance competitions. The Rialto skating rink had music by the Rialto Rink Band from 2pm to 7pm on Monday and Tuesday nights. The Georgians led by Eric Gill, played at St George's Hall and probably got their name from that residency, although it may have been because of the national Georgians dance band. There was a lot to do mid-week in October, with tea and evening dances at the Albany, as well as dances at the Rialto, Acomb Adult School, Strensall camp.

Kit Kat Band in 1930s. L to R back - Andrew Mackintosh, bass, Ted Rowell, piano, George Smith, tenor, Victor Parker, trumpet, Harry Berriman, drums, Fred Gofton, Dick Culley. L to R front - Eric Ward, guitar, Ernie Angel in white coat. Recording at the Piccadilly recording studios in York which was run by Ernie Angel. A number of York musicians made recordings at this studio. *(Courtesy Yorkshire Evening Press from Eric Ward)*

In April 1933 the Grand Ballroom in Clarence Street hosted an Easter dance with music by the Grand Kit Kat Orchestra run by Ted Rowell, (see photo). The Kit Kat Club was one of the more lavish and exclusive clubs that sprang up in London's West End after the First World War, with many jazz bands playing there. George Fisher, an American musician who settled in Britain, and his Kit Kat Band were playing at the club in 1930. The York Kit Kat Band were playing at Rowntree dining hall in the early 1930s and it is quite likely that the Kit Kat chocolate bar was given its name at that time by shrewd marketing men who realised that Kit Kat was an up to date word with jazz overtones. A new sensation in April 1933 was the appearance at the Rialto of Mrs Jack Hylton And Her band (she had started out as Ennis Parkes, singing with Jack Hylton's band).

The Melody Maker dance championships were held at the Rialto in the 1930s, and individual players won cups and prizes. In July 1934 the Rialtonians won the East Yorkshire Dance Band Contest at the Spa Hall in Bridlington for the second year in succession. They received a silver cup, to be kept permanently, a banner and a gold and silver medal for each member of the band. The judges were Matheson Brook, Dan Ingham and Con Lamprecht. Four out of the six prizes for best individual players (each receiving a 'wristlet watch') were won

The Rialtonians at the East Yorkshire Dance Band Championships 1938. The photo includes - Pete Harrison, bass, Jack Potter, drums, George Bennett, guitar, Eric Betts, piano, Jock Grant, baritone sax, Len Cundall, sax and band leader, being presented with the cup, Curly Cowell, trumpet, Bob Ashton, tenor sax, Hugh Robertson, trombone, George Smith, alto sax, Derek Dunning, alto sax. *(Courtesy Hilda Bennett)*

by George Barnes (piano), Les 'Curly' Cowell (trumpet), Jock Grant (saxophone) and Jack Potter (drums).

Elated by their success, the Rialtonians visited London in August 1934 to record some of their songs at Octocross Records. A York girl, Peggy Inglis, accompanied them and sang one of the vocal choruses. Ursula Greville, director of the gramophone company, prophesied a future in opera for Peggy. She told Mr Prendergast, who accompanied the orchestra, that he had discovered 'a natural singer'. Through this meeting, Peggy was promised a small part in Covent Garden opera in 1935 if she would go to London for tuition. The Rialtonians were congratulated on making six records under trying conditions. They were in a soundproof studio from 9.30am to 7.30pm and the place was very warm. The numbers were A Thousand Goodnights, Jealousy, Dancing In The Moonlight, Riding Around In The Rain, Madonna Mine and Speak To Me Of Love. They were billed as 'J Prendergast and the Rialtonians', with Mr Prendergast as director, and the rest of the band listed as Les Cowell, Hugh Robertson, Oliver Winder, George Robson, George Barnes, Len Cundall and Jack Potter, with Peggy Inglis on vocals. They were the only York dance band ever to record commercially. They had already recorded I Can't Give You Anything But Love and Sympathetic Smile with Kitty Kelly. The band's career continued and they played regularly at the Rialto as well as the Assembly Rooms. In 1938 they entered their third national competition, and George Bennett, a fairly new member, won an individual award for guitar. The reviewer stated, 'Using the unusual instrumentation of four rhythm and three brass against one alto sax, this band can compliment itself on the way it prevented the sax from being overpowered without any loss of dynamics or tonal brilliance from the brass, or suggestion that it was having to play down to keep under the one sax. This result was achieved by skilful employment of harmonies'.

May Queen's Dance poster, Exhibition Buildings 1936. Featuring Jack Bartley and His Band, and the Rialtonians.
(Courtesy Christine Lancaster)

George Bennett's wife Hilda recalls:

It was a musical family, his father played the violin, his sister played the piano, George played the guitar. He was in the Rialtonians from being 17 and he later played the double bass. There were special dances like the Boxing morning dance from 12.15 to 4am.

My husband's good friend was Len Cundall. I heard from his mother that Len used to come and pick him up in this sports car and away they'd go, his white scarf flying in the wind. It was great for him. That was his life, music and the Rialtonians. I remember when they broadcast from the De Grey Rooms in 1941, we stood outside and listened. A man called Gordon Reed, he played at the Hammersmith Palais in London, and he came down to York. Jack Stone was in the air force and all these army fellas came along, they were all professional players and wanted to play somewhere, and they all came to the De Grey Rooms. [The broadcast in November was of York City Police Concert Band and included Bob Halford, Bert Keech, Will Acton, Derek Dunning, George Bennett, Sid Dale, and other friends and extra musicians].

The Rialtonians and friends off duty. George Bennett is third from left on back row, and George Robson, far right on front row. *(Courtesy Hilda Bennett)*

Len Edwards Band, Terry's Ballroom c1930. L to R - Jack Potter (drums), Les Cowell, Oliver Winder, Len Cundall (bass), George Robson and George Barnes.

(Courtesy Mary Cundall)

Norman Henderson who was born in 1908, was at university with George Barnes, pianist for the Rialtonians:

He had formed a band whilst he was at Nunthorpe School with Len Cundall, Jack Potter and Curly Cowell and it was known as the Len Edwards Orchestra. [Len Cundall's middle name was Edward]. But later they became associated with Oliver Winder who was billed as Oliver Winder And His Saxes. Oliver's father was a partner with Jack Prendergast, the owner of the Rialto, so eventually these lads became the Rialtonians with others added later.

They formed a jazz band when they were at Nunthorpe and they even played for dances for the scholars in the late 1920s. They went to Russells cycle shop in Clifford Street. I remember buying records there around the early 1930s.

I think I got these lads their first job, it would be 1931, 'cos I'd gone to Archbishop Holgate's Grammar School and the Old Boys were having a dance and I went to buy the ticket and happened to say to the person who was running the dance, 'Who's your dance band?' He says, 'I don't know. I've been let down'. I said, 'I think I can do something for you'. So I immediately went round to see George Barnes and said, 'Can you provide an orchestra for a dance?' 'Certainly'. Six men, 3/6d an hour for six hours, eight till two. I think that was the first commercial dance they did. So it progressed from there.

When I became a head teacher of Fishergate Evening Institute, I used to run dances there in the school hall once a month from 1937. You had your students and they brought their pals in. We were always pretty well filled up. I had to pay the band and the caretaker of the school for looking after it. And I got a band called the Metronomes, Charlie Tennant on the drums, Dick Mawtus was piano and I ran a dance from seven till ten and I paid the band 30 bob.

Jack Potter who played drums with the Rialtonians, and later with the Assembly Players, spent some years playing for musical productions for Rowntree youth club. Clary Clay went on to play piano in many York venues and became an arranger for musical societies in York and Hartlepool where he moved later in life. The trombonist was Hugh Robertson and, after serving in the war, he opened his own music shop in Pavement in 1946.

Charlie Druggitt who played with Eric Gill and the Georgians, recalls:

I went on saxophone in 1931. He came to the Rialto, Coleman Hawkins, and after that, I decided I wanted to play. I was taught by a Mr Temple, somewhere down Heworth. I'd go once a week then practise on my own. Coleman was my idol, I thought he was a marvellous style. I went and asked him about different reeds but he said 'Oh, any old reed, any old reed'. I was playing in a dance band when I was about 17, and then I started with Eric, with little jobs, and gradually built up until we got better jobs. There was Wilf Whitwell, Reg Cooper

Dick Mawtus And His Metronomes, with Dick Mawtus on piano. 1930s.

(Courtesy Judith Carr)

played violin, Chick Ward on bass, Eric on piano, and Arthur Berriman on trumpet. We played all over York. But mainly Rowntree's. My first sax was a Selmer, and then I went on to a Con. Then I finished up with Pan American, that was the last one I had. I didn't go on clarinet, I went on soprano, it was handier.

Eric Gill was very strict. He was a marvellous pianist but if you didn't get that right, you'd had your chips. Eric was our regular singer but I sang occasionally. When I was young, of course, young and in my prime. You went to the pictures, and you came back singing, what had been on, you'd enjoyed it, the tunes were absolutely fantastic. We had some marvellous times. You know the Bluecoats School, we'd play for them when they had a party. Later on we played all over the place, and put extra men in on trombones and made it a bigger ensemble all round. It was a lovely, lovely time, and then the war came, 1939, and I was called up.

I'll tell you this much, the time I've had as regards playing, I've enjoyed every minute of it. I've been at work while eight o'clock, gone from eight 'till 12 and done a job somewhere. Our signature tune was Dancing In The Dark, start off with it, finish off with it, after your last waltz. There's something about the music we played that you'll never forget.

Charlie's brother-in-law Freddie Graysmark started playing in 1935:

Ray Archer and the Modernists 1935. Back - Freddie Graysmark, drums, Ray Archer, piano. Front - Billy Steel, Ossie Moffatt, Stan Archer.

Freddie Graysmark on drums. 1935.
(Courtesy Freddie Graysmark)

I lived at Huntington Road, and there was a chap near us, and he worked at the Empire in the pit. Drummer. He only charged 7/6d. a lesson, so I thought it would be interesting to learn to play. It was Dick Tomes, great chap. I was about 17 and then I bought my first set of drums, it took a lot of doing, I had to buy them on hire purchase. Ray Archer was grand, he had a marvellous quiff of hair and he was a great pianist. He lived at Avenue Terrace, Clifton, and I just heard about it and went to see him, and I was lucky, he invited me in, and it was a five-piece band, Ray Archer And The Modernists. There were little jobs that we did round York.

This was in the days before people had cars, and Freddie recalls that his father:

had a carrier bike for the butcher's shop, so I'd to put the two cases at the front, cycle to the ruddy job from Wilton Rise to Clifton, and I had me bass drum on the back.

The band would practise over the shop. Freddie's sister, Doreen (who is the wife of Charlie Druggitt) remembers:

Our sitting room was over the shop, it was a big room, and they got permission from the police, which you had to do in those days, for 'em to practise. It was once in three weeks, something like that, and all the band'd go up there. I played the piano, and all the kids outside would be in the street dancing.

Like many others, Freddie was called up, but he managed to continue playing during the war:

The RAF promised to pay for me drums going over, in 1940 when I got called up, and so we formed a little five-piece band over in Belfast and, of course, we entertained the officers, sergeants, and other ranks. They wanted somebody to be on the square, they hadn't got a drummer, so there was about a thousand men on the square and every morning you had to be there first thing on this little podium and they gave you a drum so I went and I got threepence a day extra for that. And a badge as well.

Tony Lister and Irene Deane giving demonstration at Rialto Ballroom. Tony Lister was MC at the Rialto. He had been to London to be coached by M. Pierre and qualified as a teacher of dancing. Yorkshire Evening Press October 1933.
(Courtesy of City of York Library)

I got a nice set of drums, £36. And a marvellous cymbal it was. Lovely, made in Turkey. You could play on any kit, but that one just suited my style and everything was handy, the high hat cymbal at the side for the left foot and the snare drum and your temple blocks.

A concert at St. George's Hall in aid of film trade charities in the late 1930s featured Ray Archer And The Modernists as well as the Rialtonians augmented orchestra, led by Len Cundall, who 'presented a jam session in typical style and featured special numbers for Reg Ingle, Hugh Robertson, Nell Robinson and 11 year old Joyce Barbour. Bill Richardson played both the accordion and the piano in great style. With him in an effective two piano cocktail was Eric Betts'.

In January 1935 the newspapers were advertising afternoon tea dances at the Rialto, and later the GPO Workers Great Novelty Dance, with waltz and foxtrot competitions and dancing from 8pm to 2am for the sum of 2/-. Another dance that month, this time at the Exhibition Buildings, catered for 1500 people, dancing to Norman Holmes's Dance Band and a special accordion band. In October a dance at the Folk Hall, New Earswick, to Ted Rowell's band, had 'the two Leslies' - Leslie Sarony and Leslie Holmes - judging a ladies' ankle competition and at Acomb Adult School Tony Lister held a series of dances as well as continuing private lessons in ballroom dancing at the Creamery Restaurant.

Wallace Rockett (known as Wally) was one of the few musicians in the York area to 'hit the big time'. He was the youngest of three brothers, and was born in Selby in 1918. His brothers Barry and John were nearly ten years older than him and became top quality musicians running bands on the continent through the 1930s. Both of their parents had been amateur musicians and ran their own dance band with two violins. John, who played banjo and piano, and Barry, who played violin and saxophone, were both classically trained, but Wally was self-taught. He played his first musical engagement on the piano at the age of nine in Selby in a family group and after that he played the drums at the age of 13 for a short time in the Baths Hall, Selby, with the rest of his family, but his first official gig was at the Rialto in 1932 when he was 14.

As well as playing the piano, he graduated to violin and saxophone but then specialised in clarinet, and it was on this instrument that he later made his name. When he left school he played sax with a Selby band, the Melodians, and from there he joined a band in Leeds playing saxophone, violin, clarinet and xylophone. His brothers were very impressed with his progress and invited him to play on tour in Europe and on the cruise liners. He returned to tour England and formed his own band in Eastbourne at the age of 21. He was about to sign a contract to take his band to the Prince's Restaurant in the West End of London when war broke out and so he joined the army. At the end of the war he was able to join Harry Roy's band. He also studied music theory at the London College of Music. He played with the Harry Parry Sextet where he stayed for two years before he left to form his own band again in

Wally Rockett and Orchestra accompanying Pearl Bailey 1950. *(Courtesy Michael Cole)*

the mid 1940s. He recalled 'We passed the BBC audition and then oh boy, did that phone ring'. He went on to play at some of London's most exclusive West End clubs and restaurants. One of his favourite jobs was as musical director at the American club headquarters at Winfield House in London, the former home of millionairess Barbara Hutton. After an engagement playing for Princess Margaret's birthday, he recalled:

'I did a lot of touring with the band, including Windsor Castle. I played quite a few wrong notes here and there, and the Queen had a quiet look at me, but being from Selby I just pressed on. If it was good enough for Selby baths, it was good enough for Windsor Castle'.

In 1956 Wally returned to Selby, having given up music and turned to his second love, that of painting.

During the 1930s national accordion bands became a new attraction, with many band leaders touring the country. The most famous was probably Primo Scala And His Accordion Band (one of the pseudonyms of Harold Bidgood). One of the few female musicians at this time in York was Molly Robinson:

We were the youngest accordion band in England and we were called the Six Minor Chords. There was Dennis Cussins, whose father was Cussins and Lights,

Five of the Six Minor Chords. L to R - Dennis Cussins, Marjorie Harrison, Jackie Bosomworth, Molly Burley (later Robinson), Roy Fowlston. *(Courtesy Molly Robinson)*

there was my cousin Marjorie Harrison, Jackie Bosomworth whose father was a butcher on Heslington Road, then Roy Fowlston and Ray Bardy, two cousins. We used to play regularly at the Co-op children's Christmas party. We were only kids ourselves and we were too young to be paid so we would get a box of chocolates occasionally, if we were lucky. Some were elaborate, expensive boxes, some were a box of Black Magic, a little quarter-pounder. But maybe the music mistress would get paid, you see.

I started off playing the piano when I was seven and my music teacher taught me for about six months and then she went off ill and died so I never touched the piano again till I was about ten. This piano teacher, Mrs Griffiths, to get music into me she'd sit with a ruler at the keyboard and I used to catch it pretty regular, so it went in hard. But she did get me through, I think I sat two exams, and one I passed with honours. And because I'd done well she persuaded my father to buy an accordion and she would teach me within a year and so I was 12 when I really went out with the band.

We had about two years of it, going various places. The height of ambition, we played at the Albert Hall at Leeds. We played many times at Rowntree Theatre, and in the workhouse. That was comical. We were told we were going to play for some children but it was at the workhouse, we couldn't fathom that out. When we got there, there was old ladies sat there knitting, twiddling little things round and they're all a bit cuckoo. But we enjoyed it, we went back two or three times and had a really good night. They really appreciated us going. And then after that we'd get taken round the back and you know the meat plates you see in farmhouses hung up, there'd be an enormous plate like that of potted meat sandwiches, and a big enamel jug of cocoa, that was our reward.

Kathy Butler was one of Mrs Griffiths' pupils in the senior band and then Kath broke away and she developed her own band and played a lot of dances in and around York, under Kathy And Her Millionaires. In something like 1936 [for the new King's accession], we went to many NAAFIs that day, or street parties, some were in the halls and some were in the street.

Accordion music is easier to read, 'cos you've only really one hand to read. You're supposed to read the other hands, but when you've got it in your ears you know which chord goes with which. I did find that the accordion helped me to play the piano an awful lot, because frankly, I have a good ear for music. You see accordion is chords. When you press one button you get three or four notes into making the chord, so if I played that and that, it was same as playing say a G on the accordion and put the right hand to it, and I was away.

I went to Leeds with me dad, and we collected Marjorie's and mine from a place that sold accordions and harps. Ours were new. They weren't cheap, those were £80. But then when we got the bigger ones, I think mine was about £120, but one of 'em was second hand, and I think it was the bigger one. The king accordion, was a Ranco, and I always wanted a Ranco, and I did play one in t'middle of Layerthorpe. There was a second hand shop there, and it was a friend of mine that ran it, and I went in to say hello one day, he says, 'Come here, I've got sommat for you, there's an accordion there. Give us a tune', and there's me stood in there playing. It was a Ranco, but I couldn't afford it then

There isn't a comfortable one to hold. The thing we got the bigger one for mainly, it had what they called a coupler on it, and you could play the same note, but an octave higher. Some have a double coupler on that you can play an octave higher or an octave lower. You don't really consider the weight when you're buying 'em. I hate to see somebody with about 20 buttons, because that's only a little accordion, with a little keyboard, and I think, 'Well, you silly so and so, you'll never play that'. A lot of people have 40.

You've got to have a certain size, and I think about 80 is the least you can have in size, to get a suitable keyboard to play. But if you get 120 you can more or less play anything. I tell you who I started following, we had some Charlie Kunz records, and I liked his rhythm. So I modelled my playing on Charlie Kunz, and I got away with it. I have little musical concerts in me head. One of my bosses said later, 'You never put wireless on in this car Molly'. I said 'No, I don't need the wireless on in me car, I've got one in me head'. I listen to the music, not really knowing that I'm listening, but that tune will go in.

I have a tendency to play it just as I've heard it, not what the music says, or anything like that. If I can't get it in me ear, I can't play it. But if I've got that rhythm, and I get it in me ear, I'm away, I can play it. Me fingers sort of do it instinctively. We have a Chet Atkins record, I daren't play it, it's fatal. I can't sit still, and I'm bouncing about, even on me own, and I notice that my fingers are going on to what would be the notes, of what's being played, not tapping me hand, me fingers are going, so that's how I play.

My mum used to make our clothes. The music mistress wanted us in trousers with the flare at the side, we did eventually get that, but my mother made the dresses. She was a good dressmaker, she felt that white was a bit plain and ordinary so there would be a bit of red on those dresses. And we had matching shoes, matching socks, matching bows, and we had nice tiaras on, an auntie bought us those, but while we were at the workhouse, somebody pinched mine. The hats were from the music mistress, she provided those. The lads were in blue satin shirts, fluffy shirts, more a blouse thing, fastened up to the neck.

Doug Green Band. Clifton Cinema Ballroom, c1950. L to R - Bobby Ward, Arthur Burcombe, Doug Green and Albert Jackson.

Several new bands appeared around this time, with the Blues at St Lawrence's Hall, the Broadway Revels Band in Wigginton, the Embassy dance band at the Bell Farm social hall and Bob Mason and his Piccadilly Music Weavers appearing in Osbaldwick. According to local historian Syd Heppell, the leader Bob and his brother Bill lived and rehearsed in St George's Terrace, Piccadilly. Bob asked Syd to play the bass fiddle but Syd confessed he was not musical, saying, 'The only way you're gonna get me in your band is if I play piano and you put the handle on the outside'. After the war Bob moved to Seaton Ross and took the licence of the Blacksmith's Arms, which later became the Bomber's Arms, as many of the airmen used it as their local during the war. In the 1960s, Bill Mason and his nephew Ken, would play music again. (See volume two).

In 1938 ballroom dancing took place every Tuesday night at the Tudor café in Davygate, and even the hall in Alma Terrace held a carnival night with spot prizes and a crooning competition! Many firms formed their own bands to play for functions, like the Postonians Dance Orchestra who played at the post office dance at the Albany.

Arthur Burcombe remembers:

I was in Harry Warrington's Strict Tempo Band. We played two nights a week at the Co-op, it was always packed. The roughest place I know was the Clifton Ballroom. They'd get a bus load in from Walmgate, and they got the police in. Turfed them all out and as soon as they came out, they came in the back way round again. We'd been jumped off the stage, had to stop 'em fighting on the floor. I think they went for a fight, they liked it. The girls would jump on the stairs, screaming and enjoying it. They quietened it in the end, and nobody would go. They said 'I'm not coming here, dead place'!'

Arthur often played at Acomb Church Hall before the war and during it:

The band there used to go for a drink at the interval and forget to come back so we got the job! My two nephews would come and see us there and they once had a little note which my missus had given them to take to the butchers. It had written on it 'bits for the dog'. They handed the note to Hugh Robertson and said, 'Will you do this?' and he thought it was a request for a song! He was proper put out!

We had a trumpet player, he was very good but if anybody came up and touched the microphone, oh 'Spoiling my solo', so keen. Everything had to be just so! And if there's a part and it hadn't much melody in the trumpet, 'I'm not playing that'. I said, 'What's up with it? It's all music, it's part of the show, like a pattern, you don't have wiggly things all over, you have plain things'.

Just after the war bands seemed to go barmy, four or five saxes belting it. Before the war it was gentler. They've got mouthpieces to play louder more easily but they sound hard. However good a saxophone is, if it has a bad mouthpiece, it's bad. And the reed is important, it has to suit.

There was a dancing school wanting some records to do a little bit of demonstration so we went to Cussins and Lights and it was wax records. We played a tango and a quickstep, about four or five of us, and when it was made they said we could buy one if we liked. 'What, paying for your own record? You can keep your record'. But the dancing class used to use it, it had the right number of bars and it was made for the job, it came over nice.

Arthur Burcombe played bass fiddle and banjo, but he enjoyed playing viola:

The music I liked best was theatre work, in the pit and you could play all the fancy bits, and then you could see the show and get paid for it as well. I played for amateur shows and some of the professional shows.

To play in the pit at the theatre, musicians had to be members of the Musicians' Union, which was beneficial as the union ensured that the proper rate for the job was given. Lots of people say, 'Oh music it's nothing, it's not a job' and want you for nothing. But you got the full rates when you played theatres. That means the best men will get the job, which they deserve.

Clarice Tudor, neé Turner, worked in music hall with her two sisters, Doris and Phyllis. In 1934 the sisters opened a dance studio in York:

We called ourselves the Three Graces. It was Nat Day, that booked us in London, he gave us the name, he must have thought he could book us at that and so we stuck to it. We used to travel

The Three Graces, Leeds, 1920s. L to R - Phyllis, Clarice Turner, and Doris at the front.
(Courtesy Clarice Tudor, neé Turner)

The Three Graces, London 1932. L to R - Doris, Clarice and Phyllis Turner.

(Courtesy Clarice Tudor)

everywhere. We had a 12-minute act, different dances and we sang a bit. We did character dancing, kicking and singing point numbers like I Want A Little Boy To Fall In Love With Me. We did cabaret too as well, we'd go to the Connaught Rooms in London and dance at dinners. We played at the Empire, one show was with Jimmy Jewell.

Once we were waiting for a train to go to Scotland for a show and we didn't know our way to the station, so we followed the tram lines. And when we got there, one of the station men was sorry for us. It was the middle of the night and he brought us a pillow and made us comfortable in one of the waiting rooms. Once we went to sleep, we put our hair in curlers and when we woke up there was a cup of tea for each of us and people would be standing on the platform 'cos they hadn't got a seat 'cos we were lying on it.

We got all our bookings through an agent. Ten per cent we had to pay them and when we were not doing very well, some tourers said to us, 'Well girls do you put any money in the envelope when you send your dates that you want?' We said that we paid ten per cent commission. 'Oh you want to put a bit of money in for the girl that opens the letter'. We learnt all these things as we went along. You had to put the money in and not to mention it, so some person wouldn't throw your envelope away. But we earned really rather a lot of money, about £20 a week for the three of us though we used to take £16 sometimes. I remember going to Ireland and they wanted us to stay another week and we thought it was lovely because they gave us £20 to stay another week. We used to earn more money than the average girl.

Once the dance studio was opened in Clifford Street, the dancers would do their performances in the Empire. Our studio was across the road and we would dress in the studio and then a policeman would come and see us across the road. We'd pack the Empire. I think we were the first theatre dancing school in York. We taught tap and ballet and the dances you see on the stage. And ballroom. I'd have the gentlemen, my younger sister Doris taught the women. Then we had cabaret class and we taught tap. We taught Isobel Dunn. She came in slippers.

I took most of the acrobatic classes, high kicking and stage dancing, and Doris used to teach the ballet. She was a beautiful dancer and I had to kill myself to do what she did. I wasn't so good but I earned my living with her as a sister turn and my eldest sister Phyllis who'd do the business. For stage dancing we'd have anybody that came. I think we could have up to 20 but we had some private pupils that came specially on their own. We had a class of little ones that would sit down and kick. We had them from three. If they paid weekly the cabaret class was 1/6d but when they paid termly it was 25/-. I didn't like teaching ballroom but we did do, especially during the war. We used to use records, we couldn't afford a pianist then.

Fred Kell became conductor of the Empire Orchestra on its opening night in 1902 and was still playing lead violin in the 1930s. The Empire was the second music hall in England to be heard over the air. Fred's elder son Reginald Kell took up the clarinet and went on to become professor at the Royal Academy of Music, whereas his younger son Alwyn toured as principal clarinet with the Junior London Philharmonic Orchestra and later the London Symphony Orchestra before losing his life in the Second World War. Reg Kell went over to America where he became tutor to Benny Goodman for classical music on clarinet. As well as the full Empire Orchestra, Fred also conducted the Clarilyn Sextette (named after his house in Dringhouses) which played light music in the intervals, and comprised of five stringed instruments and a clarinet. In 1938 alone he wrote more than 300 sheets of music. He retired in 1946. From 1919 to 1930 he had also run a Royal British Legion military band in York which competed in national band competitions in Manchester and came in the first three every year for ten years.

Trevor Bousfield, one of the York 'trumpet twins', says:

Reginald Kell was probably the finest musician to have originated from York. He was an international clarinettist whose records with the London orchestras and in particular the New York Philharmonic Orchestra are now collectors' items. He died in 1981 aged 75, and no one had heard him perform for 22 years, having spent his early years with the finest orchestra in the world. He was born at Bishopthorpe Road and was mostly self taught with the help of his father Frederick, the York Symphony Orchestra conductor 1932-5.

As well as the plethora of dance bands in this era, there were other types of popular music, not necessarily for dancing. Wilf Bannister who was born in 1916 played banjo in York from the mid 1930s:

I bought a little George Formby banjo, I used to try singing those songs, but I wanted one with a bit more range. I found with a big banjo you could play the melody and the accompaniment, whereas the George Formby banjo was just for accompaniment to vocals. I got an old second hand one, and I found I was doing very well on it. I heard about the Banjo Club in York and I joined them about 1935 and I learnt a lot more from them. I wasn't reading music then, but I could read symbols.

They did really old songs, My Old Man Said Follow The Van, Don't Dilly Dally, that kind of thing. I used to know a kid called Ted Proud, he was already in the band, and when I got talking to him he said, 'Why don't you come and join up with us?', and I went for an audition and they realised that I didn't read music then, but they said I was very good for a second banjo. I improved quite a lot then. I used to play two or three solos.

We had quite a good time there. I think I'm the last banjoist in York now that belonged to the BMG Club [Banjo, Mandolin and Guitar Club]. There was George Spindler, Ted Ulliott, Harry Cole, Harold Taylor, he was the guitarist. And he won the DFC for missions over Germany. I used to go with him in his car to the club.

The club, a branch of the national society, practised in a pub in St Sampson's Square, but after that we started practising in the Black Horse in Monkgate, opposite York County Hospital. Later we went round York playing at the old folks' homes, seven banjoists, three mandolin players, two guitarists and a pianist. A rally was held nearly every year, at Worsley, Manchester, I think it broke up just after the war. [This was a national competition and Wilf was awarded certificates from the British Federation of Banjoists].

During the war, Wilf was on war work on Knavesmire with the rocket battery, but he still found time to play the banjo. George Spindler started up the club again in 1946. It went out of existence in 1952 but was re-formed in 1957. In 1966 membership had dwindled somewhat, most members were over 50 but their youngest member was an 11 year old girl. In 1968 the York Banjo,

York City Harmonica Band 1930s. Wilf Bannister is far right on third row from top.
(Courtesy Wilf Bannister)

67

Mandolin and Guitar Orchestra came first in a contest of the northern section of the BMG groups. There were also individual awards to some of the guitarists. The local branch was still around in the 1970s holding rallies in the Folk Hall, New Earswick.

Wilf was also a member of York Harmonica Band as a teenager. It met at the Friends' Meeting House in Clifford Street:

There was a loud speaker on the end of me harmonica. I was playing with Samuel Gawthorne in their own band. He had two daughters that played the accordion, and they were very good. They joined in with the Harmonica Band, they'd drown each other out. And this was well before I knew about the banjo. We met at the Friends' Meeting House.

The 1930s was very much the heyday in York for dance bands. During the war music would be important for different reasons, to keep up morale being one of the chief ones. The heady carefree days of the 'jazz age' were over. They would return in a different format ten years after the war ended, but that was still a long, long way away.

CHAPTER THREE. I'LL BE SEEING YOU
Wartime

In September 1939, the Second World War began. The Rialtonians Orchestra was still playing for dances at the Rialto on Wednesdays, Fridays and Saturdays, but the times had to change and dances lasted from 7pm to 9.50pm due to the blackout. Audiences were told that 'gas masks are to be brought and carried'. Many York musicians answered the country's call and went off to serve in the army, navy and air force. Many were able to join service bands in other parts of the world, and the personnel of York dance bands varied as members of armed forces stationed near the city took the opportunity to sit in with the bands.

Ben Jowett, stationed with the air force at Melbourne, recalls how York dance bands were so desperate for players that he and fellow airman and musician, Harry Zeissman, were driven back to the base after gigs. He played with Bert Keech and with Johnny Sutton at the Co-op and the Albany. He says:

When I look back it's like a dream. In York on a Saturday night, everyone who passed you seemed to be in uniform, huge amount of air force, scattering of Americans, some land girls, ATS and WRENs. The streets were milling with people, they were highly exciting times.

In the 1930s cinemas began to provide music between films with the new Wurlitzer organs, and these would take on a greater significance during the war. In March 1940 Miles Wilde became the new organist at the Regal Cinema in Piccadilly. He had been the boy organist in Alfred Wilde's York Quintet at the close of the First World War when he was 14 and his first professional engagement was playing the organ on Easter Monday 1919 at the Picture House in Coney Street. He studied under Reginald Rose, York organist and music teacher, and also played at the Tower Cinema and St George's Cinema in Castlegate. From 1927 he worked in various cinemas throughout England and was recording organist at Shepherd's Bush Studios for two years where he played the soundtracks for various films including some by Alfred Hitchcock. It was Miles who played the organ music for the lying-in-state of King George V. Although he was the Regal organist, he also played at more than 1,000 variety shows at the Rialto.

Meanwhile, the Rialto had its own organist, Edward Farley. He was the first organist at the Regal in the 1930s before moving to the Rialto. At the Regal he had buglers and drummers of all the Yorkshire regiments on the stage at one performance, and after war broke out he produced two special concerts at the

Rialto. One of these featured more than 100 members of the services. Throughout the winter of 1939-40, he played the organ every Sunday night at special concerts 'in connection with the Government's scheme of Sunday entertainment for the troops' and even played in his gas mask during one of the 'carry your masks' campaigns. Sometimes the concerts would feature big names, but often there were local entertainers, such as comedians, dancers, acrobats, musicians, and ventriloquists, each week's entertainment being billed as 'another programme to brighten the home front'.

Farley made a feature at the cinema of getting the audience to sing bright songs. During his five years at the Rialto he played 1,250 interludes, and was one of the first cinema organists to have a microphone installed and lead the audience in singing. His final event before leaving York for London in 1940 was a ball in the De Grey Rooms for the Lord Mayor's Spitfire Fund, with music played by the Aero Notes, an RAF station dance band. Four years later he returned to York to play organ at the Rialto and Clifton cinemas.

From the beginning of the war, there were weekly concerts for troops at the Melbourne Chapel Schoolrooms. Jack Buchanan, star of musical comedy and films and great friend of Jack Prendergast, also came to the Rialto in 1940 in aid of the Lord Mayor's Comforts For The Troops Fund, only days after returning from entertaining troops in France. In March 1941 the Odeon Cinema presented a concert featuring Henry Hall And His Orchestra, one of the most popular national dance bands at the time.

ENSA (the Entertainments National Service Association) did an invaluable job in taking music and entertainment all over Britain and much further afield, keeping the troops in touch with home. Concerts and dancing to big bands could help ordinary people forget for a while that they were in the middle of a huge conflict and that tomorrow a bomb might drop on their homes or their loved ones might not return from the front line. The BBC produced Music While You Work in 1940 to lift the spirits of factory workers (mostly in munitions works), and they looked forward to that time in the afternoon when the music would start. This not only kept up morale but subconsciously made the workers improve their performance. The BBC would broadcast live, with Workers' Playtime from different factory canteens at lunchtime. It was an important aid to the war effort.

Concert parties, which had been fashionable during the First World War, were formed again with performers of various ages. The Yorkshire Evening Press in October 1939 appealed for amateur talent to come forward to join concert parties and entertain the troops. A northern branch of ENSA formed a committee with the aim of having 12 different concert parties in York, providing enough volunteers to enable each group to perform once a month.

Rowntree Round-up Concert Party from Cocoa Works magazine 1947.
(Courtesy Alwyn Fletcher)

In the early part of the war, Rowntree employees had their own Rowntree Round-up Concert Party. An issue of the Cocoa Works magazine in 1947 stated that 'they played two or three times a week in all conditions, from a stage of schoolroom desks to a private theatre in a country house, at anti-aircraft and searchlight posts and military camps, and in the mobile theatre - a converted bus which usually accommodated two or three audiences per night'. The party gave about 300 performances and 'surmounted many difficulties including halls without lights, stages without stability and pianos without strings. They were at times treated royally, and on one occasion they performed the notable feat of eating fried eggs with their fingers. They made friends everywhere'. The original producer was Dennis Nicholls who eventually left for National Service, and was replaced by Mr J Watson.

Audrey Halder's mother Elsie Hornby, who was born in 1904, was taught to play the piano and then had her voice trained. Her parents encouraged her to sing when she was quite young:

and then she went into the Amateurs. As she got into her early twenties she started to sing in clubs in the Yorkshire area though at the same time she had a job. But singing was her life. Her father used to take her everywhere, he would go to all of the gigs with her and make sure that she was safe. Travelled all over, coming back after midnight on the milk train. Then war broke out, and the concert parties started. She would sing with them. They were known as the White Rose Concert Party and they all wore a badge with the white rose on. They had a bus and it was convertible, into a theatre inside. They had a stage at one end and the audience could come in and watch the show, if there wasn't a theatre or suitable venue at the air force or army bases. They would do that for charity. There were no signposts and everything was pitch dark you didn't even know where you were going, apart from the bus driver, because of the secrecy thing. You'll remember Bensons' Bikes in Goodramgate, Tommy Benson, he played the banjo, and then there were a couple of sisters called Maher, Winnie and Margaret, they were singers. There was Harold Hatfield who played the mouth organ and Nancy Barrett who was known as York's Gracie Fields. They travelled around all over the bases. I remember going to one air force base when there was a raid on and they couldn't perform obviously. Everybody just disappeared, went to man the guns and everything and we were left in this hut, it was quite scary at the time, but everybody just laughed about it. It was the Dunkirk spirit.

Valerie Mountain recalls:

I joined a concert party with Bobby Hirst. His father had the Digger-Bell Concert Party, and I used to go out with 'em entertaining troops. We had a proper bus, with a stage and a piano in the back. We'd go to ack-ack sites and army camps and get in about two in the morning, and I'd be dropping asleep at school the next day. He was a policeman was Fred, Digger Hirst, and Don Bell. I played piano for 'em. I was only 12.

They really were the best times of my life, I met some lovely people. And I was full of confidence then, I'd play for anybody when I was young. We used to have a brooch with a white rose on, VES, Voluntary Entertainment Service, Northern Command. We didn't get paid, but the experience you got was worth more than money. It was a fella called Harold Brown that drove the bus, it was just a single decker and the seats would turn round the other way because the stage was at the back. Not that we ever used it for a performance, 'cos we always went to a village hall, or an army or air force camp like Elvington.

York City Police Concert Party had started up in the spring of 1938 and gave ten concerts for charity in the winter months of 1938-9. The party initially consisted of Bob Halford, Operator Pat White, PC Brown, Engineer Butler, PC Jack Cox, Engineer Reinhard, PC Clarke, Sergeant Albert Wilkinson, PC Fred Hirst and his son Bobby, who was to become a well-known musician in York in the 1950s, but later others joined. Charles Barnard, a plain clothes policeman,

York City Police Concert Party. Yorkshire Evening Press April 1939. Back row L to R - Bob Halford, Pat White, K Brown, C Butler, Jack Cox. Seated L to R - PC Clarke, Engineer Reinhard, Audrey Thackray, Mrs Moore, Master Bobby Hirst, PC Fred Hirst.
(Courtesy City of York Library)

had a strong baritone voice which made him a keen member of the concert party. The police concert party was certainly a favourite with York audiences and during its existence, members performed for audiences ranging from six people at an ack-ack post to a thousand at an ITC gathering. One of the period's best-loved musicians came to prominence through the concert parties. Bob Halford had first played in public in 1928 and the following year he joined the Kit Kat Band at the Grand Ballroom. He also occasionally sat in with the Rialtonians. His brother Dave Halford recalls Bob's talent:

He went to the Empire and there was a competition for singers, he won that. Somebody asked him to go fulltime with a band, but he couldn't - the police you see, he wouldn't leave that. He'd go to Leeds and see bands and if there were competitions on, he'd win them. He sang like Webster Booth. Sometimes he'd take me with him. We had a car between us, a Ford 8, with the wheel at the back. We went to Butlins, Ken Brown, him and me, at Skegness. Al Bowlly was there singing. There was another one there, Mantovani. Him and Ken Brown played Bob and I at table tennis. Bob could have gone there, he could have got a job as a red coat.

Girls would say to me, 'Can you get me a date with your brother?' I used to say, 'No, I can't'. And in the Assembly Rooms, one of the girls in the bar was always after him. He was in the band playing, and she'd say, 'Get me a date with your Bob'. He was such a good singer you see. They went round doing these concert parties, monologues were popular and they went to dinners, Frank Dobson, Jack Cox and Bob. When Bob was singing, we thought it was great because we were getting free drinks all night! They used to perform, get on the piano with Bob singing, and me sitting watching and having a drink with them. He was a good singer, a crooner.

Bob actually began singing when he was young, as his widow Jean Halford explains:

Bob and Dave had learnt to play banjos and Bob then began singing 'cos it was really singing that he was most interested in. He joined one or two choirs and then got interested in the band scene and taught himself the saxophone and the first gig he did was at Appleton Roebuck and he went on the back of somebody's motorbike so he thought he'd 'arrived'. He was not more than 17 then.

Police Concert Party 1941. L to R - Ken Brown, Bob Halford, Charles Butler.
(Courtesy Jean Halford)

He got into the Assembly Players and they were doing a lot of work. Although he was on the police, he used to manage when he was on shifts to work it so that he could play, which didn't actually do him an awful lot of good to be honest, but he liked it so much that he did it. He actually ran the Assembly Players, did all the bookings for them, but he played with anybody, they all did, if Doug Green wanted somebody he'd go, and they all mixed up together. They played at New Earswick the longest, it was a very good time, a lot of years. And it was packed every Saturday night. Jack Potter, Eric Betts, George Smith and Clary Clay. They were all good but Clary Clay was exceptional 'cos he could play anything, anytime, anywhere, just sit down and play anything you wanted.

Bob modelled himself on different people at different times, Bing Crosby was one. He was very popular and he used to compere as well with the dances, and sing, and tell jokes. He was playing virtually every night. People would say 'I don't know how you can stick it when he's out all the time', but it didn't bother me because I knew that he wanted to play. And I wanted him to play. He just loved being out in the scene. But he didn't want to play at home. So he wasn't what you might call a dedicated musician at heart but he did love music and when he couldn't do it anymore, I don't know whether that did have anything to do with his illness but you can imagine.

I didn't know him when he was 18, he'd get up on the stage and go in for these competitions singing and the only thing he did was have a record and sing along with one of the famous singers, learn it that way and then go and sing, and he had a good voice. He must have been very extrovert really. He was a bit of a heart-throb at one time and knew it. He was big-headed in a way but he was so nice with it that you could take it.

Running a band was not always easy:

Bob was electrocuted one night! With a microphone. I think it was at Earswick. He was knocked to the floor with it but he was all right afterwards. I can remember times when somebody couldn't come at the last minute, and then, 'Oh terrible' because most of the people who were good were playing so if you were left at the last minute without anybody it was a disaster. And there was a wonderful pianist but not reliable and Bob used to say that musical talent is like a lot of talents, it drops on anybody, and if you're not reliable, you do all right for yourself but you're no good for band work.

Bob Carter also played with the Assembly Players on clarinet and saxophone. He was a nurse at Clifton Hospital for most of his working life until he retired in 1975. He was in the hospital dance band and was very interested in choral music and sang bass in the choir as well as playing the organ for both St Luke's Church in Clifton and the hospital chapel.

In December 1939, Kathy (Butler) And Her Millionaires appeared at the Rialto and Kathy sang and led her band. During the war there was more opportunity for women musicians to play in dance bands, like the nationally known Ivy Benson and her all-woman band. Kathy was given the chance to take centre stage and play at many local dance halls in the city.

She went on to be involved with various aspects of showbusiness - television, variety, summer seasons, revues, cabarets and pantomime. She was a recording artist for Doric Music and later she and Claud Morris ran Doric Music from their home in Green Dykes Lane.

Other musicians started out with Kathy, such as Bobby Hirst, and Eddie Lamb, drummer and leader of the Ambassadors dance band at the Albany dance hall, who began his musical career with Kathy's accordion band before the war:

The drummer, a lad called Falconer, was leaving to join the RAF. Somebody said there was a job going so I applied and I was with Kathy for a couple of years. We played cinemas, the Rialto, the Regent, anywhere. I wasn't crazy about accordion bands, there isn't enough tone contrast, as opposed to reeds and trumpets but you got a background of playing with a group. She was very popular in York was Kathy.

I remember being a kid in Hull and getting a biscuit tin and turning it upside down and putting nails on top of the tin and getting two pieces of firewood and playing drums on the floor there, sounds ridiculous, but it worked. I used to listen to all the big bands on radio, Ambrose, Geraldo. (Much later I was at Caesar's Palace when I was drumming there and Ted Ray the comedian asked how did I get interested in drums. I used to listen to Maxie Bacon the drummer with Ambrose. I said I thought the world of him and a few nights later Ted Ray called me into his dressing room and he said 'There's somebody I'd like you to meet' and behind the door was Maxie Bacon. That's the kind of fellow Ted Ray was).

I used to go for lessons a couple of times a week to the drummer in the pit orchestra at the Empire and he taught me reading. He was a very good drummer, and to improve the reading I joined a brass band. I played cornet but I used the brass band as a means of improving my reading.

George Roberts and I played at the Albany during the interval when the band took their break, him on piano, me on drums, and eventually the drummer left the Albany. They asked me if I would go there and I did and stayed 15 years.

Eddie Lamb singing at the Albany in the 1940s, with Eric Dawson on sax.
(Courtesy Eddie Lamb)

George believed in a Sunday morning rehearsal and we met Eddie Thompson, a tenor sax player, in King's Square and he said, 'Have you heard we're at war with Germany?' Charles Atkinson, who bought the Albany in 1942 said he inherited a dance hall, all the crockery and café paraphernalia and a drummer. I stayed with him until I went south in 1955 and we became great friends.

Other nationalities starting coming in, you'd get the French from Elvington, you'd get the Canadians, but there wasn't any trouble in those days. Just after I left in 1955 was when all the fights started in the dance halls. It never happened while we were there. Everybody was out for a good time. Originally we were alto, tenor, trumpet, piano, bass and drums. But we built it up until we had three saxes, three brass, piano, bass and drums. In fact on occasion we'd have four saxes. We did introduce a gimmick which I pinched from a band in Rochdale, what they called a bike race. They would pick all the slow foxtrots from the Top 20 and just play one chorus of each. Everybody was dancing round, singing their hearts out because they knew the tunes. That was very popular. Most of the musicians there were in reserved occupations. I worked for the Air Ministry at Cooke, Troughton and Simms, I was a member of the Aeronautical Inspections Departments. We'd be working 7.30 in the morning to 7.30 at night, and then you'd have 30 minutes to get home, change into evening dress, and get to the Albany, quite fast.

Dance bands and dance halls played a vital part particularly in a garrison town like York with aerodromes and camps springing up all around it. They caught the bus into York and came to the dance halls. Mondays at the Albany were medium but all the other nights were absolutely jam-packed, they'd be queuing to get in. I think it was licensed to hold 400 and it was the best dance floor in York, and if you walked across it when nobody was in, the floor actually sprang.

It was our job to keep them happy so we always thought that when they left, a happy crowd left, which is why there was no bother, it was desperately

The Ambassadors at the Albany. Eddie Lamb on drums, Bob Halford second from left, Bob Carter, far right.

(Courtesy Jean Halford)

important. And we'd get visiting musicians, and members of the forces and you always had to keep up a certain number in the band, shuttling people about all the time. Morale was very important. Then when somebody's drummer was ill or on holiday, they'd say, 'Can you do next Tuesday?' which was our night off from the Albany. I played with most musicians in York I think. I played with Bert Keech once at the Retreat for their annual do.

Dickie Bailey was a character off stage but on stage he was a very professional musician. He played everything except drums and bass, and was highly intelligent apart from being technically superb. For instance he would bring a euphonium, because he always played in a brass band as well, and play euphonium in a slow number, against three or four saxes and the sound was breathtaking. Whoever thought of putting euphonium against three or four saxes, only Dickie!

I think now they get wound up with this throbbing beat all night in clubs and when they come out they're still wound up. Instead of calm, relaxed and happy like we used to send them home.

The big band stuff was disciplined, and classical is disciplined music but this stuff that goes on now is a reflection of our times, bang, bang, bang, no discipline in it. And bebop, they turned a lot of chords on their blinking head, you got augmented 11s. Who the hell ever heard of an augmented 11? You'd have your band built up into tiers, that's tiers not tears, and your saxes then your trumpets then your trombones, and right at the top was the drummer. We had a very big band at the Royal Hall in Harrogate one night and I was right at the top. I was above but near to Dickie Bailey and I kept looking at Dickie because his chair was getting near to the back edge of the dias he was sitting on. I was getting very anxious but we'd disciplined the band whenever an instrumentalist was taking his solo, that the band looked at him which focused the audience's attention to that particular musician. We were playing American Patrol and I'm worrying about Dickie and when it came to the drum break, I edged back and I fell flat on my back on the stage about 12 feet below and there was all the band focused looking at the drummer who wasn't there. And I was lying screaming with laughter on my back.

Charles Atkinson ran the Albany Ballroom in the 1940s and 1950s, and gave dancing lessons and demonstrations of ballroom dancing. He actually became acting Wing Commander with No 4 Group Bomber Command of the RAF during the Second World War. Eddie had a good working relationship with Charles:

Eddie Lamb & His Music at RAF dance 1940s. Eddie Lamb, drums, Bobby Hirst, piano,
Derek Dunning, alto, Derek Mackfall, trumpet, Phil Jackson, bass.

(Courtesy Derek Mackfall)

*When I first joined it was called the Ambassadors. Then when Charles took over
he said, 'Why don't you call it Eddie Lamb & His Music?' so I did. I turned pro
at the Albany because it became very stressful working five nights a week. There
was a lot to do. And rehearse Sunday mornings half past ten to half past twelve.*

*We had ties on at the Albany, always. A bit more casual if we were at some
station, air force or army, but always at the Albany it was evening dress. When
I left in 1955, bebop was just coming in, which I blame for destroying the big
band thing, the average public couldn't understand bebop. I think that's what
pushed them back to the simple rock 'n' roll three chords stuff. Some musician
once described it as the three chord trick, simple music, because they'd been
completely baffled by bebop.*

*It was strict tempo dancing, maybe 34 bars a minute for a slow foxtrot and we
once held the area star championship at the Albany where the professionals
came and danced from the various regions. You always started with a
quickstep, a foxtrot, modern waltz, repeated that, stick a tango in, or a rumba,
and always traditionally finished with the last waltz. And that would be my
band's signature tune, The Whippoorwill Song. We're Poor Little Lambs Who've
Lost Their Way. We used to do the odd comic number to keep the people
entertained, always in strict dance time. I remember one night, I was doing*

George Formby Concert Party at Express Theatre in Lille, France. March 1940. Harry Warrington on far right. *(Courtesy Liz Calpin)*

April Showers, and I had a hose pipe stuck down my trousers and coming out of my leg into a bucket at the back and one of the musicians when I was singing would get a funnel, stick it in the top of the hosepipe and pour water into it and one night the hosepipe didn't hit the bucket and it fused all the lights on the stage and Charles Atkinson's brother, the disciplinarian, was not amused.

I used to do a number Papa Do, and Dickie was the biggest punster in the world, and I announced it one night and Dickie said 'Where the hell's Papa Do?' but one night instead of finishing on a long note for two bars, I did a bit of ad libbing, and Dickie played harmony with my ad libbing. He'd never heard it before, that's a marriage of musicians.

Some people went further afield with ENSA like Harry Warrington. On March 6, 1940, he left England for Calais with a concert party touring France, headed by George Formby. Luggage was restricted and it had to be deposited and registered the previous day at the Theatre Royal in Drury Lane. Harry was accompanied by three others from York - Dorothy Beamer, Henry Wheeler and Guy Masheeder. Their luggage included one alto saxophone, clarinet, double bass, drum kit comprising console, drum and three cases, and an accordion.

Harry lived and breathed music but he was a modest man and never boasted about his achievements. His daughter Liz Calpin remembers asking:

*'What did you do in the War dad?', and he never really said. It was only as
he got older that he became proud of his link with George Formby. But it was
something to do with Jack Prendergast, and his contacts at the Rialto that got
me dad, and Harry Wheeler, and the other two that went to France.*

*From 1934 he had a car, a Morris 8, just a tiny little black thing, and they'd
go to dances, and very few of the musicians had cars, so he'd pick them all
up along with the equipment. Harry Wheeler, who lived up Fulford, played
double bass, and that would go on the top. Cars in those days were not
reliable like they are now, and the lights, me mother used to say it was like a
couple of candles, so it must have been absolutely straining with great big
men, boxes of instruments and music.*

Wal Walsh spent his war as an army musician. He joined the army in 1937 at the
age of 14, as a band boy:

*I always reckon the 1930s and the 1940s were the best time for the music.
They knew how to write a melody in them days. It was quite normal,
somebody going along the street, singing a song, the latest, whatever that was.*

*And then the radio, that came into being in the 1930s, and most of 'em at the
start were portables, and you had accumulators because the electric mains
didn't come until half way through the 1930s.*

*During the war the Americans came over and they did a lot to improve
things. They brought their arrangements for the big band stuff, Glenn Miller,
and everybody was playing that then. It was real lovely music.*

*In those days, music was quite strong in schools, and you started off your
music in the choir in church. You started from seven years of age learning to
read music. This was about 1930. You started off at the tonic solfa, then you
went on to reading orthodox music like treble clef, bass clef and sight reading
it from a copy, and it was really good training. And having had that right
from seven I was all right when I was accepted as a band lad in the army,
because I could read music .*

*Well it was like all the kids want to play guitar now, mine was the saxophone,
the up and coming thing in those days. I was only a little lad and I started
off on the soprano saxophone. But the fingering's the same for all of them.
Then when I got a bit bigger I went on to the alto, and then the tenor, and in
the finish your saxophone player was expected to blow all the saxophones
from the baritone up to the soprano. The alto's my favourite, but I like tenor,
and I like playing t'baritone as well.*

If you played the sax, you were expected to play the clarinet as well. It was lovely, the clarinet. You all started off liking the saxophone, but you got to like the clarinet too. It had a much bigger range, and you got fellas like Artie Shaw and Benny Goodman coming up and playing, so you wanted to play like them. And there's the old Mozart stuff, you got to like classical as well.

In the army the dance stuff was secondary, because you had to have the entertainment side. They were big bands in them days, 'cos the army could afford to have 'em. They could afford the full lot whereas, just getting your own little group going depended how much they were going to pay you. In the 1940s for a four hour dance, you'd get 30 bob, £1.50.

When you got playing in the band, the army provided the initial instruments, they were good, mostly from Boosey and Hawkes, they had all the army contracts. The ones I learnt on were the old 20th century, quite good solid, hard wearing instruments. But most sax players got their own. I had a Bucher. And it was the best sax I ever had. I got it in India. You could buy 'em through the band fund. I was in Calcutta and we used to go down to Rahna The Mystery to buy reeds. The army issued you one a month, but everybody used to buy their own 'cos they varied, the reeds. Some people liked 'em hard, some liked soft, you got different tones out of the different types. They were about half a crown for six.

The saxophone cost me 100 rupees, a rupee in them days was 1/6d. It was second-hand, it had been well blown in. When the Japanese started, they shipped us off, packed all the instruments in and we went to Burma. When I came back on me way back home, I wanted me sax, and I found out it had been sold back to the shop where I'd got it, and the money had gone into the band fund. So I went down to Rahna, and he says 'Well I can't let you have it back, I've sold it'. And I'll tell you, there was a Fred Hartley Quintet, used to be a regular broadcasting band, a famous outfit of the time and one of them had bought it.

Wal eventually came back to the barracks in York, and continued with music:

Bert Keech, when he was short of a sax, he'd come down to the barracks and it was TBTB (Thirty Bob Taxi Back). I did quite a few jobs for Hughie Robertson. I didn't have me own instrument then, and so I said to Hughie, 'Can you get us a sax cheap?' He got us a sax and a clarinet, and he got us a job at Albany to go with it. And that's when I finished up playing with Eddie. When Eddie left, Sid Watson was on piano and Sid took over the Albany band. And I worked there for quite a few years 'till it folded.

At the end of the war, the army were short of musicians. I should have finished somewhere about 1946 but they asked you to sign on for another two years, to keep the bands going. And so Ron [his brother] and myself and Henry Thomson, we took on this extra two years, and they gave you about 250 quid, and then when you'd done your two years, they gave you another 250 quid. Mind you, by the time we'd done the extra two years, the Korean War was on, and everybody was kept in. I think it was Coronation year when I got out and I'd done about 16 years.

They always said an English band, no matter how good, they didn't have the swing that the Americans did. And the BBC tried to do it with Ted Heath and they were pretty good, but they just didn't have that American sound. You could have a written arrangement and give it to an American band, with the same instruments, five saxes, six brass, and full rhythm section, and give it to an English band, and both play it, and it would sound different. It was something in the music that English bands couldn't get. Mind you we had some very good small bands like Sid Phillips, with six pieces. And some of our jazz outfits were good, we could never get that big band thing that the Americans could get.

Good music, good musicians, but maybe they were too exact, where the Americans looked to have a rapport playing with each other. And they feel for each other, and that's the difference. But a lot of English fellas went over to America, and they fitted in.

Now Reginald Kell, he was the fella that Benny Goodman got to coach him. And Artie Shaw had a lovely sounding clarinet and Benny sounded that little bit harsh to me, but it's good, and it really gets him going and his execution's magnificent, and it's all off the cuff as well. But he wanted the classical, and he got Reginald Kell to take him on. Lovely slow vibrato, that was what he was noted for, because it was frowned on was vibrato by the old school, they liked it real straight, but he could do it and it makes it warm. And of course saxes always have done that, and it used to be marked on your part, whether to play it just a straight note, or a vibrato, and you do it with your lip. You've got to be very careful and put it in at the right places.

That's what Glenn Miller's saxes were doing, the vibratos were all going together. And that's how he got going. Particularly when he had the clarinet going up on the top as well, and the clarinet had the vibrato, and you got that lovely sound of all the saxes, and the clarinet on the top.

The De Grey Rooms is always remembered as one of the favourite wartime dance halls. Edith Keech, the wife of Bert, recalls the days when they lived there:

I was married on April 9, 1941, and we opened the De Grey Rooms on the 12th which was Easter Monday. Bert was a great pianist, he had his own band, and he used to love to play at intervals without the full band. We had dancing until 2 o'clock sometimes. And you didn't get to bed until about three, and then I was up at seven. I sometimes wonder how I did it. He had a band before we were married, and he used to play at the Folk Hall. Frankie Brown on drums, somebody called Elliott on trombone, Bob Halford.

On VE Night, it was absolutely wonderful, everybody behaved themselves, it was great. And Bert said, 'I've charged you all these years, everybody comes in free'. He used to run dances and give the proceeds to the County Hospital. Geoff Love, he was in Bert's band, he was a lovely boy, he lived at the time in Walpole Street, he was in the army. [He later enjoyed great success with the Geoff Love Orchestra].

For dancing we'd have about 300. Oh we had to refuse people. And by the Monday before a Saturday we were sold out.

Jack Carr came to York in 1937. Within a short time he had formed the Melody Aces comprised of piano, drums, guitar, trumpet, violin, alto and tenor saxophones. After regularly playing at the village hall in Osbaldwick, he secured a Saturday night residency at the Co-op ballroom, which held 600 dancers. He left to go into the army in 1940 but the Melody Aces under the leadership of Jack's brother Cyril continued playing in York. For example, in February and March 1942, they played at dances at English Martyrs' church hall, the Regent, Davy Hall, Rowntree, the Railway Institute, the Co-op Hall for an Aid To Russia dance, the City Arms, a stage show at the Regal cinema and New Earswick Folk Hall.

Jack was stationed in the Middle East and his diary for 1943 records how he sent songs home by airgraph, a kind of telegram, such as a new song he had come across called Sweetheart My Own. Officially no musical instruments were allowed in the airmen's kit, but most musicians managed to smuggle their instruments with them. Others bought instruments out there. He continued to play his clarinet and saxophone at the RAF camps, and in his spare time began to learn the trumpet in June 1943. By August he was blowing bugle calls and in September he sent an airgraph back to his fiancée Joan of a new waltz The Bells Will Be Ringing For You'. He began composing more tunes, including When The Moon Shines Over The Desert, which he sent home and which was played by the organist at the Regal Cinema. He sold

Jack Carr and His Melody Aces. Jack on clarinet and Cyril Carr on tenor sax. Other surnames unknown. *(Courtesy Joan Carr)*

the trumpet in October and played the piano in a local hotel various nights that month and the next, but on November 6, he bought a violin.

Joan would send out the Melody Maker from home as well as a violin tutor and brother Cyril sent all the latest information about the Melody Aces. In late 1944 Jack sent his violin and soprano sax home, to keep them safe as well as 'my new foxtrot' home to Joan.

In the years after the war the Melody Aces became the house band for Betty's Ballroom. Sometimes a smaller ensemble would play where only four or five-piece bands were required. One night Jack and his wife were dancing in the Dorchester Hotel until 1am then Jack had to catch a train back to York to play at a farmers' ball in Helmsley. In the late 1950s and 1960s as music began to change, Jack's Quartet had a residency on Saturday nights at Everingham Hall which had been turned into a country club.

Joan Carr recalls:

He'd started before the war, he was in the army for six years. When he came back he started playing regularly, about four nights a week, in various halls, mainly Bettys, Terry's, the Queen's Hotel in Leeds, Thirsk and Helmsley, the Black Swan. He had a pool of musicians, about 10 or 12. He didn't take them all on each occasion but if one person couldn't fill in another person did. They wore ordinary evening dress. He was quite fussy about that. It all had to be quite immaculate. And if anyone turned up with a soiled shirt they were immediately sent home to change. Nobody was doing this to earn a living. They were all doing it as a hobby really. That went on for a great many years. Obviously, busy at Christmas and New Year, and all that sort of thing, so I had a few very lonely holiday times but I didn't really mind because I knew he loved it. He'd had an absolutely dreadful war and this gave him many pleasures. He carried on until about 1980.

There was a well-known Lord Mayor in York called Jack Wood. And he forgot to book the band for one of his rugby do's, and John's band was playing in Bettys and he got this frenzied phone call from Jack, to say everybody was there and had had their dinner and there was nothing happening in the way of a band. He said, John I didn't tell you, I'm terribly sorry, and of course John, who liked Jack very much indeed, said, 'Oh we'll sort it out worry not'. So he came rushing home for a duplicate set of music, and about a half an hour behind time they did get going.

Sheila White recalls dancing at this time:

We danced on a lunchtime at Rowntree's in the dining hall, it was part and parcel of the workers relaxation. I'd be about 16. Mr Pulleyn would put these big 78 records on and we'd do the modern steps.

I went to the Co-op, the Assembly Rooms when it was a big one and the Albany where my friend Eddie Lamb was the drummer and the band leader, and the De Grey Rooms. But the De Grey Rooms was a bit pricey, I think it was about half a crown whereas the [Co-op] Stores was about a shilling.

It was funny at the Albany, the lady there had this little tiny bedroom fire of coal and girls would take tongs and put them in the fire and tong their hair up so that you were always nice before you went in. We did the waltz and tango, foxtrot, maxina that was one, oh and then they used to do polyglide. We jived too, the Americans fetched that.

Eddie used to get up and croon and he had a beautiful voice. Well everybody fell in love with Eddie. They'd stand at the bandstand you know and do this to him and he used to sing to them all. Bob Halford was same. He was very quiet but had a beautiful voice, I think he sang in St George's Choir.

When Tony Lister was at the Clifton, he had 'process of elimination' dances and you went in and he touched you on your shoulder and you'd to sit down. One

Sheila White, second from right, at Marks & Spencer staff dance 1948 in Assembly Rooms.
(Courtesy Sheila White)

year the partner I had and myself won it with the tango Jealousy. I got a zipper bag with Max Factor makeup in and my partner got a wallet with a £5 note.

We all went out, five or six of us together. Kathy Jefferson, Nancy, and Ellen Coates who always collected me, and we'd go for Renee Milner and then for Renee Murray. We all went together, we came home together. We never came home with any men.

We had Music While You Work at Rowntree's and Hannah, a girl from Selby, we'd give her a list and she'd put the records on and we'd sing. When the bell went you'd to stop singing. When the music was on we were working like mad. It keeps you going, stirs you up. We'd be on six to two so when it came on at half past ten, it was like having a boost. Then in the afternoon when you got to about three, you were flagging a bit and then the music came on, set you up again. Well they used to play marches for the soldiers to get them going didn't they? We loved it, yes, music was a big contributor.

Chris Poole recalls watching dance bands when he was 18 in 1945:

My favourite place was the De Grey Rooms. That was the Bert Keech era, he had his own band, and he was a lovely pianist. He was an enormous man, and at the interval when we all went for coffee, or another drink, he would sit and play but he had to stretch his arms out because his stomach was so great he couldn't get to the keyboard. But he was a wonderful man.

There was a lovely little intimate place, the Albany, in Goodramgate, and that was one of the sprung dancehalls. Underneath the floor a man put a lot of compression springs, so that when you danced, the whole floor would bounce up and down and so there was no fatigue with dancing because it was so nice and light. We'd sit round on little seats and see which was the prettiest girl, or fella and then you would have a dance. If you saw a pretty girl dancing with another fella you could always tap him on the shoulder and say, 'Excuse me' and they quite accepted that you wanted to change partners.

It was a lot of fun. And fun was the main thing of that society. After the awful times of the 14-18 War and the Depression, and the awful gloom that set on, we tried to bubble ourselves up to make everything happy again, and all the songs were very upbeat, Happy Days Are Here Again.

There were often little dance schools, and you would go along with these prim sort of ladies, how to hold your hand, and how to put white gloves on, side together, side step forward, and, graceful sort of dancing. But in the 1930s and 1940s, the Americans came, and they were a great influence with the jitterbug and the jive and that changed things.

The Ken Parks winning dance formation team, Butlin's camp, Filey c1953. Men - Jimmy Malone, Tony Hoar, Alan Smith, David Gowland. Women - back row Marlene Gregory, Rita Storbridge, Muriel Crayce. Front row - Maureen Joy with Billy Butlin.

(Courtesy Frank and Muriel Day)

Ken Parks had a dancing school in High Ousegate above Burton's, and we did formation dancing and used to compete all over the place. He had teams that went into Come Dancing.

Terry's was a lovely place in which to dance. Beautiful panelled floor, panelled walls, maybe just two or three people in the band, string, bass, piano. Always we'd get dressed up for it. But as a young man, it was principally dance music. That was the idiom of the day, the popular songs, the fun songs, they got together in cinemas and community singing was very popular, and even newspapers had songs in like the News Of The World. No, no, A Thousand Times No, You Cannot Buy My Caress. It was a sort of bonding, all the chaps and all the girls, if you could get a good sing-song, and it cheered you up when things weren't awfully good. The Sweetest Song In The World, You're As Pretty As A Picture, Has Anyone Ever Told You Before?

When the television came, people had pianos, they don't use them, they just dump wonderful pieces of music by the ton, lovely covers and everything. It was that time when people didn't want to know about yesterday, they were all looking forward to tomorrow, more optimistic.

May Passmore and her daughter Trudy were both in ENSA but never together. May remembers:

When I joined ENSA I had to go and pick four people up from different parts of London in a van, and then we went to Bedford - and I had travelled all night, hadn't been to bed or anything and I had to take them to do a munitions show and at night we did a show for the army. And for the first fortnight we had a munitions show nearly every day and a show every night, and I didn't know whether I was on my head or my heels. And I was the driver, there was only me who could drive.

We were in a Ford 8 van, we travelled with a mini piano and all our luggage, to different camps every week. We went all over. I thought I had been everywhere, until I went with ENSA - and I found out I'd been nowhere! We travelled by train and car when we were on the music halls. That was nothing compared with what we went to with ENSA. I used to work with a comedian, we did songs altogether, and I was in the sketches, I had nine changes in one hour! I sang all the popular songs like Begin The Beguine.

We went to so many out of the way places where there was a camp - or even seven men, on a gun site. And we went farther than John O'Groats, down to Land's End. Up in the Orkneys we went to a camp, did the show, and when we came out it was snowing heavens high and we had to turn back, and we went into this NAAFI, and all the soldiers had gone out and the two people who were running it were just clearing up. The fire was nearly out, and it was cold, but they took us in and they gave us some tea, and we had to go back to the camp. They took us into a hut where the NAAFI girls were all asleep and they had khaki scarves all around their faces because some of the windows were out, and we had just what we stood up in. We were five days there, and we couldn't get out. We were in Africa for six months, and when we were going up the African coast, I was sick for four days! And when we stopped, and I got dressed, and I sat on a seat on the ship before we could get off it, and they took us in taxis to a camp, and I had the most gorgeous meal I'd had in my life! We went to West Africa, Freetown, we were there for a month, and we worked at the Garrison Theatre. And then we went to Takaradi, Gambia, Nigeria, up into the pygmy country, and up into the Sahara Desert, we used to watch the camel train coming in from Egypt. And we bought quite a lot of leather things that the camel trains brought over. I was with ENSA until 1946.

But Trudy was 40 years abroad, and she was quite a star, she was in South Africa and in Singapore for about 16 years. Penang, Bangkok, lots of places.

How she went with ENSA was, she was a pianist to Danny Malone, when she was 14, and then when she left him she was a pianist to Norma Dawn, and she was playing in Islington, and a man came to the stage door and asked her

if she would like to join ENSA and of course she had to write to me, to ask me if she could go. She was 17 then. And when she was finished with ENSA she went with Combined Services Entertainment. And they played in Germany after the war was over in a revue called Come To The Show. When she was in Singapore she had this offer to go in this cabaret. And they released her from CSE, and then they wrote to me and said they were sorry to let her go because she was the youngest and most glamorous pianist they had.

Trudy Luker in Singapore. 1960s.
(Courtesy Trudy Luker)

Trudy Luker taking off with ENSA, second down on right, from Picture Post September 1945. *(Courtesy Trudy Luker)*

During the Second World War, it was very difficult for ordinary people to travel so various towns organised Holidays At Home Month with different events and activities taking place during the summer to entertain local people.

In July and August 1942 open-air dances were held three times a week and attracted large crowds. The local ARP dance band played at the first dance which was held in West Bank Park and the West Yorkshire regimental dance band played at the dances in Rowntree Park, with Bert Keech and his band playing in both Rowntree Park and the Homestead. Tickets were sixpence each. The ground staff for each park had worked hard to improve the lawns to make them as good as possible for the dancers.

By 1944 there was such demand for these events that a big top was erected in Bootham Park grounds on the site of the York Gala, a marquee which had a pitch-pine floor especially for dancing. A number of concerts took place and dances were held on Monday, Wednesday, Friday and Saturday of each week. The marquee could accommodate 1,000 and there were also coloured umbrellas and deck chairs, (loaned by Great Yarmouth) outside, where refreshments were served. The most ambitious programme was in the summer of 1944 when 40 different concert parties were engaged to entertain, including the famous national concert party, the Roosters. The opening dance

Holidays At Home, dancing in the Big Top, Bootham Park 1944.

(Courtesy York City Archives)

on July 15, attracted 900 dancers, which was probably the biggest number for any dance in the city, who were delighted with the beautifully polished floor and the decorations of fairy lights, flags and tubular illuminations. Music was by the dance orchestra of the King's Royal Rifle Corps. There were also afternoon dances on Wednesdays and Saturdays.

At the end of the month, the figures showed that more than 13,000 dancers had danced in the big top to 11 different first class dance orchestras, with nearly 4,000 dancing at the open air dances. Although the month of events had been splendid and people looked forward to sampling them again, it was a much greater relief that the following summer of 1945 saw the end of the war.

Kathy Butler in two of the roles she played during her varied career.

Wartime songs when heard today can still convey the spirit of the time. People who were present during the war enjoy sing-songs from the 1940s because it reminds them of a time when emotions were heightened, though their memories may be sad as well as happy. Dancing was a crucial part of trying to enjoy oneself today, 'for tomorrow we may die'. Songs such as I'll Be Seeing You and We'll Meet Again conveyed the pain of parting, but We'll Gather Lilacs In The Spring Again, I'll Never Smile Again Until I Smile At You and There'll Be Bluebirds Over The White Cliffs Of Dover encouraged hope and spoke of a future where peace would reign.

CHAPTER FOUR.   I'M PLAYING AT SEVEN
The Post War Era

In 1945 and 1946, after the war had ended, the musicians came home. Many of the international big name bands had disbanded by this time. One reason for this was the four-year strike by American musicians who refused to make records, except for V discs specifically for the armed forces. Singing groups started to take the place of bands and when the dispute ended, the singers were the main attraction, with bands an accompaniment.

But in York dance bands were as popular as ever. The name which is really synonymous with dance bands in York, and particularly the De Grey Rooms after the war, is Johnny Sutton, who came to dance music from brass bands. A photograph of the York Cocoa Works Brass Band in 1903 shows his father Edward Sutton playing in the band which he had helped to form. He played cornet and later tenor horn. Fifty years later he was still playing in the brass band, along with his two sons, Johnny and Ted, who were both taught the cornet by their father. Edward Sutton was born in Hull and was originally in the Welton Brass Band near Brough. Nearly half the members of that band were from the Sutton family and at one time there were ten Suttons in the band.

Trevor Bousfield recalls how Johnny started:

Johnny was introduced to the cocoa works band by his father in 1921 as a cornet player and he played regularly with the band until the attractions of other types of music led him away during the period of the war, when the band activities were limited. When Johnny was 19, he would attend dances with other people of his age and one evening the Sutton boys had decided to give band practice a miss in favour of a local dance. Johnny was passing away the time at home by running down the yard at the rear of his house and jumping on to the stone window ledge. Suddenly his foot slipped on the window ledge, throwing him forward, his right hand breaking the glass as it went through the window and as he fell backwards from the window ledge, his right hand was badly torn as it returned over the jagged edges of the glass. Makeshift tourniquets were applied in an attempt to stop the haemorrhage, urgent attempts were made to get him to hospital but in the end he had to walk from the Groves to the County Hospital, a distance of three quarters of a mile with a towel wrapped around his raised arm.

He spent three weeks in hospital and 18 months as an outpatient, and the accident left him without sufficient control of the fingers of his right hand to

play a valved instrument. His solution was typical of Johnny's determination.
He used his left hand over the bell to reach the valves.

The accident did not stop Johnny from playing. He was obviously a man dedicated to music and to sharing his love of music with others. Numerous people talk of how Johnny let them sit in with his band and how this gradually improved their playing. The most famous of them all is the international composer and arranger John Barry, the son of Jack Prendergast who owned the Rialto. He was recently in York to receive the Freedom of the City and he told me that his apprenticeship with the Modernaires, for whom he played trumpet in his early days, was a very good training ground for his later career. He said:

I loved Johnny, he was the best. He knew how to run an orchestra.

Keith Laycock, who lived at the Shoulder of Mutton pub in Heworth, tells of how Johnny brought fellow musicians from brass bands and elsewhere, to rehearse in the hut behind the pub in 1945. This really was the birthplace of the Modernaires. It was the only big dance orchestra in York, as other dance bands tended to be six or eight-piece. Keith's parents, Eric and Esme Laycock, were in the Benny Connell Band before the war and so he had been brought up in a musical family. His father played saxophone and his mother played piano and accordion:

Johnny Sutton's Modernaires at the De Grey Rooms, 1950s. L to R: Henry Thomson, Mick Smith, bass, Terry Shackleton, drums, Ron Backhouse, Brian Parker, Bob Scott, trombone, at back Ken Wray, Barry Prendergast (John Barry), trumpets.

I used to go with 'em during the war. My sister went to the next door neighbour and I went with them. I started playing drums. They were working at some aircraft works and couldn't get to the dance until about nine o'clock, so they taught me to play the drums sufficiently to start it off until they got there.

After the war:

Musicians would come into the pub. My father was playing with the Assembly Players at the Folk Hall then. Johnny Sutton cottoned on to the idea of using the hut for a rehearsal band. He wanted to get his rehearsal pupils in there, with a nucleus of a band. He had about four trumpet players, a trombone player, and the drummer.

This band began to play regularly at the Co-op Hall. In March 1949 Bill Serby became 'Director of the Bert Keech Orchestra' in the De Grey Rooms. Bill explained that his initial line-up was a rhythm section, three saxes and himself on trumpet. He got the job there when he arrived for an audition to join the current band. He was kept waiting for some time and was then told that the 'house band' had been sacked, and Bert Keech intended bringing in a band from Birmingham. Bill Serby offered to form a band instead and Bert agreed. This band also played at a club in Coney Street, the Flying Services Club and did Sunday night jazz gigs at a pub on the outskirts of York. Band members included Ken Kenyon, Will Acton, Dennis Goodsall on alto, with Gordon Cottom playing piano, and Horace Tappin on sax. In October 1949 Bill was asked to join the Vic Lewis Orchestra so he left York at that point, and he later played with the famous Ken Mackintosh.

From November 1949 to January 1950, Jimmie Honeyman was resident at the De Grey Rooms and it was in 1950 that Johnny Sutton's Modernaires took the residency although other bands still played there occasionally, including Albert Honeyman and his band (who had no connection with Jimmie). Albert Honeyman ran a band under his own name from 1953 to 1963 based in Wetherby, but often played York venues including Terry's and the Station Hotel. York band members included George Roberts, Pete Williams, Gordon Cottom and Keith Laycock. After 1963 he changed his professional name to Peter Stuart, ran a seven-piece outfit and played the trombone and sang. He described his band as 'the best in the county', a claim endorsed by Keith Laycock who said that the band had great stage presence and was very well organised. Mr Honeyman explained that his band used individual arrangements and did not buy them off the shelf. He later worked on the QE2 and spent many years working the cruise ships. He was in his early 20s when he ran his first band, and by 2003 he will have been running dance bands for 50 years.

Trevor Bousfield describes the De Grey Rooms as:

the dancing centre of York. As you walked up the staircase into the first floor ballroom, the band could be seen on stage in the left hand corner with saxophones and trombones on the front row, trumpets elevated at the rear, with the drums, acoustic bass and grand piano occupying the remainder of a small stage. Low lighting revealed seats all the way round the wooden sprung floor as people danced to the sounds of the big band era. The music was purchased for 3/6d, piano score and parts at Banks music shop. Johnny's music library contained all the popular tunes, standard arrangements from such bands as Glenn Miller, Stan Kenton, Duke Ellington, Lionel Hampton, Ted Heath, Tommy Dorsey, Les Brown, Count Basie, Sid Phillips, Harry James and Woody Herman. The most popular music was that of Glenn Miller, numbers such as Little Brown Jug, Tuxedo Junction, Moonlight Serenade, American Patrol and Pennsylvania 65000. Most of this music would be played at every dance along with such pieces as Tenderly (waltz), and Harlem Nocturne (foxtrot) with a most haunting alto sax solo. Some of the music in the library was in such frequent use that it became very dilapidated, such pieces as Solitude, Satin Doll, Hamp's Boogie Woogie, Woodchopper's Ball, Hot Toddy, The Hawk Talks, I've Got My Love To Keep Me Warm, I Get A Kick Out Of You, I'm In The Mood For Love. This then would be the sound as you climbed the elegant curved staircase to the ballroom at the De Grey Rooms.

During the period when Johnny Sutton's dance band played there, he gave the opportunity to many young players from the cocoa works band to change their style and play the modern music of the day. The greatest problems facing the brass band player, wishing to make this change, were their rapid style of vibrato and the non-diaphragmatic style of production. Another problem was the need to play for long periods at a time with very few rests in between. Dances were usually held between 8pm and midnight, or from 9pm to 1am, and those players with the 'smile and press' technique, were unable to sustain any high register over this length of time. Added to this was the need to play notes considerably higher than those experienced in the brass band, such as 'super F' and 'super G'. Some managed to make the transition but those players unable to control their vibrato were unsuccessful. But the cocoa works band did not view favourably those who had left their ranks for the more popular events of the day, though it turned out to be a forward move in their development as some of those players with this added experience later returned to the brass bands when ballroom lost its popularity, and helped to introduce a much broader repertoire of music.

Alan Sutton, Johnny's son, now lives in Australia. He recalls being interested in music from the age of eight or nine:

I always remember it at home because they would have rehearsals in the front room, the brass section one night and the sax section another. I started practising trombone about 10 or 11 years of age. I played with the brass band, probably up to being about 16, then I bought my own trombone. It was a toss up between buying a trombone or a motorcycle, and I was persuaded to buy the trombone because dad was looking at me to carry on the tradition in the dance band.

The De Grey Rooms was the place to be. I'd go at 15 or 16, and listen to the band and the crowds were just unbelievable. There was a couple actually that used to come early on, they'd be there spot on 8 o'clock, waiting for the band to start. They did amateur dancing, and later on became professionals. But they used to come in so that they could dance to the music dad was providing because he was very strict on his tempos. He was absolutely fanatical about it, he would look at his watch and count out how many bars per minute he was playing. And if it was wrong he would readjust it. Round about 10 o'clock it'd start filling up, and then by about 10.30 it was shuffle time. People would jive but you couldn't jive in the middle of the ballroom, and if you'd been caught, me dad would come off the stand immediately and drag them into a corner.

Dad stayed with the brass band during the war years. That was when he became interested in dance music. He would be going round with different musicians to army and RAF camps, entertaining.

There was a man who played tenor sax, Gerry Allen, who did some excellent arranging. Jack Prendergast, the owner of the Rialto, asked dad to listen to his son Barry [John Barry]. Dad had a listen to him, and he thought that the best that he could do, would be a third trumpet player in a big band. But he did like his arrangements, so whenever Barry knocked out a new arrangement he'd bring them along and they'd try them .

You'd always have somebody that would come along and sit in dad's band. He'd have a listen to make sure that they weren't going to make the band sound not right. Then he'd say, 'Okay, come along to rehearsals'. Because although the band played Wednesdays, Fridays and Saturdays, it still had a Sunday morning rehearsal. Two hours, going through new arrangements and everything. Even after Dad had actually played it properly the night before, he would rehearse it the following day if it didn't sound right, and he was very pernickety when he came to rehearsing a band.

Music was his life, that was all he lived and breathed for. When they discovered he had angina, the doctors said he had to stop playing. And he came to me and said that he would rather play his trumpet and die earlier than live six years longer and be bloody miserable all the time.

Modernaires rehearsal at Shoulder of Mutton 1949. Back L to R - Geoff Towse, Malcolm Tindall, Leo Burrows, friend, Bill Ibbotson, friend, Bert Thompson, Johnny Sutton. Front L to R - Ron Backhouse, Alan Stillborn, Ken Wray, unknown serviceman.

(Courtesy Alan Sutton)

Even when Johnny was ill, he would not refuse to help any would-be musician and was asked to go into schools:

They rang dad up, and said they wanted to buy some instruments, would he go along and advise. Then they rang and said they'd got the instruments, now they needed someone to teach them to play. Would he be interested? And he went along, and gave his time for nothing. When his lung cancer got that bad that he couldn't drive, they used to send a taxi for him and he'd take his oxygen bottle with him. And he'd go and teach the kids how to play. He'd gone back to Rowntrees Cocoa Works Band, he was the conductor there, and they also formulated the younger brass band and had a lot of young people. Tony Whitehead asked me one night where my dad was and I said, 'He's got nine young fellows rehearsing', and Tony just turned round, and said, 'Your dad will just never give up will he?' That's all he lived for. He mainly wanted to pass on his knowledge, and his expertise in the music.

When the union rate went up, probably sixpence an hour or something, and the guys in the band would say, 'We want this rise', he said, 'I can ask Bert [Keech] for extra money and I know he's gonna turn round and say 'no', he'll just say one of the members of the band will have to go to pay the others' wages. It's up to you guys what you want to do. Stick together as a unit, and enjoy your music, as well as getting paid for it. Or whether you wanna go to the stage where it becomes a money matter, and then you blokes decide who goes, I'm not going to decide who's going'.

I don't know if there must have been ill feeling along the line, because I'm given to understand that Geoff and Ken went to Bert and indicated that they were prepared to give him a small band. In other words they were prepared to carve up the band. Bert replied, 'Well you'd better talk to my musical director'. 'Who's that?' 'Johnny'. It was something that Bert had obviously thought of very quickly on the spot, because he wanted me dad there because he knew what his capabilities were.

With the trombone I sort of worked at it and it was one of those things where I just couldn't keep an interest, I didn't have the flare for it. Brian came in and took over from me. I used to spend most of me time at the De Grey Rooms and on a Friday night, they did what was called a midnight waltz. The piano would sit there and everybody'd get off the stand. And I'd go and fiddle around with Leo's drums, and play a waltz tempo thing. We did a Boxing Day morning 12 o'clock till 4 am. Leo turned up but he was not well. Dad rang around trying to get a drummer. Couldn't get one, so Leo suggested that I did the job. I'd got the bass drum in the right place and the high hat in the right place and so I took that on board and went out. Eventually I suggested I should get a drum kit and I picked up a cheap kit for 20 quid from a bloke then built it up by adding bits and pieces. I just used to practise and practise and eventually I'd do one night a week at the De Grey Rooms. Noel Porter would do the other nights, and then, in 1963 when we actually finished at the De Grey Rooms, I went to Bridlington and did the job at the Spa Ballroom with him.

I don't have a great technique, but I've got the ability to hold the band to the tempo that's been set. And I suppose having dad breathing down me neck, when I was learning, I'm able to maintain that dance tempo. Because he was a stickler for tempo, it's probably something that's rubbed off and I've got the ability from my dad.

I went to see a lot of these big bands. Stan Kenton used it as an orchestra, so he got the full sound of an orchestra. That's why my dad would never go out with less than nine, because the band, had to sound as a band. Three saxes, two trumpets, one trombone, three rhythm.

Some of the young musicians who would eventually graduate to the big bands, started out at the Old Priory Youth Club Band, like Gerry Allen, who became known not only for his musicianship but also for doing arrangements:

Old Priory Youth Club Band using the equipment of Bert Keech Band playing in the interval at the De Grey Rooms 1946. All musicians were in their teens. L to R - Denis Goodwin, piano, Taffy Jones, Derek Parker, Arthur Jones, alto. Keith Laycock on bass, Leo Burrows on drums. *(Courtesy Arthur Jones)*

Group from New Rialtonians at the Rialto c1953. L to R - Geoff Knaggs, Denis Wright and Leo Burrows. *(Courtesy Denis Wright)*

I didn't start on clarinet until 1947, as I didn't seem to be able to raise any cash to buy an instrument, although I was interested in music from an early age, and all I could do at the time was to make a flute affair out of a tube and drill holes in it, and get a tune out of that. And then the first introduction to music was to go to the library and get a book on music theory, I started to study theory before I had an instrument, and then I managed to get the money together to buy a clarinet. I'd heard all this music on the radio and I was absolutely bowled over by it, I knew that that's what I wanted to play.

So I started to get lessons from Derek Dunning, I approached him and he got me into this Old Priory Youth Club Band on clarinet, but playing on tenor sax parts, which wasn't very satisfactory. I said it wasn't working very well, so he says, 'I'll lend you a tenor sax' and I was much better. I remember doing a job in Redeness Street, I think it's been demolished now, but that was the first job I ever did with this band. I wouldn't use the word competent, they were better than me when I joined, but we were just rough and ready I suppose. It was a good start and then shortly after that I was called up for National Service. I never stopped playing once since I first started in 1947, never once dropped. I took my clarinet with me and I was in the band at Sutton on Hull. I joined the Modernaires in 1950 and started doing arrangements for them in about 1952.

But what happened that was additional, was that on Sunday evenings the De Grey Rooms band was augmented at the Rialto for a Sunday night show, under the name of the New Rialtonians. John Barry was playing with us at the De Grey Rooms and it was his involvement with his father, that's how it came about.

Another time he came to me to do an arrangement for him did John Barry, I thought that was rather nice. And now look where he is. That was a trumpet solo with the Rialtonians. He asked me down to his house in Fulford, and we went through and sorted it out, and I did an arrangement which he played. It was called I Can't Begin To Tell You. And then I took a postal course from Bill Russo, Stan Kenton's trombone player, he was in Germany, and I think John Barry took the same course. I was keen to be a band arranger, I didn't think I wanted to compose, so I packed it in. I wanted to break into arranging, and make it a profession.

When you first start you don't know how it's going to sound, so you listen eagerly to the first arrangement, and unfortunately it never does sound how you think it ought to and eventually it comes into place exactly how it's going to sound. I use a piano mainly and once I've got the chords right, I know when I'm writing it down how it's going to sound with the band, through experience.

I went to the Graham band at the Rialto Ballroom at Liverpool and that was really marvellous and they used to do Music While You Work broadcasts. I did some arrangements for them as well, and they were very appreciative. I was there about six months, and then my mother was very poorly so I packed my job in and went home, which I've regretted, I think really I ought to have stuck with it. With hindsight I would have needed a bit more experience, I was a bit green really. I think the arrangements kept me in and I learnt a lot while I was there.

Things got a bit better at home, so I took a job at Redcar with Danny Mitchell and Pete Ball and I was there for about six months, and then I had to pack in that. Danny Mitchell's daughter was the first alto with Ivy Benson, and she was having a baby. She wanted to come back so her dad wanted to give her a job in the band, so it was first in last out, so it was me. Then I came back to York, and I thought that really I'd had enough. It's risky because if somebody comes along that they like better than you, you're just out, and that's it. There's no contracts, it's a dirty business, you just go. When I was with the Graham band, the leader fancied another tenor who was leaving somewhere else, so one of the tenors had to go, but I was doing the arrangements, although the first tenor was better than me, this activity kept me on.

Gerry found that there was a massive difference between playing semi-professionally in York and in a professional outfit:

It's mainly the discipline. Local bands tend to be over-enthusiastic, and too loud, everybody's over blowing and tries to get their own sound heard above everybody else. The rhythm section has to be really soft, and listen to the front line, the front line has to bring the volume down, and listen to everybody in balance, get the vibratos matched and balanced, and if everybody's blowing loud, that's all ruined. A professional band has all this discipline, that the local band doesn't have.

But in the York band, there was more enjoyment:

Well we laughed more than when you're with a professional band, because you couldn't relax, you had to be on your toes all the time. Whereas when you come back here you could relax, and just have a good time. But Johnny was strict, and that band was pretty good, probably hasn't been surpassed in York. Jimmy Lally's arrangements were the most popular. Because you could play them from a small combination to a large combination, and they'd still sound good, even played with two or three instruments.

When I went with the professional band, they knew that I was more or less a beginner, although they liked the arrangements, and tried to get away with not paying me much at all. When I left the band he wrote to me trying to get me

New Rialtonians at Rialto c 1953. L to R - Geoff Knaggs, piano, saxes - Gil Fox, Gerry Wakefield, John Greenwell, Gerry Allen, non-player sitting in, Denis Wright, bass, Leo Burrows, drums, trumpets - Johnny Sutton, Derek Mackfall, unknown, Pete Mortimer, trombones - non-player sitting in, Ron Backhouse, George Thompson, serving member of army station at Strensall sitting in.
(Courtesy Alan Sutton)

to write more arrangements, and I did one for a broadcast for the BBC. At one time I just worked from home doing arrangements. I advertised in the Melody Maker for work, and sold arrangements to various people around the country.

I was listening to the big bands on record, on radio, and I was learning their sounds, and how they were doing arrangements, and I was trying to get better harmonies, richer harmonies, and trying to get the art of the day into my arrangements. Overall good arrangements with interesting harmonies, by not using the chords that were written for the tune, and putting my own harmonies to it, inventing new chords, chord changes, so that it sounded quite different and more exciting than just the standard melody. You've got to compose the introduction, and then maybe compose a counter melody, which is totally different to the melody of the tune, and then compose a bridge passage, and then quite often alter the tune as well, to something a bit different, so in a way it is composing. In the Rialtonians we had singers, and I did arrangements for the vocals on those concerts. I did about 40 arrangements for Johnny Sutton while I was there.

At the De Grey Rooms, we started off playing Stan Kenton numbers, which were very ambitious. The first three numbers were Kenton numbers, which you'd never get away with in later years, and when it came to coming off the stand you could hardly get out, the crowds were absolutely teeming, and I had to fight my way off the stand at the interval. To me that was absolutely marvellous. And we had band jackets, it seemed very professional when I was just starting out. Those days were never to be the same. It gradually got less and less, from 1950.

There were fights at all the dances occasionally. Even the De Grey Rooms had problems. I remember when Bert Keech was there, there was a lad causing trouble, and Bert sat on him until the police came. There was a Scottish lad, he terrorised the place. He took a vendetta against the band because he'd been barred, but he'd be waiting for us outside when we were trying to leave the dance hall, ready to rough us up. Denis Wright had a scooter, and he rode out. I had a scooter as well, and I rode out, and he took a run, a fist at me, and nearly knocked me off it, but I managed to keep hold on.

It takes a lot of energy to play. But you get used to it, and then you can take it in your stride. I remember once I did two jobs in one night, each of four hours, when I was in the RAF at Hull and we did the station dance from eight 'till 12, and then a job in the Odeon Cinema for a staff dance, and that was from one o'clock 'till four o'clock.

Playing is the number one for me, but there was a buzz from doing arrangements, but playing preferably, more fun. If a solo is a good one, that really sets you up for the day, but if it's a bad one, you're really down in the dumps, so it's very satisfying, if luck's with you, and it turns out to be a good one.

Like Gerry, Arthur Jones began to play after the war. In 1945 he had music lessons, though he explains that 'sitting in with a band' was the best apprenticeship:

My father was a sax player in the army and during the war he played in the Post Office Military Band. I used to go along on Sunday mornings and sit with him and watch him play, and he had this alto sax and it was under the sideboard, and he gave up playing for some reason. When I was 14 I kept nattering to play this saxophone and eventually he gave in, and said, 'I'll let you have it on condition that you go to a proper sax player and have lessons'.

I had a paper round, so I went to Jimmy Cave, and it was half-a-crown a lesson, for half an hour, and I'd cycle from Heworth, to Fulford on a Sunday morning. He'd sit me in his front room, and stick the orchestration parts up, and I would play second, and he would play the lead. And one day he said to me, ' Do you fancy coming and sitting in with a band?' I was a bit frightened but I said I'd try.

The band was Ted Rowell's. They played at Rowntree's and I sat in and they made me welcome. It was my first job. Then I met Eric Gill, and got in the band and I stopped with them for three years. Eric was a good solid pianist, and a good teacher and I learnt a lot from him.

I used to play with all the young lads in the youth club, and we had a nice little Dixieland band and I played clarinet in that, Denis Goodwin played piano, Keith Laycock on bass, Duncan Cooper played trumpet. We enjoyed that and that got me playing a bit and reading, and when a job came up at the Albany in Goodramgate, I applied for that, and I got it. Dickie Bailey was absolutely brilliant. I did a lot of work with him. If you couldn't get a trumpet player, he'd come with his trombone. A trombone's written in the bass clef, and the trumpet part's written in the treble clef, but Dickie could just sit there and blow them off, some of them were really difficult but he could extemporise. I'd be sitting at the side playing alto parts and he'd be playing trombone parts, and there'd be a trumpet player there. And Dickie would say 'I'll take the middle eight', and he used to lean over, and play the middle eight of the tune from the alto part. And when I stopped I said 'Dickie, how do you read, when I'm in E flat, you're in

B flat?' and he had some sort of formula that he played treble clef in bass clef and he added some sharps somewhere along the line. [Len Cundall said about Dickie Bailey that if he stuck a mouthpiece on a piece of lead piping, he'd get a good sound!]

And I joined the Ambassadors as it was then, with Eddie Lamb that ran it, and Geoff Knaggs on piano, and I stopped there for two years until National Service. I managed to keep playing in the army, and when I came out I kicked around with different bands and then there came along two young lads, the Bousfields, trumpet twins, and they'd won a contest on the television, and I joined them, and played with them for a few years.

After that I started freelancing. I was a reasonably good reader, and I could get by, and I came to play with all the different bands. I'd sat in with Johnny Sutton, so the phone used to ring and I'd end up playing alto at the De Grey Rooms. We had our own little Archer Street, in York [a London street where musicians would go and wait for band leaders who needed a player, rather like a musical hiring fair]. It was called the Half Moon in Blake Street and there was a lot of musicians about and most of the lads would get themselves down into town about seven o'clock and have a beer before they went on the job. And you'd be having a drink, and somebody would sidle up and say, 'Are you doing anything a week on Friday, can you help me out?' By quarter to eight the place was cleared. Dancing was still very popular, and there was a lot of work.

Old Priory Youth Club Band c1949. Back - Johnny Burton, drums, Keith Laycock, bass, Laurie Leaf, piano. Front - Arthur Jones, sax on far right. *(Courtesy Keith Laycock)*

I used to get me reeds from Hugh Robertson, they were 1/9d. each. And one day I went in and there was this lovely alto sax. It was 1946 and there was nothing about, no new instruments, but this sax, a Martin alto, a beautiful thing. He said, 'It's £35'. I was earning about 7/6d a week as a watchmaker's apprentice! But I was getting 30/- a week playing. So he said 'Why don't you take it and pay me so much a week?' So I did and after 35 weeks it was mine. But sadly I lost it years later in the fire in Christie's Ballroom, upstairs in the old Grand Cinema. We played there two or three nights a week, and we'd leave our instruments on the stand, which was a bit foolish. It was heartbreaking for me, as I'd just started in business, and I'd very little money, and my sax needed overhauling and I'd taken it to Kitchens in Leeds. It had been overhauled and I played it one night and it played beautifully, it was a dream, but I lost it in the fire. We got them made up eventually. I bought a Selmer balanced action alto which was a dream one, and we'd get quite a lot of work with Victor Sylvester. Whenever Victor played, he needed a house band and he'd say, 'I want that band'. And we'd go along.

I remember John Barry, he used to hang around, if you were playing at the Assembly Rooms, you'd probably see him standing behind a pillar or something, listening to the band. He was dead keen on the bands in the early 1950s, and would go along to Johnny Sutton on a Sunday morning.

Johnny was a marvellous man, a very good reader. And he helped you out, and could tell you things, and the lads did respect him. He always insisted that the band must rehearse and to make sure the lads turned up he used to pay them their wages on a Sunday morning. I was big mates with Leo Burrows, and he said that John Barry had gone in, one Sunday morning, and he'd done an arrangement, and asked John to play it, and he called it the De Grey Stomp. The lads played it and said it was great and I think that was the start of John Barry doing his arrangements. It was a great library that Johnny had. All the standards and all the Cole Porters, and Gerry Allen did a lot of arrangements.

There were some really good musicians about. Derek Dunning could play like Charlie Parker, I admired him and I did a lot of work with Dunning. He'd think nothing to having five bands out on one night, so you never knew where you were if you were with Derek. You'd just get a phone call, 'Can you go to so and so?' On most occasions I'd be at the Assembly Rooms and I played with Freddy Mills, who was lead alto there. Sometimes the band would set off and there'd be no sign of Derek and he'd be somewhere else, seeing to the other bands, and we'd be playing away, probably a quickstep, and suddenly there was an alto playing, he was running round the music, he was brilliant at it was Dunning, and he'd be standing in front of the band and he'd stop there for half an hour, and then he'd disappear and he'd go somewhere else and do the same thing there.

There were some times you used to be so thrilled with the stuff you played. We did a lot of Count Basie, One O'clock Jump, and they were absolutely beautiful to play. When you play in a big band and you have the brass behind you, and they're all round you playing, I can't explain the feeling, it's absolutely out of this world. I'd think 'All this, and money too' but I'd have done it for nothing. Music is a drug and when a lot of the lads gave it up, I think they would miss it. They were certainly good times.

Lew Skords also began playing in 1946 and enjoyed a variety of music over the next few years, but his interest in music began before that:

It was before the war, and the radio was on, and somebody introduced Duke Ellington, A Train. Just like that, it got through to me. I'd never heard anything like it, and that was my initiation. But there was no scope at all to play it. Old Priory Youth Club started a band there. We were kids playing for dancing in the youth club, and as a novelty in various church halls.

I learnt piano at a very early age. I was locked in the room and had to play scales. The hard work stuff, and I got a whipping if I didn't, if I tried to jump the gun, very strict my old man. He played flute and drum. I think he was a drum major in the Coldstream Guards in his early days. Very straight up and down. But he softened a bit, whenever I was playing jazz in our front room he couldn't resist, he came in to try the drums.

Derek Dunning (on clarinet) and musicians, including Will Acton on bass.

(Courtesy Paul Acton)

111

I went into the air force on National Service in 1947. Up to then, I was a pianist only, and then I went into the air force and found myself at a station where the Squadronaires had been based, and they had just disbanded from there. One looks to see, are there any musicians in this place? 'Yes, but you can't be in our dance band unless you go on parade, so you've got to have something you can carry about', and I picked the trombone. And that was marvellous, they were two great years where I learnt the trombone.

I came out in 1950 and we started to play Dixieland jazz in the front room of my hall, very loud of course, and it was heard on the street, and a musician who lived 200 yards away, he was playing piano with this band. Sid Watson. And he said, 'Do you want to come and play?' The band was at the Co-op in Railway Street on Thursday and Saturday evenings.

Dancing was thriving. That's where all the young lads and girls went. What we liked to play we called standards. There was quality in a lot of those songs, a lot were American, Noel Coward wrote one or two. They were the bread and butter of an orchestra's library. The pops that came along with the films, they didn't last long, here today and gone. The bands were a good vehicle for anyone who was jazz inclined, but you had to tread a thin line between doing what you wanted to and being totally selfish, and being able to play for people to dance to. They were a bit of a hybrid in some ways, but at the Co-op we got away with it.

If you know music, to learn another instrument isn't that bad really, if you know what the music is, and you've got an ear. Trombone was one of those instruments, not mechanical, you've got to be able to pitch it, like a violin. You've got to have a good ear. Commander Sim, the Musical Director of the Royal Air Force, he used to go round the camps and see the various big bands. Wherever we went he got all the musicians to tune the orchestra, and I got it spot on, and he said to me 'Young man, you've got a wonderful ear, but believe me it will be a torture to you in your musical career'. And it has been. If it's out of tune, it drives me mad, it's a plague, it is honestly, being out of tune.

Mention singing in York in the late 1940s and the name that springs to everyone's lips is Neville England:

I didn't take singing lessons until I played a part in Gilbert and Sullivan, there was a bit of a dispute on as to whether I was singing baritone. Arthur Taylor used to play in a band at the Albany Hall and I'd vocalise there, it was all just fun really. And he said, 'I don't think you're singing in the right voice'. And he was ultimately proved to be right.

112

I was using my lower register all the time and he said, 'You've got a lovely top register, you should be making more of it'. So I took lessons from Robert Naylor, an understudy for Richard Tauber, in Harrrogate. And I kept the dance band scene up. But I've never treated life, or singing, seriously. It's been good to me. I used to enjoy myself.

Neville played a lot with Derek Dunning:

He was a brilliant alto sax player. Valerie Mountain played the piano often, she was very good, and when the dance had finished, the audience liked me to sing some opera, which I enjoyed and they enjoyed so I was asked repeatedly for it. I remember at the Assembly Rooms, on nights we weren't playing, and other organisations were providing the music, a lad called Brian Sutcliffe. He was very good.

In August 1958 the Yorkshire Evening Press reported how Neville England was appearing at the Assembly Rooms with the resident dance band, and as the dance ended with the last waltz just before midnight, and the dancers were about to leave, 'suddenly and unexpectedly the pianist Valerie Mountain began to play the introduction to 'Donna e Mobile' and Neville joined in and sang an aria and the pair gave a short recital of pieces'.

Percy Dinsdale learnt to play in the York City Brass Band then at 16 moved to the Eric Gill Band in 1949, on trumpet:

Assembly Rooms 1950s. L to R - Jack Wood, Lord Mayor, and Neville England.
(Courtesy Neville England)

113

Brian Sutcliffe singing with the Modernaires at the Assembly Rooms c 1958. *(Courtesy Brian Sutcliffe)*

There was Eric on piano, Chick Ward on bass, Freddie Carney on drums, Arthur Jones and Wilf Whitwell on sax, Charlie Druggitt on tenor sax. We were playing quite a lot at Rowntrees in the dining block. And we would go out once or twice in the week to the RAF stations or the villages.

Percy's sister Grace, who later married Ted Pratt, was also keen on music and she was the only girl in the brass band, as well as playing in dance bands. In the 1970s she had her own band, the G Set, which was very popular. She and Ted met on Christmas Eve 1956 when they found themselves seated next to each other in a band. Ted had begun playing trumpet in 1945 as a band boy when he was 16 with an army band. He spent the latter part of his life teaching brass and woodwind instruments in secondary schools and in about 1985, he founded the New Modernaires, who still play together today. Percy recalls:

My sister was a very good cornet player. She followed me you see, I wasn't amused at the time because it was no place for girls in those days. I suppose I did feel that that she was imposing into a male environment. Silly, but that's the way young lads think. She played solo cornet with the Railway Institute and moved across to Rowntree's after a lot of years. And she played with some of the York dance bands as well, like Doug Green and Billy Davis, and quite regularly with Jack Carr And His Melody Aces.

After Ted Pratt died in 1997, Ernie Wilson became leader of the New Modernaires until his death at the age of 70 in March 1998. He was very keen on jazz and in the 1950s had played in small jazz bands in the city. At Ernie's funeral, the new leader of the Modernaires, John Greenwell, led the band in a selection of Ernie's favourite tunes as a celebration of his life. John Greenwell started playing in 1936 when he was only ten:

My parents were interested in music and they bought me a piano accordion and that's how I got started. I graduated from the small piano accordions to a full sized one. I did play in a little five piece-band, led by a chap called George Long. He was the pianist, he was very good but the rest of the band were hopeless. We played at the Friends' Meeting House in Clifford Street, and then in Colliergate at the Drill Hall. We didn't have any orchestrations we just took a piece of sheet music, which was produced in those days, and just played from that.

Then I went to see a chap called Hughie Robertson who played at the Co-op, and said, 'I play the piano accordion, do you think I could sit in with your band?' 'Aye, it's possible, come and see me in my shop next week.' I went in and he said, 'Never mind your piano accordion this is what you should be playing,' and brought out an alto saxophone. And as it happened, quite by chance, a guy walked in to his shop, and Hughie said, 'Here's the very man who'll teach you how to play it.' Chap called Billy Mendez. He was in one of these small bands that went round the periphery of York in those days. And so he came down and he taught me to play the alto sax. It'd be just after the war, I'd be 18.

Billy Mendez played with a band led by a pianist called Norman Holmes, a very gentle man was Norman. Played at the better venues like the Station Hotel, dinner dances, and those kinds of functions. When I was with him he always played in a dress suit with full tails. [Norman Holmes was a pilot ace in the First World War and was shot down by Baron Von Richthofen, the Red Baron, but later flew again and was awarded the Military Cross].

The Albany, I used to go dancing there, loved listening to these bands and after I'd got a bit proficient on this sax I went to see this chap Atkinson and said, 'Could I sit in your band just to get some experience?' He said 'I'll have to ask the boys first.' I went back and he said, 'Oh yes that's fine come on in.' I was there for several years after that. Eddie Lamb was on drums, I think Godfrey Knaggs was on piano, Billy Steel was playing trumpet and Dickie Bailey. When these two departed, we got a young man called Derek Mackfall. I was studying for my professional examinations and so I had to give up for a year or two, until I qualified. And then, next thing I was invited to go to the De Grey Rooms to join Johnny Sutton. About 1953.

It was a good band at the Albany but a small one. When you went to the De Grey Rooms you got three trumpets, two trombones and five saxes. So it was a big difference. When you're on your own you can play what you want. You don't have to follow the dots immaculately. Soon as you're in a section with five saxophones you have to play what's written on that piece of paper, you can't deviate, you've no latitude whatsoever. I don't busk much. But once you've got the melody you're free to go round it if you're on your own. Soon as you're in a section you're leading it, (at least that's what I like to do). So when I was with Johnny Sutton, it was lovely leading this section. And I thoroughly enjoyed that experience, wonderful.

The Sunday night concerts at the Rialto were one-offs, we only did two or three. But when we did them, and this is the amazing part, there'd be queues right round the Rialto cinema waiting for us. The emotion that's going into your brain, it's wonderful, especially with the big bands. If I'm playing a solo I play from here [the heart]. You've got to put expression into it. It's what makes the difference between soloists and non-soloists in effect.

I've had one or two jobs with really professional big bands and I was in the section, I wasn't leading, because they had a professional leading it. I enjoyed that because they're so good. As a section man you've got to be able to hear what the leader's doing and follow him. When you're in a section you can't express yourself. You have to follow the leader. That's why I like to be the leader, then they've got to follow me.

Gerald Goodwin was another York dance band musician at this time who came to prefer working in the theatre:

I got a lesson with Len Cundall in his front room while he was getting ready to go out to a dance. After that I couldn't find a clarinet teacher anywhere. And somebody told me of an excellent clarinet player called Len Shutt, and he was playing at the Empire. I used to knock off work about an hour early on a Friday afternoon and ride down to the Empire, and have an hour and a half lesson underneath the stage. Len had played professionally from when he was 13 in theatres and cinemas, he said that the most dramatic thing that ever hit the music scene was when talking pictures came out. Every cinema of any size had an orchestra, and overnight they were all obsolete, even the smallest fleapit had a pianist, but the better ones had an orchestra, of varying sizes. But he managed to survive. And he'd played every theatre you could think of.

My dad very wisely realised that if you want to be a clarinet player the place to learn is a military band, because in a military band the clarinets are the violins of the orchestra, so I joined the territorial army, the West Yorks. I absolutely loved that, and I was in from the age of 15 to 21. We used to go playing every weekend, Morecambe and Bournemouth, this was marvellous. Whereas all the others used to go soldiering, the band would concentrate on their music and I took up the saxophone as well in my teens, so that I could play with the dance bands. Played a long time with Eric Gill.

We played at the Assembly Rooms when Victor Sylvester came. I remember saying to him, 'What do you think to us?' And he said, 'I haven't heard much, I haven't been listening', he was very diplomatic! But 'I'll tell you what, you've got a bloody good bass player'. That was Chick Ward, he had very bad hearing, but he was a wonderful player. We used to have to tic-tac the numbers to him. He just had a feel for the bass. A lovely sound. We'd play at Selby Baths 'till two o'clock in a morning, come back to York, and in Heworth he'd left his bike over a fence. And he'd take the bike out, big wide leather strap, put the string bass on his back, and then ride off home. And he was over 70 then. Amazing.

Then I started playing in the York Theatre Royal. First one I did, a three-week session and it was the most embarrassing in my life. When the big companies used to come here, the D'oyly Carte Opera Company, they'd bring all the principals - first violin, first flute, first clarinet - and then they'd pick up locals wherever they could, and I was asked to play second clarinet. The Gilbert and Sullivan week was very intensive, because I'd skive off work to get to practice, they did a different show every night, and a rehearsal on a morning, it was all really like lightning. The following week it was the Rambert Ballet Company, and they didn't bring a clarinet and I had to play the ballet music which was fantastically difficult, and I was totally out of my depth - managed the week, but it was unbelievably embarrassing. I've done a ten-week stint at the Theatre Royal and I had 13 years at pantomimes, which was fantastic, I couldn't possibly stand it if I was playing in a straight show for that length of time, but for pantomime you are interacting, joining in all the time, it's good fun. And we had some good players in the pit.

Lots of jazz players are very good musicians all round, but how good you are is recognised by how good you do your solo stint - 16 bars, 32 bars, eight-bar solos. But a lot of jazz musicians, if they're honest, would say that they're not brilliant readers. And also straight players, like myself, are no good at doing ad lib solos. Valerie Mountain can play away all day, she has a beautiful ear, excellent pitch but she does not read music, and she doesn't have to, she reads chords. And I know others, like Brian Parker, brilliant musician, can read anything that's put in front of him, but he is not an ad lib solo player. It's just the difference.

During the war Tiddy Mead played piano and recorder, and reached a good standard:

When I was 16, about 1943, I was at Nunthorpe School, and my dad came in with two clarinets one night, he'd got them from a fella at work. I managed to make 'em squeak, and make some notes out of it, and my interest was started, and I couldn't leave the damn things alone after that.

At school we formed a little band, which was frowned upon at that time. The headmaster didn't like the idea, only the drop-outs did that sort of thing, and so there was a bit of hassle going on, but in the class there was a lad with a saxophone for sale.

Saxophones just seemed to jell with me and I neglected the clarinet and persevered with the saxophone until you couldn't keep me off the damn thing. Then I left school and went on the railway which was fortunate because I was exempt from National Service, and I didn't realise but it opened up the field for this playing.

My aunt was going out with a trumpet player called Vic Parker, who played with Ted Rowell at the Rowntree's dance on a Saturday night. She mentioned that I was doing very well on clarinet and saxophone. He said, 'Brilliant. I'm just the one to deal with it, I'll have a word with Ted', and then I joined that band, and sat beside Jimmy Cave. I subsequently took over from him and became a member of Ted Rowell's band, and that was the start of me going into the dance band field. And I'd got the classical side with the orchestra but couldn't cope with them both, and I dropped that and became an out and out member of Ted Rowell.

Ted Rowell Band at Coach and Horses, Jubbergate. February 1947. Front L to R - Dickie Bailey, trombone, Arthur Berriman, trumpet, Tiddy Mead, sax and clarinet, Ted Rowell, piano. Back L to R - Harry Berriman, drums, Stan Cole, bass.   *(Courtesy Tiddy Mead)*

Ted's was a very good band, he was very dedicated on piano, and like all the other bands at that time you were here, there and everywhere. Then he got a regular spot at the Railway Institute on a Saturday night. The De Grey Rooms was the big hot spot in York, second to that was the Co-op in Railway Street, where the Revels were. So his band never quite reached the heights of the other two, and in the process, I was gigging around, because if Ted didn't have a job I was asked by others to help out, so I was beginning to hear other bands, play with other bands. That's how I met them, all these different people. I think I depped with every band in York! It gave me experience, sight-reading was no problem to me, because I'd been brought up that way. I'm not a busker, my teaching was that if you had music, you played music, you didn't extemporise.

The first formation dancing I ever saw was at Full Sutton aerodrome. They were Poles, and I went playing with Ted Rowell and they all got dressed in their national dress and it was a gorgeous sight. And they did formation dancing, and that's the first time I ever came across it, and it was a sight to behold. I'd only be about 20 at the time and it made an impression on me. These women came out in their national dress costume and they all danced, and oh it was a pleasure to play, it really was.

Then I joined the Revels. It was run by Hugh Robertson. Harry Warrington was his side kick and that ran into some long sessions and they got this regular job at Pocklington. At the same time Hugh Robertson had climbed his ladder in business and so he packed in playing and the band became Harry Warrington's. I was five or six years at Pocklington, we had every Saturday

Ted Rowell Band c1948. Ted Rowell, piano, Harry Berriman, drums. L to R -Arthur Berriman, trumpet, Tiddy Mead, alto, Gordon Knight, tenor. *(Courtesy Tiddy Mead)*

Norman Holmes Dance Band. L to R - Unknown, Billy Mendez, Norman Holmes, Harry Wheeler, unknown, Harold Arthur. *(Courtesy Christine Lancaster)*

night and practically all the private jobs that went into the Oak House. Billy Hall used to do a couple of nice vocals with the Revels. Miss Otis Regrets, I liked him doing that one.

When the Revels finished at Pocklington they came back into York doing private work, a lot of masonic work and Licensed Victuallers' do's. Every lodge used to have dinner dances, and the big connection with Masonic Lodges was Norman Holmes. The women folk loved him, his drummer was a lad called Harold Arthur. And Norman decided he was going to pack in playing, and he handed the band over to Harold Arthur [this was the County Players, which started in the early 1950s].

And in that band was a lad who taught me saxophone, Harry Strain, and he wanted me to turn pro, but I couldn't leave home, my dad was very ill, and we needed the money, couldn't take the risk. But Johnny Sutton came then on the scene with a young band, which won the championship at the Riley Smith Hall in Tadcaster in 1949.

That was the only big band there was, and to be quite honest, he couldn't have done that if he'd been in the Union, he couldn't have got the money in them days. Most bands were running at six, seven or eight pieces, that was the average. I've been down on a Sunday morning with rehearsals, and I've seen those lads ending with £2 for working three nights a week. I used to say to

120

Geoff Towse, 'I wouldn't do this lad, not for that amount, I can get that for one night, come on, it's silly'. But they were really into big band music, they liked Stan Kenton and all the big stuff.

I went to see Derek Dunning when he won the competition at Belle Vue in Manchester, because I was taking lessons off him on clarinet, and I was teaching him to read music! We did another contest at the Rialto and it was Tye Bruce and a makeshift band that did it. We didn't get any award as such. We got a couple of commendations of players.

There was good rivalry at that time, but there were dance halls all over. You didn't have enough bands to cover the amount of halls. Every village hall had a dance, it was the only form of entertainment. Radio had got stale, television hadn't really come on the scene, and so dancing and cinema was life, that's how the girls met the lads, the meeting place was the dance hall.

I had about four or five years with Eric Gill. He'd taken over Huby on a Saturday night, from the Trumpet Twins, and I joined him. When Huby packed up he went in at Gallery Golf. Horace Tappin came in after me, and then when Eric died, Horace took it from there.

The Eric Gill Band, led by Eric on piano, was legendary in York. He had formed a band as a young man in 1936 and played throughout York and district. He died in 1976 at the age of only 56.

Tiddy believes that York has had some very good musicians:

Ted Pratt, of course, was way out on his own on trumpet. Brian Parker was a tremendous trombonist, very talented lad. Derek Dunning was very accomplished, and Bobby Hirst was really good. Gordon Cottom, a very nice pianist and Geoff Knaggs was another wonderful pianist.

When you get a small band you've all got to work damned hard, because it's on your shoulders. Because you didn't get covered up by other people, that's one of the big differences. You get a five-piece sax section, and one person in that section is a leader, the first alto. Now if he isn't good, the sax section is rubbish, the other lads can be good players, but if he isn't good and doesn't lead 'em right, it's dead as a bloody dodo. The other ones can be good or indifferent but he's the one that matters. That's where the responsibility lies. So in a small band you work a damn sight harder, than you would when you're sat in with these sort of people. I used to work hard because I was the leader of six, so whatever I did, whatever time I went into, I put emphasis on loud and soft, they had to go with me, I was the one that was leading them.

121

In a small band, if you only have a trumpet, alto, piano, bass, drums, then those two front line men had a lot of hard work to do. Then you get one in, could be a tenor saxophone, so that was a little bit of support for the alto player, but really that was about your nucleus. So that's where the difference comes in between small bands, and big bands. A small bandsman really has a lot of work to do. When you did old time [dancing] in the early stages, the eight-some reels, they were killers. When you have to play a wind instrument for that, you want lungs like nobody's business, and you've got to gallop like hell. And they go on a long time, they really do.

All big bands had arrangements whereby you had solo passages, and then when you come to solos they had to stand up and do them, and that comes down to the ability of the person in question. Sometimes you'd get a good player but put him up on his feet, and he's gone. It's like putting a singer on stage. They could be a damn good singer until you put 'em on a stage in front of a microphone and a load of people and it just folds up. Nerves could do that. So it isn't always the best player who is taking the solo. When you're in a big band you have to conform to the dynamics, what's on the music, when you're in a small outfit you please yourself. But when I stand up and take a solo with them, I play it in tempo but I play it my way.

Tiddy Mead expresses himself through his music so that his instrument becomes an extension of his person:

I play as I feel. I never honestly will play a tune twice the same. It depends on how I feel, what I'm thinking. So if I want to play softly I play softly, if I want to play loud, I play loud, if I want to basically cry down the instrument, I cry down the instrument, and I talk when I'm playing, I'm speaking through the instrument, or singing through the instrument. That's my way of playing, I'll be honest with you, I say 'This is me, listen to me'. I can't avoid it.

Valerie Mountain was one of the few women musicians in York at this time:

My father Herbert Danby was a good amateur. He played in Stan Shouksmith's Harmonica Band, about 20 of 'em on mouth organs, and me dad also played mandolin, and piano accordion, and violin a bit squeakily.

I did have lessons, 'cos I could play when I was about three years old. When they showed me a piano, I sat and played it, but me mother wanted me to have lessons from a lady for 1/- an hour. She taught me for about four years, and she said she just couldn't teach me any more because I could pick things up quicker than she could. I'm a busker, and I can read, but I'd rather not read. And when she played a piece through to me, I'd memorise it, and play it back to her, even though I couldn't read it.

I met my husband in 1945. I was 15, and he was a drummer, and we met at the church hall. He had a band and his pianist couldn't get one night, so the accordionist Len Hall, had rung me up and asked if I could go, and that's when I met me husband. I did this job to fill in that night, and then later on I joined his band. Len Hall, me on piano, Bob Brown on tenor and Bunny Hall on trumpet. And I loved Bob Brown, what a player. They used to look after me, make a fuss of me, 'cos I was only 15. But you weren't threatened in those days, you could go anywhere.

Don Hattee played Hawaiian guitar, with a rhythm guitar Bob Goodall. My favourite tune of the time was Harbour Lights, and I says to me husband, 'Go and ask if they can play Harbour Lights. So he went up and asked. 'No, we don't know that one'. 'Well she'll play it for you then'. I got up and played it and they said, 'We've been looking for a pianist, will you join our band?', so that was the first band I played with after I got married, 1949. Probably Don Hattee And His Serenaders. We played at the Post Office Club, and then they brought in a jazz guitarist, Pete Sparling. Bob Goodall was as near Django Reinhardt as you're ever gonna get, and when he and Pete got going, it was fantastic.

We lived up South Bank and we went to the Winning Post for a drink and they had a lovely grand piano in a bay window and I'd sit and play. My husband liked me to play piano and he was a friend of Derek Dunning's before I even knew him. I remember Derek coming into the Winning Post and saying, 'Will you join my band Val?', and if it had been Ted Heath, or Joe Loss I couldn't have been more excited. That would be about 1950 and I was so thrilled 'cos in those days it was a lovely band, and played at the Assembly Rooms. I'd play the odd waltz, or tango on accordion. I've always had problems, because they're so heavy. So many couplers on, it's beautiful, and I know where all the notes, bass, counter bass, minors, diminished, but it's not easy to play one, it's too heavy.

In those days, it was every Saturday at the Assembly Rooms, and maybe the Windmill on Blossom Street, we had a few jobs there. And these posh jobs. I remember once playing at Grantley Hall near Ripon, and it had midnight blue velvet curtains and a white grand piano, I'll never forget that job, it was so beautiful, and if I remember right, it was a Polish audience, and I knew the Polish National Anthem, and I played it for 'em, and nobody sang, but they stood to attention.

We did lots of lovely work, 'cos Derek knew a lot of the nobility, we played for Colonel Legard at Malton, Major Hillary Pearson-Adams, at Brandsby Hall, we even played for the Duchess of Kent at a hunt ball. The only trouble was it'd get to two o'clock and, 'Can you go on for another couple of hours?', and we'd be out of breath by this time, and I'd three children to get off to school. But we'd some lovely jobs.

And I was available for anybody else that wanted me as well, the Tony Whitehead Band, and I did a bit of work with Jack Carr, he could charm the birds off the trees. He had a nice drummer, Terry Shackleton, I can't remember who was on bass, Jack on this wailing sax, and me on piano, playing Bettys Ballroom mainly.

I wanted to be a jazz person, and Bobby Hirst tried his best to teach me, but you've either got it, or you haven't. I can play most any tune you ask, but I can't play jazz. You had to be better than the fellas, to get the work. The only other woman musician I knew, at the time, was a lady called Jessie. She used to play at Knavesmire Hotel, a real Winifred Atwell-type pianist, but we were about the only two, all the rest were fellas. A woman was taken on as a last resort, they'd try all these third rate fellas, and if they couldn't go they'd get me. But that's why I was so honoured when Derek came and asked me to join his band, me, not some fella. They had the Melody Maker Championships at Belle Vue in Manchester. What a night, there was Bobby Hirst on piano, Derek on alto and clarinet, Lou Pearce on bass, and Tony Jones on drums, and they were the jazz set-up in York in those days. Fabulous.

Derek Dunning Band in September 1944.   English Martyrs' Church Hall.   L to R - Tony Jones, drums, Lou Pearce, bass, Bobby Hirst, piano, and Derek Dunning.

(Courtesy Val Mountain)

We had a very nice uniform with the Dunning Band. I had a black pleated skirt, red coat with black lapels, and Derek Dunning Orchestra badge across there, a white shirt and black tie. You felt good, 'cos you were with the Dunning Band.

The Assembly Rooms held 450 people and with the back place open it held 650 people. On a Saturday night that queue would be right the way round into Museum Street waiting for tickets to get in, so, it was very popular. In those days there wasn't the entertainment in pubs and clubs. Pubs then, you went for a pint, and a game of dominoes and darts. You didn't have all these quiz shows, and karaoke and entertainment. Your main entertainment on a Saturday night was a dance, be it a village hall dance, or Assembly Rooms.

Dickie Bailey was fantastic. Derek used to get him in occasionally and one night we were doing a tune, and Derek pointed at Dickie to do a solo, and Dickie played twenty-four solos of this tune, and wouldn't sit down, but never repeated himself. Derek was going purple, 'Sit down will you?' You were only supposed to stand up and do one chorus, he just closed his eyes, and he was away was Dickie. He could pick a mouthpiece up and play that without an instrument attached. He used to take snuff, and he'd say, 'Have a pinch of snuff Val, clear your head out'.

In the band you always had a solo and if it was a modern waltz, they'd say, 'You play a modern waltz while we find some music', so I'd rattle off a few of me own tunes, that I liked. Once Derek got the crowd, he didn't want to let 'em go, so he never had a cut off point. He'd say, 'We'll be back in 20 minutes', and we kept going. All the trumpets and saxes went so there'd be bass, drums, piano and Derek, but he always kept it going 'till the rest of them came back and then you went off to have your supper. It was a hard working band.

It was not easy for women to get into music, probably because they would have had to make a choice between career and family. It was difficult to manage both, whereas men did not have that problem.

Oh yes, it definitely was a man's world, and I don't think I've ever gone looking for a job yet. What jobs I've had, people have asked me to do, I've never touted for jobs. Somebody would ring me up and say 'Can you come and play the piano?' I don't ever remember applying for anything.

Gordon Cottom was a pianist, but later he came to play the vibes:

I always have been interested in dance music, I remember at school we had a piano in the class room, and me and another lad called Henderson used to play duets. Hold That Tiger and all that sort of stuff! And once the headmaster came back from his lunch early and caught us - oh dearie me! I can't remember what we got for that.

I played for Bill Serby at the De Grey Rooms, he was an excellent trumpet player. It was all the rage, one trumpet and five saxes and the rhythm section. Geoff and I were the leaders of the Modernaires after 1953. I was supposed to be the musical director. I bought sheet music from Banks, for our ordinary music, I used to go to Leeds to buy the latest, because they were coming out thick and fast in those days, I'd get two or three arrangements every week. And we'd all pay so much a week between us to buy these things. I'd get these on Wednesday afternoons, come back and we were rehearsing them on Wednesday night. I sometimes sang with the Modernaires, duets with Margaret Cairns like Baby It's Cold Outside.

I'd double on vibes. I had some Ajax vibes, I even took those to the Chase with me when I started there. Then Philip Morris, [who owned the Chase], bought me new Premier vibes, they were just there for me one Saturday when I rolled up. He was a kind man, I nearly dropped through the floor when he said they were mine. Afterwards we used to do gigs at Tadcaster, and I played with Tony Whitehead at the Craiglands Hotel, at Ilkley. I'd bomb over there three times a week, playing piano.

Music has been a big part of Gordon's life. He even wrote his own song, Funny What Love Can Do:

When I was playing solo at Middlethorpe, at the beginning I'd play four nights there, but it tailed off towards the end, but I could please myself what I played. One person in particular said, 'I've never, ever heard a restaurant pianist play like you before, with your heart and soul in it'. I said, 'As long as I know there is just one person listening that's good enough for me'.

In the years following the war, dance competitions were very important. The Derek Dunning Swing Quartet won the Melody Maker West Yorkshire Dance Band Championships in Bradford in June 1945 and he was judged the best alto sax player. One of the judges was Ted Heath. On September 13, the Melody Maker South-East Yorkshire championships were held in Doncaster and this time the Derek Dunning Quintette took part, with Derek winning the prize for best alto sax. In February 1946, Derek Dunning's Swing Sextet won first prize at the Melody Maker East Yorkshire Dance Band Contest in Hull. Derek played alto saxophone and clarinet.

In a programme at the Rialto in 1947, two York dance bands competed with other bands from Yorkshire. The Tye Bruce Orchestra with five saxophones, French horn, trumpet, piano, bass and drums played East Of The Sun, a slow foxtrot, Santa Lucia, a waltz, and Disc Jockey Jump, a quickstep. The other band was the Leithart Quintet led by Bobby Hirst and featured tenor sax, trombone, piano, bass and drums. Their offering consisted of a slow foxtrot,

Over The Rainbow, a waltz, Tenderly, and a quickstep, High On An Open Mike. The competition was adjudicated by Dick Katz of the Duke Ellington Orchestra and Keith Bird, lead tenor saxophone with Geraldo And His Orchestra.

On Friday May 7, 1948 the Melody Maker Central Yorkshire District Dance Band Championship was held at the Astoria Ballroom in Leeds. Eight bands from Yorkshire competed and the Modernaires led by Johnny Sutton won the contest. The adjudicators were Edgar Jackson, of the Melody Maker and Alfie Noakes, the famous lead trumpeter with the Geraldo orchestra.

The 1950 New Musical Express North Yorkshire Dance Band Championship took place on Sunday May 14, at the Rialto. There were three York dance bands taking part, the Leithart Quartet led by Bobby Hirst, the Terry Barnett Quartet (run by Terry Shackleton) who also featured a four-piece band, (tenor sax, piano, bass and drums), and the Modernaires Dance Orchestra, a 15 piece band, featuring five saxophones, three trumpets, three trombones, piano, guitar, bass and drums. Their repertoire was quite ambitious with Ad Lib Frolic for the slow foxtrot, Far Away Places for the waltz, and Stan Kenton's Intermission Riff for the quickstep. Johnny Sutton's orchestra was by far the

Derek Dunning Swing Sextet winning competition in Hull 1946. L too R - Will Acton, Ken Kenyon, Len Cundall, Billy Steel, Derek Dunning and Sid Dale.

(Courtesy Angela Dunning)

Sax section of the Modernaires at De Grey Rooms c1951. L to R - Henry Thomson, Pete Frost, Geoff Towse, Bill Ibbotson, Gerry Allen. *(Courtesy Bob Scott)*

biggest in the contest, with most of the others being either four or six-piece bands. Also appearing that evening were Kathleen Stobart (acclaimed as 'the world's greatest girl tenor saxophonist') And Her New Music, a seven-piece dance band, and the Johnny Dankworth Seven with Kathy Stobart and Johnny as judges. Brian Parker recalls that the Modernaires won, and the judges 'said very nice things to us'. I recently saw the Humphrey Lyttelton Band playing in Beverley, and Kathy 'still blows a mean tune' on the baritone sax. She has fond memories of the contest, especially as her husband, Bert Courtley, played trumpet with her band at that event.

Pete Williams recalls that the Leithart Quartet, comprised at this time of Bobby Hirst on piano, Ray Backhouse on bass, Ray Phillips on drums and Dickie Bailey on trombone, won the North Eastern Band Championships at the Rialto, judged by Harry Gold. They played Kiss Me Again, Blue Moon and a Dickie Bailey original called Ha! During their performance, neither Dickie nor Bobby had a note of music in front of them.

In 1953 the Modernaires split, seemingly because of arguments over money. Geoff Towse and Gordon Cottom and some other members left and kept the name of the Modernaires. The other half of the band stayed at the De Grey Rooms under the name of Johnny Sutton And His Band.

Being married to a musician was not easy. Wives and also children have to accept the role that music played in many a man's life. Some wives were not very understanding. But others like Bob Halford's wife and Harry Warrington's wife came to accept the loneliness and were willing to encourage their husbands. Harry's daughter Sue Baker explains:

She spent a lot of time of her own, and at times like New Year's Eve, he was never there. It was the music, he would have gone if they weren't paying him anything, he just loved it. But it's no good for family life isn't playing, not for the ones that are left at home. I wouldn't have liked it if I was me mother, and if there was any family thing that was going on, he never would give up his playing.

He used to get invited to lots of parties 'cos in those days more people had pianos than they do now, and he'd get invited so he could play the piano. And even if he wasn't meant to be playing, he gravitated towards the corner where the piano was, and once he got there, he never came out. He was shy really in lots of ways. He got more pleasure from playing and entertaining them, I think he'd rather play than speak.

Her sister Liz Calpin agrees:

We grew up never expecting him to be there, he was never at home on Bonfire Night, somebody else, like an uncle, always had to let your fireworks off. He was never there at Christmas, but we just accepted that if it was some family function, he would shoot off at quarter to seven because he's playing. It didn't seem funny to me, that was our lives. He never gave up his playing, he was

The Revels. L to R - Hugh Robertson, trombone, Bunny Hall, trumpet, unknown, bass unknown, Tony Whitehead, drums, unknown, Les Kirkpatrick, tenor, Harry Warrington, piano.   *(Courtesy Liz Calpin)*

129

always off to do it, it was like a drug. I think if you've got a talent then, you use it don't you, and get pleasure from it and everything else fits round it. Me mother could take it or leave it but me dad certainly couldn't leave it.

When I was a kid, we had an old 78, and I was with him when they made it, with Robinson Roses on one side, and I think it was somewhere in Piccadilly in those days and you went and paid, and you made your record.

But he was a very quiet man, and although he had his own orchestra, he never fronted it, just played the piano, and the announcements were always made by somebody else. We knew it was his band, because he used to have to ring round at home to get people to play, and then pay the money out. But if you walked into a dance hall and they were playing, you wouldn't have known it was me dad's band. He was a very shy person really. It wouldn't occur to you to tell him not to go, because all our lives it had been paramount, his playing. Long before he died, we used to say on his tombstone we'll put, 'Oh count me out, I'm playing at seven'.

CHAPTER FIVE. CAN YOU FEEL IT?
Jazz in York

'Music is your own experience, your thoughts, your wisdom. If you don't live it, it won't come out of your horn'. Charlie Parker.

Jazz musicians say that you have to feel the music, to dig inside yourself to find what's there before you can tell a story. Nat Hentoff described Dizzy Gillespie's playing as if 'he were feeling so good that he had to let some joy out or he'd explode. He made me feel glad just to be listening, he played as if he had just found out he was going to live forever. Hearing Dizzy was like getting a transfusion. The thing that makes jazz so exciting is that you never know when that time is going to come when everyone in a group is on fire. You're cooking when you can play everything that jumps into your mind, when your fingers practically go where they're supposed to before you're even aware what you're going to play next, and when that happens your horn is a part of you. And when everyone in a jazz combo is at that level, the experience is the most exciting I know'.

Jazz is not easy to define. People seem to love it or hate it. In the early part of the 20th century, it was coming over from America and having a huge effect on musicians and listeners in Britain but what was labelled jazz then has no relation to what came later. It was a music which, by its very nature, was open to constant change and development. Following the Second World War, there were musicians in York who began to love it. One of the main people was Bobby Hirst. Lew Skords explains how Bobby and others started a jazz club above the Drill Hall:

It was a very nice little spot, but we had to get permission from the Chief Constable, and of course in those days jazz was synonymous with drugs, booze and you name it. But we had a good spell going there for a while. They weren't thick on the ground the jazz venues. Any sign of 'it' and they'd raid the place, stop it before it's started in other words.

I liked playing Dixieland which you don't hear at all now, it's disappeared. It's trad now, but Dixieland was very good, it was very loose, swinging. And mainstream, that's what I like. Getting towards the modern style.

Just as in the 1920s when jazz was arriving from America, there was a deep mistrust that the music would somehow 'corrupt'. In 1955 when various York pubs applied for Sunday music licences, they had to assure the magistrates that there would be 'no jazz bands'. So it was quite daring to offer a jazz club in

131

these premises. Although York musicians admitted to enjoying a few drinks, they knew nothing of drugs at this time, though American jazz musicians like Louis Armstrong were renowned for smoking cannabis, and perhaps it was this that made people wary of jazz clubs.

Another place that did offer jazz, was the Golden Fleece in Pavement. Lew went there:

Now that really was alive, it had a hell of a lot of atmosphere. If I couldn't get in I used to go creeping round the backyard, through Fossgate. That was really jumping. And that was where one of the geniuses of music used to play. Dickie Bailey. Not just my words, but the top pros who came to judge the Melody Maker contest. He walked away with the Individual Musician Award. Eccentric, mad as a hatter, but brilliant musician.

It's the window to a musician's soul, music, without any doubt. If you've got anything to say, it'll come through your music. And jazz, that's the vehicle for your emotions to come out.

When it starts to swing and it all comes together, so it excites the band, then it gets to the people. You don't learn it, you either can or you can't. When it's very good and it goes right through the band, that's a night you'll never forget. It's marvellous. If it doesn't communicate to the audience, they don't come in.

Trombones come in a few different bores. I played a large bore, a custom made trombone. I wanted that to get a good tone for jazz. It's not the easiest thing to play, to use an instrument like that in a trombone section of four, blowing lead. Normally a lead trombone plays a small or medium bore. Easier to reach the top, and easier to blow. I was on a very hard game. I had to blow half an hour at home, every night, just to keep my lip on top form to get the top notes. You had to hit some high notes in the dance band, the band was playing copies of professional band music. Count Basie originals and Glenn Miller originals.

If there was a good piano, you'd find the musicians, that's what determined it. We'd go around pub crawling, not to booze, to find good pianos. There was a chap, Gil Fox, best tenor player York's ever seen, we did a jazz parade at his wedding in 1953. He knocked at my door, says 'I've found the ultimate piano, let's go'. Ended up at Naburn, Blacksmith's Arms would it be. Well you can imagine, it hadn't been played since Wellington's day. I've never seen a piano like it, it was built like the Bismark. I've never ever heard a sound like it anywhere, and I've played some bloody good pianos. I'll never forget that night, I don't know whether I wept, but I should have done. It was that good!

Parade for Gil Fox's wedding at Holy Redeemer Church, Boroughbridge Road, March 1953. L to R - Stan Bowsen, cymbals, Phil Jackson, bass, Bobby Hirst, squeeze box, Ray Phillips, side drum, Derek Parker, trumpet, Denis Goodwin, trombone, Johnny Forde, bass drum. Leader - Bill Banks. *(Courtesy Mike Dann)*

Bob Scott loved jazz:

I listened to the bands on the radio, I can remember Henry Hall broadcasting. But what got me interested in jazz was a lad who became an evacuee and his father sent him to Canada, Brian Scrines. He came back in 1946, and he was courting my sister, but when he came round he brought records, which we hadn't seen. I listened to them more than my sister, and all of a sudden I got a taste for it. American records weren't readily available, there were certain restrictions. I went to Banks and also there was the one in Pavement, Hugh Robertson's, but at Banks, a chap called Cyril more or less ran the record department there. And I started buying Woody Herman, and that's what triggered me off on trombone, I heard Woody Herman, and I heard Bill Harris, and that was it.

But Jack Prendergast, who ran the Rialto and put these bands on, he objected to people going to play in a jazz club after the shows, he thought it would detract from people paying to see the show, when they could go to the jazz club and hear it for nothing. He was calling the tunes really, so they stopped doing it. The Colliergate Drill Hall, I think they had a smaller room where there was a bar, and they ran jazz in there, Bobby Hirst, Derek Dunning - the Leithart Quartet.

Dunning's band, they were all into Charlie Parker. Parker sounded way out and modern in those days, it's still very difficult to play, bebop, but it doesn't sound ultra modern. You had two schools, the New Orleans and the Dixielanders, and if you went into a pub and there was two groups they wouldn't even speak to each other. Jazz is my first love, when it comes off, whatever you're playing, you get a kick out of it.

Bob started up the 59 Jazz Club:

It was on the A59, the Hammond hotel. It did very well, I got over 400 members. They didn't attend every week. Financially it was disastrous. Probably should have been charging more, and if I had more money I would have been more certain of getting the bands there, but it became a bit of a nightmare getting a band.

Music's a funny thing to be involved with. Sometimes you set off at six o'clock in the evening, and get back in the early hours of the morning but you do it because you enjoy playing. You don't just get your instrument out and go and play, if it's a brass instrument you've got to keep your chops in. You've got to work at it. Somebody did a list of an orchestra, brass people drink pints, horns don't associate with trumpets and trombones because they think they're one cut above and they probably drink halves. And the strings don't associate with the brass at all, they look down on them, and they drink gin and tonics.

You used to get kids flocking round the stand, listening, and in those days they could recognise a good jazz solo. There was also loads of Mickey Mouse bands, playing silly music, that had a following. But the bands that were good, the best bands, these kids could stand round and when a soloist stood up, and if he was on form that night, playing a great jazz solo, they'd recognise it and go with him. What happened to the taste in music? They can't do it now. You could go out there and question about 100 people, and I bet you'd find about two who knew what a good jazz solo was.

There were dance arrangements, but in Jimmy Lally's there wasn't any scope for jazz at all. They were designed to be played by any combination, arranged in such a way that you wouldn't miss an instrument, if there wasn't one there.

You'll never make jazz popular. They didn't regard Tommy Dorsey as a jazz band, it was a swing band, but he had good jazz solos in it. I think it's what's available to the kids at the time, what the record companies and what the commercial music people push at kids. The cool school came along and just sat there and expected whoever was out there to understand and like it - but they didn't, so they went elsewhere. And what did the groups do? They stood up, and they had all these antics. After all is said and done, they were entertaining them, whether the music was sub standard or not, that's a matter of taste, and that's what pulled the kids in. And if they could stand up and entertain like the Beatles, they were on a sure winner.

Later Bob had his own band, Scott's Hardware:

Just a jazz blow, in the Black Swan. The landlord was Robert Atkinson who was a pianist. I approached him to put jazz on, on a Sunday night. He went out and bought a piano, and I had a trumpet player, and a tenor player, Dave Kendall and Dave Wheatley, both from Guiseley way. We had some good nights in there. Bobby Hirst, Mike Brown on bass and maybe other people. Jazz sessions very rarely, seem to last, they fizzle out because there's no money in it and it usually becomes a headache, and eventually you get fed up of working your socks off for nothing. York hasn't really produced a lot of jazz people, it's produced some good ones, but not in abundance.

There was the 59 club, and I arranged for a Sunday night jazz session at the pub. After we'd finished there we went to Peter Madden's, all in one night, and had another blow there. And Ken Turner's brother, who came from Canada, thought what a swinging place York is, he'd never seen anything like it. All this jazz going on! But it was only a one-off really.

The Big Coach, upstairs, I've played in a jazz session up there. The Londesboro' in Petergate had a big room at the back and they had jazz in there and the Half Moon in Blake Street had jazz sessions in the back room.

In the early 1950s Gordon Reed led the resident band at the Chase Hotel, with Harley Acton on piano. Harley had studied classical piano from the age of eight but when he heard records by jazz pianists like Count Basie and Teddy Wilson he preferred to play their kind of music. He also played solo piano in the Society Club in the early 1960s.

The Mick Smith Quartet later became resident at the Chase Hotel for 31 years. Mick Smith (who had originally played with the Modernaires on double bass) was keen on modern jazz and they played for Saturday night dinner dances. The other members of the quartet were Laurie Cleeton on piano, Frankie Martin on vocals, Ray Brown on drums. They also played jazz every Friday night at the De Grey Rooms in the late 1960s.

Brian Murphy got demobbed from National Service and in early 1950 developed his interest in live jazz:

Band at the Chase Hotel 1950. Leo Burrows, drums, Gil Fox, sax, Harley Acton, piano, Gordon Reed, MC.

(Courtesy Paul Acton)

I went to the old York Jazz Club, [above the Gunners club] the Black Swan in Coney Street. That used to be the only centre for jazz in York at that time. From the mid 1940s to the mid 1950s, we'd get band concerts at the Rialto. Ted Heath, Teddy Foster, Geraldo, and of course at the end of the performances quite a few members of the band would come down to the jazz club in Coney Street and sit in, or just sit and listen.

One night Geraldo had been playing at the Rialto, then we hot footed it down to the jazz club. And Bobby Hirst was playing at the time. And that night he was offered a job playing with the Geraldo orchestra by a member of the band, the only thing was Bob couldn't read a note of music. Had he been able to, I don't suppose there would have been any limit to where Bobby Hirst could have gone. But thankfully for York he didn't.

Brian Murphy began his singing career at the Spotted Cow Jazz Club, which is covered in volume two of this publication. He was at the venue one night with a friend.

And I just happened to say to her, 'This is absolutely marvellous, I could really sing with a group like this'. And the next thing I knew, the pianist came over, and, 'What would you like to sing?' So I reeled three numbers off the top of me head, and he said, 'Oh, this is our kind of music, we'll do all three', so that was it, from that moment I never looked back. It was the first time I'd actually sung in public, and I thoroughly enjoyed it. I had marvellous musicians, a great bunch of lads. They listened to what I was doing, I was listening to what they were doing, and the whole thing jelled, and it was absolutely great, and I was asked in fact if I'd go back and it turned out that I'd go there every Friday and Saturday night for years. The original pianist was Reg Sollitt but he moved on and we got a new pianist, another marvellous fella, Harley Acton.

And we settled down then to over a decade of absolutely marvellous weekends, we had some fantastic times, every Friday, every Saturday, and every Burns Night, irrespective of when Burns Night fell, and it was whilst I was there that I was offered my first semi-pro gig. One of the chaps who was a regular there, Ray Phillips, a drummer, said to me, 'Do you fancy joining a residency at the Chase Hotel, with Mike Smith and his band'. The Chase, I thought, was the absolute four star sort of place. A couple of weeks later he said could I do an audition, and we went through half a dozen numbers. At the end Mike Smith said 'You've got the job, when can you start?'. So for a number of years we did every Friday, Saturday, and quite often Wednesday as well, but then the rock 'n' roll era crept in, and dinner dances lost their appeal. But I learned an awful lot whilst I was there.

The personnel rotated as people went and came back and one thing and another, but the basic line-up was Mike Smith on bass, Ray Phillips was the drummer, Laurie Cleeton was piano, and then we had Joe Bulmer. He was piano, organ, and also played the vibes. Ernie Hampson was a guitar player. Joe, Laurie and Ernie, had all been professional musicians. Ernie had played for Oscar Rabin and several other bands, and moved all over the place with them, and he only came to the Chase when he retired.

Another character was Laurie. He was a Londoner but he'd been up here flying Halifaxes from Burn and Riccall, tail end of the war. He was, for a long time, Anne Shelton's accompanist.

In the Chase, Laurie would play the dinner music. Mike would tell us, 'You needn't turn up before quarter to nine lads, because they're feeding'. But Laurie was there for eight o'clock, and he would play whilst the diners were eating. And then at about quarter to nine, as the deserts were being served, we would go on and literally we would rehearse. Mike would say 'Have we got any new numbers this week, anyone who wants to try anything?'. I might suggest one and he'd say 'Right, what key is it, how shall we take it?' We'd do the stuff which we, as jazz musicians, liked. Just soft cool jazz numbers, which you couldn't play for once they started dancing. We'd do a bit of Green Dolphin Street, and a few bossa novas, and then once they started dancing, we started playing for dancing as soon as the first couple got up.

We did the Saturday gig and a couple of days early on the following week I was in town and I saw Mike Smith, and he said, 'Ray had a heart attack this morning, he just dropped down dead in his shop', so that was the end of a very great musical talent. He was a great drummer was Raymond, and he had a very dry sense of humour, and a very quick wit, he was fun to be around. Ernie was already quite elderly and he died shortly after Mike. I think I'm the sole survivor. So there's a nice little group somewhere up there, I hope they're not waiting for the singer, 'cos I'm not ready to join them yet. They were great people.

We had Ken Kenyon with us when Ray Phillips was off sick. He had a very good residency with Gordon Cottom, Tony Witham on bass, for many years at the Abbey Park Hotel on The Mount, then they had a residency in the lounge in the Post House.

At Terry's one night a fight broke out. Unfortunately it was at our end of the room, a table was knocked over and everybody stopped dancing, and the vast majority of people went to the far end of the room, and left the combatants *knocking seven bells out of each other. I didn't know what to do and Mike said, 'Keep playing lads'. And I was singing and the only people who moved were the fighters. At the end of the medley, somebody was ejected. Apologies made all round, and then we started up again!*

There was another time at the Milton Rooms, in Malton, we'd just set up, and I had a microphone stand, and thought I'd just move it a bit further back, and I stepped back, and off the edge of the stage. It was quite a drop but fortunately, up against the stage was a table with spot prizes on it, and I hit this table, which broke my fall and then I rolled off on to the floor. And I sent these presents flying. But they were very solicitous after my welfare, the lady who was organising it couldn't do enough, she wanted to buy me a brandy and everything. But I said 'No, I'm quite all right, I've fallen off the stage stone cold sober, I better not have a brandy'!

In the Black Swan, upstairs there were a couple of rooms, and one was quite large and that's where jazz was held. In the late 1940s, Bobby Hirst was there, Denis Goodwin, Mike Smith, Ray Phillips, they all used to call there, and perform. But the type of music, it depended who was playing. You see musicians have their own sort of ideas. For local people who liked their jazz, it was very well attended. If you were a good local musician then, it didn't matter whether you were a pianist, drummer, trombone player, saxophonist, 'Come and have a knock', meant get up and have a blow. But if you were an unknown quantity, they were always ready to say, 'Come up, have a go, see what you can do'.

As a singer you had to prove yourself. Every time you met a different person or you sang with a different band, you had to prove yourself. There was a feeling amongst a lot of musicians that no matter how hard you tried, singers and drummers aren't musicians. I don't know why, maybe 'cos you don't do everything to the dots, I don't know, but I've found I had to prove myself, for years.

But then after a while, it stopped. People knew me for what I could do, and from then on I would be invited. I'd visit the Black Swan in Peasholme Green for instance, and there's been jazz on, and Brian Thacker has said 'Come on, give us a song', and I think that's the highest accolade you can get, if you drop in somewhere unannounced to listen to something and then to be asked to 'Give us a song'. Without music life would have lost a lot of its colour. I owe music a great deal, not just because I enjoyed singing, but I enjoyed listening to music, for as long as I can remember.

Chase Hotel 1960s. L to R - Ken Kenyon, drums, Mick Smith, bass, Gordon Cottom, vibes, Bobby Hirst, piano, Bob Goodall, guitar.
(courtesy Gordon Cottom)

One of the first jazz pieces I ever really got to like was Struttin' At Some Barbecue and that must have been the winter of 1940, I heard it on the wireless. I was ten years old, and I remember telling my pal across the road. And that Bob Crosby one, Big Noise From Winnetka, I used to whistle that on me way to school. I'm a bit of a sentimentalist really, the Adagio from Rachmaninov's Second Symphony, third movement, brings tears to my eyes.

In the 1960s, I was in my 30s, but quite alive to everything that was going on, but the younger ones who were coming up, these groups were rebellious. This is one of their attractions, one of their gimmicks, the thing that they put out. 'We are the rebels'. Take it to an extreme you get the Sex Pistols and these rebels encouraged the younger generation who slipped in behind my generation, and their attitudes were coloured by the pop culture of the day.

You could go to the Society Club, for instance, for a good night out. You could hear first class musicians playing sophisticated, cool music, to which you could get up and dance, or if you didn't feel like dancing, you could sit, have a drink, and you didn't have to shout, you could have an ordinary conversation. Night clubs today are just places where the youngsters thrash about to psychedelic lighting and noise, a sound level which would probably give me a headache within three minutes flat. That's not entertainment as far as I'm concerned, but it's certainly a culture change of great, great proportions.

At the Chase you got an intimate much smaller group who are all dedicated jazz men. The only time we ever looked at music was if we'd got a new piece to do. We used to do a novelty section, where you had to buy it and learn how to do it because it was expected in the last half hour. But otherwise everything came from up in your head. The standard stuff, Jerome Kern, Cole Porter, Rodgers and Hammerstein, we knew the melodies backwards and so we could do our own thing. Provided you kept the tempo if they were dancing, you could do more or less as you wished with them.

George Roberts came to the Chase for three weeks as a dep, and he had quite a reputation. He wouldn't tolerate any mediocrity, if you worked with George then you had to do the job properly. I was terrified 'cos I'd heard a lot about George. One of our numbers was called the French Collection. A number of songs, Boom, Why Does My Heart Go Boom?, April In Paris. And Mike said, 'What we do George is...' and he reeled off the four numbers and the keys. And George turned to me and said 'Right kid, I want you to pay no attention to the first eight bars, and come in on the first beat of the ninth bar', and he started playing some gently swinging version of the Marseillaise, and then I lost track, I was busy counting, and I came in, bang on the dot, with April In Paris and we went through that medley, and at the end of it, he turned to me and said,

'All right lad, you'll do'. And Ray said that, from George, was praise indeed. He was like Bobby Hirst, he could play any tune, in any key, virtually in any style. He was the sort of man who could have played the Muskrat Ramble as a Viennese waltz, and it would have sounded good. He could do anything with a piano. And the idea of him playing the Marseillaise, was first of all because it bore no relation to the tune that I was going to sing, and he wanted to know if I knew the difference between eight bars, or nine bars. He was testing me I suppose and, I passed the test fortunately.

Eddie Lamb also played with George Roberts. At Caesar's Palace, George backed many international stars and Eddie recalls:

George was on stage with Johnnie Ray, and Judy Garland came in and Johnnie persuaded her to come on stage, so George has the distinction of having accompanied Judy Garland. He was a damn good pianist.

When George Roberts died early in 2002, he was described by jazz trombonist Ron Burnett as 'one of the finest musicians to come to York'.

Gerry Allen recalls that within the Modernaires, they had a small group in the 1950s, which satisfied the need of the 'jazz men' to perform:

Just clarinet, trumpet, trombone and tenor sax. At first I used to do it with Duncan Cooper, tenor sax and trumpet, we would come and do this, just the two of us, a jazz number, like Lester Leaps In. Not much good for dancing but there were so many people you couldn't really dance properly, it was a solid mass, just sort of creeping.

When the beat groups came in the mid-1960s, we noticed a sudden change, because they had a disco, and everybody got up for the disco, and hardly anybody got up for the ballroom dancing. It was a real sadness, and then gradually it reversed, the dancers found that the beat groups were limited, they couldn't offer the whole range of dances that the band could. So gradually the discos eased out a little bit, and the bands came back where they were running a band and a disco together.

In 1964 that seems to be the end of the era that I remember, that's when the Beatles came in. The De Grey Rooms finished, and dances went down, probably with the advent of television and discos. There was a sort of resurgence in the 1970s, a sudden interest in revival of Glenn Miller and that's brought the bands back. Mike Brown had a band at school, the Stars And Stripes, I helped them out a lot with getting started, and do a bit of playing with them now and then.

142

Lyn Chelin, pianist and jazz fan, traces her love of the music back to her teenage years:

My friend and I would go to the Holy Trinity Church in Micklegate, come out of there, and straight to the Golden Fleece and sit in awe of Teddy Rowell and his band, and I used to love Duke Ellington's Caravan. We would only be 14 or 15 and the music scene was great. There was a piano in every pub, and we'd go and sit on Derek Dunning's window sill where he lived, to hear him practise. He played at the Poppy Road Adult School dance then, he played all the latest music, I knew them all. There was a lot of adult school dancebands in them days, they learnt their craft there. It was before the war when I fell in love with jazz and the first record I ever heard and I thought this was marvellous, Django Reinhardt and Stéphane Grappelli.

I couldn't call myself a jazz pianist, but, that's why I got interested in Bobby Hirst, 'cos of his wonderful playing. I once played the piano with him, when he played the accordion, just the once. You don't want to know the piano when you heard Bobby play he was so great. I adored George Shearing and fell in love with Fats Waller, I liked his style, and I got a lot of his books. I played the Alligator Crawl, but Bobby played it much better.

I used to go round the schools playing for the keep fit classes. But I only used the music as a guide, 'cos through Bobby I was able to put a little bit more in. I learnt a lot from him, I couldn't do it like him, but it made me a better pianist. You can do the chords, you see I can do over an octave, and yet I've only got a tiny hand, because of my training.

Bobby was just magical on the piano, absolute magic. He could make the piano talk, and he could also make you laugh or cry. It was his first love and he could make an awful piano sound good. It came from his soul actually. He didn't know a note of music and he actually played a tune better than the music. The Warsaw Concerto, I heard the original, and I saw the film, but when Bobby played it, it was something. He played everything so much better, he was great. And the piano loved him as well. When he was at the Mount Royale he had a different tune for every regular who walked in, if it was a woman in a dress, he'd play The Lady In Red. He could play like Art Tatum, and Shearing and Brubeck.

But he was a modest man, a sensitive man, and his heart and soul were just in the piano, he had a love story with the piano, that was Bobby. And there could be bombs dropping, there could be any kind of tragedy, and Bobby would be on another planet. When he started a tune, it didn't matter what happened, he would finish it. There was no way he would have left off for anything, or anybody, that had to be finished. When you got him on song, I don't think there's anyone anywhere that could beat him. And when he was on song, people didn't shout and scream, they just sat and listened, they were just in awe. The standing ovations that he got were marvellous. He should have been a millionaire, and he died a pauper. Money didn't mean a thing to him, but he didn't need it, because with his great talent everybody loved him, he got all he needed, he got the love from everybody, he got taken to where he had to be, he got taken home, if he wanted a cigarette somebody would give him one, if he wanted a drink.

They wanted him, Geraldo and Ambrose. Won the Jazz Musician of the Year, three years running. He spent all his life with professional people, but you see they couldn't hold him. He was a free spirit, a one-off.

In December 1959 Yorkshire Evening Press journalist Stacey Brewer reviewed Bobby Hirst And His Music who played every Saturday at the Chase Hotel, by saying 'many people get the wrong idea about jazz. Their impression is of a 16-piece band with blaring brass blasting out vulgar arrangements. Those and others can learn something of the true meaning of jazz from hearing Bobby Hirst's quintet. The group consisted of Bobby on piano, Ken Kenyon on drums, Mick Smith on bass, Bob Goodall on guitar, and Gordon Cottom on vibes. Bobby was compared to the great British pianist George Shearing. Their library ranged from music from 1945-55 with some of their own arrangements. There were also two vocalists, Nancy Raymond and Brian King. The musicians explained that they had a closeness which helped their playing, 'an instantaneous affinity so necessary in the production of good jazz that it is immediately apparent'. As they explained 'we almost know what the others are thinking musically before they know it themselves'.

Bobby's daughter Ella Hirst was very close to him:

He lived for music. They say that he was the best, not only in Britain, but in Europe, they asked him to go to America. He was absolutely superb.

The first time I can remember him doing a concert was the Tempest Anderson in the Museum Gardens. I would have been 16 and he just decided to put a concert on. He didn't know how many people would come but it was absolutely packed, and it was fantastic. From 13 years old, he used to take me every Sunday to the Chase with him, and I'd have lunch while he was playing. There was my dad on piano, Mick Smith on bass, Ken Kenyon and Bob Goodall, whose nickname was 'Prof.'

He'd come round with me and my pals, it was like having an older brother. I loved the atmosphere, that went with it. In later years, he had a jazz thing going at the Black Swan and we would never miss a Sunday, because the atmosphere was absolutely electric, and I loved that. The fact that I'm called Ella says a lot, 'cos he was listening to Ella Fitzgerald records when I was born. I always think it was a good job he wasn't listening to Frank Sinatra. His favourite pianist was Art Tatum, but to me, me dad sounded just like Oscar Peterson, you couldn't tell the difference. He'd put a record on and say, 'This is Oscar Peterson', I'd say, 'No, it's you, dad'.

Everybody said when they heard him play, 'You should go to London', but he liked it up here and all his friends. The reason he didn't go to America was because, the band he was with, they wouldn't let me father in, because he'd once written to the Communist Party for some information. Never a member but they wouldn't give him a visa, but he was in South Africa and Tenerife for two years. He was a gypsy at heart was me dad, he never settled long enough in one place. He went to Portugal to live for a while, he would go and play his jazz, get the money, come back home.

There was also a bloke called Ken Doughty, he had a club called the Caribbean on Tadcaster Road, and Bob played the piano there. They used to get a load of famous people, the big stars. And the annexe to the Caribbean was the Boulevard, the very first nightclub in York. Before that we'd had youth clubs, art school dances, but this was a big deal. I remember it opening. Bob, being Bob, had connections, he said, 'Don't worry, I know there's thousands want to go, but I've got you four tickets for the opening night', and in we went. It was a group called Peter Jay And The Jaywalkers. We were just so chuffed that it was somebody a bit famous. And Peter Jay signed his autograph on me bosom. There was American singers and all the big names from London were there and Bob worked with a load.

He used to play this tune called Never On A Sunday and deliberately hit the wrong notes, and everybody was in on the joke, like when Les Dawson played the piano. One night these Americans came in they said, 'What are they paying this chap for, he can't play properly?' They came back next year and said, 'We've come to see the bloke that hits all the bum notes', and they didn't realise that it was just a joke.

There was this time when he was playing in a concert, and he suffered from the most terrible gout. On the piano you've got to work the pedals, and he'd said to Lyn Chelin, 'We're booked out, and I can't touch the pedals with me feet', 'cos he got it so bad, but there was no way was he was gonna let anybody down. So he told Lyn and they worked out between 'em that before the curtains went back, she would scurry in, get underneath the piano, so nobody could see her, and with her being a really good pianist as well, she knew which bits to push, so she did and he's playing away, and Lyn's pushing the pedals around.

He had to keep a real straight face, she's there giggling and laughing on her hands and knees doing all that.

Once me dad and Leo Burrows were playing in a club in London. Leo's giving it this, and this one particular bloke, every time he got up and went to the toilet he would hit the cymbal. Leo was a big man and he lost his temper, and he went to this chap and said, 'If you do that again, I'll shove this drum stick as far up as... so knock it off'. And that was that. Playing away, and then the bloke came up and paid 'em and says, 'There's a couple of gentlemen here want you to go and have a drink with 'em'. So they went and had a drink and it was the Krays. And this bloke with 'em who'd hit Leo's cymbal, he's there picking his teeth with a toothpick and he says to Leo, 'What did you say to me, if I hit your cymbal again, you'd do what?' Now Leo can't lose face, he says, 'I said I'll stick my drumstick as far...' 'You don't know me, you know Mr. Kray and Mr. Kray, well I'm their minder. Do you still think you could?' And Leo daren't back down, and Leo said 'I'll tell you what, I probably couldn't but I'd have a bloody good go'. This bloke said, 'Shake hands mate'. Round of whiskies all round.

My dad's favourite was Body And Soul and if anybody said, 'Play what you want to play Bob', that's the one he would play and mine was always Lullaby Of Birdland. He used to play that for me.

When her father died, Ella put his obituary in the press and it read 'When a jazzman testifies, a faithless man believes'.

Ella recalls:

And that crematorium was packed, standing room only, and people outside. I've never seen so many people. Everybody knew Bobby Hirst.

Val Mountain played at the Colliergate jazz venue in 1953:

We had a jazz band there called the Ghosts, Derek Parker on trumpet, Leo Burrows on drums, Phil Jackson on bass. And I played at the Society Club for three or four years. I can't remember how I got the job, I think maybe Bobby had it first, 'cos he used to come in, and we'd sit and play duets at the piano. Trouble was, you never knew when you were going home. With a band job you knew it was eight to 12, but there, it was 'till everybody had had all they wanted to drink, then they'd go home. It was pretty exclusive. You went up this beautiful staircase, and it was all like a different world, lovely red velvet and chandeliers.

Bobby was eccentric. He took me round to his house and I couldn't believe that there was nothing to tell me that a genius lived there. He never had a piano. I says, 'You, the finest pianist in this land, and you haven't got a piano?'

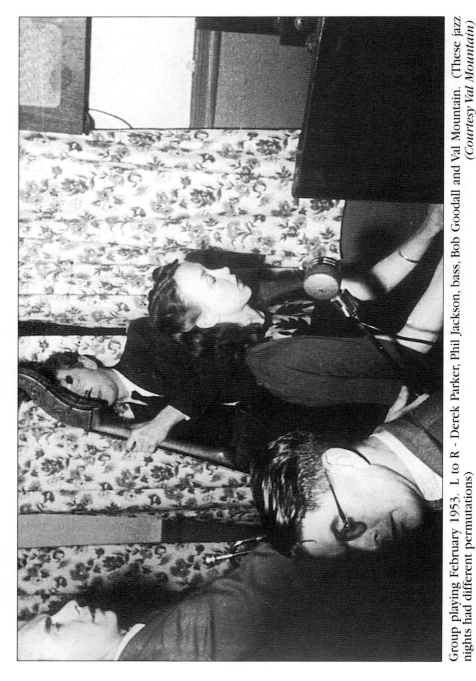

Group playing February 1953. L to R - Derek Parker, Phil Jackson, bass, Bob Goodall and Val Mountain. (These jazz nights had different permutations) *(Courtesy Val Mountain)*

Band playing at Civic Restaurant at Festival Hall, Market Place, New Year's Eve. 1955. Bob Goodall, guitar, Morris Toes?, drums, Val Mountain, accordion.

(Courtesy Val Mountain)

'No, I go and play other people's'. And he went out for a packet of fags one day and met up with Ray Phillips, the drummer and Ray was off to London so Bobby went with him, came back at the end of the week, and his wife just looked up and said, 'Did you get your cigarettes?' That was Bobby.

Walter Davy recalls loving jazz in the 1950s:

As a child, during the war, it was when all the American, Canadian servicemen were over here, and it was on the radio, the Glenn Miller style, the big band, that's when I first got interested. I liked the arrangements that were on the go and there were some very very good musicians. I was a big Artie Shaw fan, and the drumming of Gene Krupa, people like that. I was brought up on this, and I have very nostalgic thoughts of the war. I know it's a sad thing but at the same time it brought some music out that I enjoyed.

My sister's boyfriend was in the Canadian Air Force, we had a party, it was Doreen's birthday, and I can always recall going out of our house looking down Thorpe Street, they were taking almost all the whole street up, coming up to our house. And if you can visualise a three bedroomed terrace house in Thorpe Street, the back door open and all the Glenn Miller sounds on. It was a wonderful memorable night, and it sticks in the mind.

As you probably know Bettys was the 'in place', the atmosphere bubbled. And York seemed to be buzzing. I started going out listening to music, we went to a jazz club, and this was after Mr Prendergast, who brought some fantastic bands to York, musicians which I was very interested in, he pulled all the best bands in the country and some from America. What we latched on to, there was a public house called the Sea Horse, then it changed its name to the Shire Horses. We had the York Jazz Club up there, they weren't wild, but they let their hair down, you got 'em really into a jam session and the best comes out of them sometimes. It'd be very early 1950s, we had some of Ted Heath's top musicians there, Vic Lewis and Harry Gold And His Pieces of Eight. All the top instrumentalists would come over. They got the griff of it and instead of going in the Edinburgh Arms, as most musicians do, they want a fix after they've indulged there, in those days Sunday was Sunday, it was 10.30pm bang, but the jazz club allowed this extension.

One or two friends of mine came, Glenn Moses, Johnny Armgill, Joyce and Nan Smith. That was the Sunday night scene for us, which we looked forward to. This wasn't on every week, it was whenever he brought a big band, so we were very restricted. But at that time they struck up a jazz group who were very good, the Leithart Quartet, Derek Dunning was the leader, Bobby Hirst, and a friend of mine called Gil Fox. He was a clarinettist. They had this gig at RAF Linton and it was a hot sunny night, and Gil was telling us they'd gone there and it was stupefyingly warm, because everything was like tin roofs and Nissen huts and it was packed. They were playing and they got the nod, 'Shall we take our coats off?' 'Yes, certainly', so they all agreed and took their coats off, and when Bobby took his off, he was sat there with a green vest on, long thin white arms, and just a dicky front on! Everybody broke up! They said he just brought the house down, he never cracked on to anybody, he just went along with them, just take our coats off, so they all agreed. And that was Bobby.

Oral historian Mike Race was very keen on jazz:

My parents were always singing in the house, there was always music, Henry Hall or Harry Roy. My mother was always showing me the latest dance steps and my dad had won Charleston competitions. So I grew up liking popular music, and at work I got friendly with a chap who had a saxophone, and I bought this Boosey and Hawkes alto sax. Albert Cole, a chap I liked very much, said he would give me a few lessons. And then I set out on my own, practising in our back bedroom for about half an hour a night doing arpeggio scales, playing jazzy type numbers, Honeysuckle Rose, Sweet Georgia Brown, easy to play stuff. I had some friends who were also interested in jazz, and we'd have a session on a Sunday afternoon at St George's Youth Club, in Margaret Street. But it never developed beyond that. I enjoyed going to concerts at the Rialto and listening to the big bands and hearing the best musicians, and I set myself against those and thought, 'My goodness, I'm not very good' and consequently didn't take the thing further forward.

There were a lot of big bands travelling around in those days, each having its own little gimmick. Eric Delaney and his band, his drummer had two large kettle drums as part of his drum kit, and it gave his band a slightly different sound, he'd bring this kettle drum in quite a lot into his arrangements. Bands were always striving to be different. The heyday for me was about 1955, I was

16. A couple of years later I went to see Lionel Hampton who had a tremendous band, a really thrilling driving band, really rhythmic, but it was poorly attended. And Stan Kenton in 1956 was great.

I'd go to St. George's Youth Club dance on Sunday night, to records, and there was this very trendy couple. He'd come in very tight trousers, he was about 18 or 19 and I'd be 15. He was Mr Cool, this chap, with his dark slicked-back hair, brothel creeper shoes, drape jacket and drainpipe trousers, and he'd be bopping with his head down, shoulders square, toes pointed with his silent, enigmatic, gum-chewing, blonde girlfriend who he spun round with her full skirt billowing out. On hearing the music, Mick the elderly caretaker would rush in saying, 'Stop that, we're having none of this bobbing about in here'. Joe Cool and girlfriend never turned a hair!

A different generation was coming along, the bands that had played in the 1930s, people had really enjoyed them during the war but new people were coming on the scene and rock 'n' roll was starting to appear. People like Elvis Presley, Cliff Richard, they were starting to catch the imagination of the young people, and there wasn't room for both - big bands and rock 'n' roll. People lost interest in big bands generally but there were always enthusiasts who carried it forward, people like myself who were still as interested in the 1960s, 1970s and 1980s just as much as in the 1950s.

It may be that there are individuals who spark these things off. Innovative people, people with imagination, with talent, who want to go in a different direction, who try something, and people listen to them and it gradually grows. It gets bigger and bigger, and leaves everything else behind. I did enjoy rock 'n' roll as a young bloke, going to see Rock Around The Clock with Bill Haley. I don't think that the two are mutually exclusive. The only thing is my interest in big bands probably continued where a lot of people changed altogether.

I think it is louder now, I think there is more accentuation on the beat, on the rhythm, rather than the tune. When I hear music being played in discos and such like, they are not singing along to a tune, they are almost vibrating to the beat, it's the rhythm that's driving.

Cool jazz came out in the 1950s, there was the Modern Jazz Quartet, and there was some thinking that jazz wasn't intellectually stimulating, so these four black musicians decided to bring jazz to a new level, and they started to play a more cerebral jazz. It wasn't to enliven you or stir you emotionally into a fever, it was jazz, but played in a cool fashion. There was traditional jazz which originated in New Orleans. That started to get a big following again in

150

the mid 1950s. The Clifton Ballroom attracted bands who played traditional jazz, and the aficionados of this music wore baggy sweaters, duffle coats. Modern jazz followers were more introverted, more intellectual, they wore fashionable loose fitting gabardine suits listened to Jazz At The Philharmonic with Lester Young, Charlie 'Bird' Parker, and Dizzy Gillespie.

The Stan Kenton outfit was my favourite big band, music with an edge, sometimes dissonant, and Woody Herman And His Herd was another swinging big band with a jazz feel. Perhaps my favourite type of jazz was 'cool', also named West Coast jazz because it originated in California. For many years I had a record by the Gerry Mulligan Quartet which I almost wore out.

Some of the lads started buying guitars, and started playing Cliff Richard numbers and things, when I was in the army. The lads I had played with formed a little skiffle group, Phil Scott played tea-chest bass, Affie McClay played the wash board, a chap called Walter Harrison played the clarinet, and the most talented of the group, Mick Brown, played the piano. In the army, one of our regiment could play guitar and he was very popular. In 1958 we all sang Cliff Richard's Living Doll as we rolled along in the back of a truck on a journey from Belfast to Derry. The world was turning from black and white to colour and excitement. Music would never be the same again.

On Saturday nights, I always went out in a shirt and tie, a sports coat or suit. In 1957 I'd wear a long Donegal tweed drape jacket, what you called a finger tip drape, so that when you put your hands down by your side the jacket came to your finger tips. 16 inch bottoms on your trousers, which was fairly conservative really, if you were really daring you wore 12 inch bottoms. You were really considered the bees-knees if you did that. But also you were a little bit outside, a bit of a rebel. And black square toed shoes before winkle-pickers came in, and a slim Jim narrow tie. Things changed a bit in that era, over to the Italian look about 1960.

We'd perhaps go to the pictures first, say about six o'clock, come out about nine o'clock, go to a fashionable pub, perhaps the Starre in Stonegate, and then about 10 o'clock we'd go in the Assembly Rooms.

Certainly jazz had many strands in the 1950s, swing, mainstream and contemporary jazz, revivalist bands playing traditional, bebop and cool, and Latin influenced music. The greatest enthusiasm seemed to be for the big bands, the Musicians' Union had relaxed its ban on American musicians working in this country and we were able to see and hear the great performers. Cool jazz could be a bit 'posey', people thought of themselves as being a bit more intellectual. Miles Davis, Chico Hamilton, people like Chet Baker, and I suppose Dave Brubeck would be called cool.

Despite all these different categories, Eddie Lamb believes that jazz is so universal that it unites like-minded people wherever they are:

Music has been terribly important to me. If we go to a restaurant and there's music in the background, it's no good talking to me. I'm listening to the damn music.

I've heard jazz all over the world, heard it in New Orleans. I sat in with a band in Italy, and my Italian isn't that good and their English was non-existent but we got on. That's jazz.

The thing about playing is you get on the stand with all the cares in the world you know, from your ordinary day to day life but the minute you start playing they all drop away. You concentrate on one thing, that's the music, and your playing. I can still get lumps in my throat listening to music. La Boheme the first opera I ever saw in Covent Garden. There's one chord in there that really gets me. I couldn't imagine life without music.

CHAPTER SIX. MAGIC MOMENTS
The 1950s

As the 1950s dawned, dance bands continued to be popular though soon there would something to challenge their supremacy, and the decade would bring huge changes in the world of music.

Robert Atkinson began to play piano in dance bands in the 1950s:

I can thank my parents because they loved musical evenings. I never felt inhibited in having to accompany people. My sister had a very nice singing voice. I have a brother who used to play the violin excellently. And the Light Opera often came round to our house. My father would get the whisky bottle out and we'd have musical soirees. A chap came into the village shouting 'Anybody here play the piano?' and I said I did and he took me along to the band hut and they auditioned me. That was my first introduction to any form of strict rhythm music because until then I'd been classically trained. I wasn't particularly good at this style of music because to be good at dance music you really need to be able to extemporise, and to have a jazzy feel about you. But because I could read they could put any music in front of me. When I was demobbed in 1955, I was then called upon by one or two local band leaders to sit in with them.

The band leaders had a pad of music. This was like gold dust. They were quite valuable, perhaps 200 orchestrations for the piano, for various saxophones, for the trumpet, for the drums and they looked after these very closely. When you went to play at the dance they would give you this pad and call out number 37, 58, it was usually a quick step you started with. The orchestration was actually for a full dance band but you were very rarely playing with that so it was up to the pianist to fill in.

There was a small group called The County Players. Their main venue was at Fulford Golf Club. It was only four or five-piece band. Very much dinner jacket and rather genteel. Musically we weren't any great shapes but our faces fitted for the type of places we were playing in. It was run by a chap called Harold Arthur and then he amalgamated with another band run by Harry Warrington, who was the pianist so I was out on my ear. But that's when Derek Dunning picked me up. And from then it graduated that Derek would sit me in playing with the big band.

A lot of the pianos that you were expected to play had seen far better days. In fact, you'd go to some of them and the pitch was so wrong that the

County Players, The Assembly Rooms, 1970s. Front Row L to R - Bunny Hare, Billy Mendez, Bob Halford, Tiddy Mead and George Smith. Back Row - Leader Harold Arthur, Harry Warrington, bass player unknown

(Courtesy Jean Halford)

instrumentalists would have a job pitching their instruments to the piano. Quite often some of the keys didn't work. The band leaders had usually rather antiquated amplifiers, working on valves, and they'd stick the microphone into the piano and quite often get feedback. Because I was playing the piano I would sometimes be expected to play reception music while the guests arrived. Then I would have to move through and play 'food' music; background music while they ate; then move through and play with the dance band when the dance music started. Then often there was a cabaret which the pianist was called upon to accompany. And then back to dancing for the last part of the night, which was fairly tiring because it meant you could start at six o'clock in the evening and not finish till two!

I had a formal education on the piano. I passed a lot of top examinations and I usually used to get a hundred per cent on sight reading. But this had a down side to it. If a piece of music was in front of me I more-or-less felt it commanded me. Whereas, a person who was self-taught had a much freer expression in their mode of play.

The music that we played from the pads was by and large Cole Porter, Irving Berlin, Gershwin. And you were romantic in those days, and you'd get the Hollywood films and it was quite nice to be playing these. I started really moving away from this scene at about the time of the Beatles, and the Rolling Stones. I felt enormous resentment when I found out the huge amounts of money that these pop groups were pulling in.

I was still playing when the twist came about, and the dance used to finish with a little ensemble, that sang The March Of The Mods. Occasionally, if it was a private dance the organiser would come up and, 'How much would you require to play for another hour?' The bands used to hate this because you had actually paced yourself. And quite often, by the time you'd played that last waltz you were ready for getting home.

We were playing at the Assembly Rooms once and round the back of the stage there were big heavy screens, about six feet high, and there were some hoodlums running around. Some of them had picked up some fire buckets full of water, and from behind the band they threw them over these screens so they went right across the front line. The saxes and trumpets had just started to play. And I was sat to one side at the piano. And of course there was an immediate silence. Derek said to me, 'Keep playing.' And the band as one, jumped up, and were going to lynch these lads that had thrown the water. There were a few punches.

Jimmy Lally must have made millions out of doing arrangements for dance band work. They were fairly straightforward to play and sometimes there

155

would be a chance for a sax player, a pianist or a trumpet player just to shine for a few bars. To get into the last chorus you had to have musicians that were competent to go into a slightly more difficult key and you needed your trumpet and three sax to cover it all. The leader would say 'intro three', so you would play the chorus three times and then a soloist would take it on and make something of it so it didn't become too boring. And this is when a good musician could shine.

I played for a small band with Mick Smith, a very nice bass player. A contract to provide music at Butlins at Filey. Ray Phillips the drummer was one of them. We used to enjoy that because that'd finish at something like half ten at night. It was while the resident Butlins band were taking their break. And that was every night of the week perhaps, for two weeks. Maybe you didn't get another job for about two or three months and you used to charge your batteries up over this time. Quite often you would get with a group of other musicians and the night was absolute beauty. But I would say two times out of three you would be very thankful when the night had finished. Occasionally it would all come together and you'd think this is absolutely marvellous.

And one of the nights was for youngsters, a party night at Brid Spa. Games and little talent competitions. I was driving there one night and the mini estate had a problem with its petrol pump and over the Wolds it packed in on me. I was in my dinner jacket. I didn't want to go climbing under the car. A taxi was coming by and it pulled up, he could see that I was having problems. He said, 'I live in Bridlington, I don't want anything for it'. And I asked him, 'Have you any children?' He said, 'Yeah, I've got four' so I said, 'If you take me straight to Brid Spa and tell them to be by the stage door I'll take them in with me, they won't have to pay'. So he phoned ahead. And when I got there his children must have told every youngster in Bridlington. I was like the Pied Piper of Hamelin, there was a queue about 50 to a 100 yards long. The authorities at Brid Spa weren't very happy about this but I says, 'I wouldn't be here and you wouldn't have the night going unless this had happened'.

One New Year's Eve Derek Dunning got a job at the hotel above the banks at Scarborough. The last one before the banks drop down to Peasholme, and it stands very much aloft up there. We arrived and there was a gale blowing and it was half an hour before we were due to go on. As we climbed out of the car, the wind got in some of the pads and blew these copies down the banks. It was like a paper chase. These pads were absolutely essential, so we were all, in the pitch dark and in our dinner jackets, climbing up and down the grassy banks trying to find all the copies that had got blown about.

It was pretty much standard ballroom dancing but occasionally you would get some pretty hot jivers and the crowd were very appreciative of this. They'd usually clear a space and egg them on. Of course, the band used to give them as much encouragement as they could, and loved to see some really hot dancing taking place.

The Assembly Rooms was something we looked forward to all week. They had the small bar in the far right-hand corner. And we were all single, so we had some money in our pockets. The favourite was to treat your girl to a Pimms. They used to churn these Pimms out by the 100. Dancing in those days, was a means of getting to know the young ladies.

Sometimes it was rather difficult to get the tempo of a popular song into a danceable rhythm. If you heard Frank Sinatra singing a dreamy-type number you were expected to play it, but if you played it at the tempo Sinatra sang, it was a dirge so you had to up-tempo it. Often you'd start playing and nobody would get up and you would feel as if you were giving a concert. You'd try a waltz, and then a jive and they just wouldn't move. What would sometimes happen, just when you were coming to the end of the third number some would start to get up. The floor would start to fill and you'd no music left in front of you. So that was when busking was required. He'd quickly say 'How High the Moon, F.' And the pianist had to take this off, and then you'd hope that some

Derek Dunning Orchestra at Kirkham Abbey 1958. L to R - Derek Dunning, clarinet, Henry Thomson, Fred Mills, Gordon Knight, saxes, Tye Bruce, trumpet, Keith Laycock, bass, Bob Goodall, guitar, Leo Burrows, drums. *(Courtesy Fred Mills)*

other members of the band would take the solo on that. The floor would fill up more and more and you might then finish up playing without music for ten minutes. Because while the floor was full the dance band leader didn't want them to return to their seats 'cos he knew he might have a job getting them up again. He'd want to keep it flowing.

Trumpet player Derek Mackfall moved to York in 1948, and recalls that there were 13 dances on a Saturday night in York in 1949. He began at the Albany that year:

For the first six months I sat at the back of the band, I was 17. The band was situated on a very small stage at that time. There was a baby grand piano on it, and Eddie on the drums, and a double bass. And I was hidden at the back, tootling away for about six months, and then Billy Steele went to Doncaster and they offered me the job. I was there for seven years, from 1949 to 1956, and I left and joined Geoff Towse with the Modernaires. They had split from Johnny Sutton, and took half the music, and some of the equipment, and went on their own. I joined them from 1956 to 1960, and in 1960 the beat groups started to come in, and they virtually put most bands out of work. In 1977 I was at the Royal Hall at Bridlington, and we did virtually all their work 'till 1979, and in those two years we played opposite Joe Loss, in the summer months, to crowds of up to 3,200, which is quite an audience.

When you look back at the bands that were playing, they were playing music that had been formulated since 1920 to 1939 when the war started. When this new style of music came in, it completely altered it. That's all everybody wanted to hear. But a lot of jazz musicians, they didn't want to know about this, 'Oh, it's rubbish'. It wasn't rubbish at all. The bands that did change were working so much, they once offered me 60 jobs between October and Christmas. And I could only do half of them, and another trumpet player I know did the other half. So we shared them between us.

You could have, if you were playing pop music, three beats in the bar, in the middle of a four-beat section, which was unheard of. 'You can't do that, you can't all of a sudden put three beats in a bar'. But what they failed to realise was that people were no longer doing foxtrots and quicksteps where the steps were all set out, they were all jigging about together, so it didn't matter whether there was three beats, two beats, or one beat in a bar. So things altered at that particular time, some bands altered, some didn't, and those that didn't I'm afraid petered out eventually.

Derek's wife Brenda Mackfall also enjoyed music:

I spent most of my youth at the Rowntree's Youth Club Dances and it was Eric Gill and the Georgians. And that was my highlight of my week. Everything was geared to going to this dance, clothes and everything was special. They had

Eric Gill And The Georgians at Linton aerodrome NAAFI c 1948. L to R - the MC, Bunny Hall, trumpet, Eric Gill, piano, Arthur Jones, sax, Eric Wakefield, bass, Wilf Whitwell, sax, unknown guitarist sitting in, Billy Addison, drums, Charlie Druggitt, tenor, Reg Cooper, violin.   *(Courtesy Arthur Jones)*

a lovely singer, a ginger haired girl, Margaret, and she was magic. And then as I got older, I started to go out more than one night which allowed me to stray as far as the Albany Ballroom, and that's where I met Derek.

He was playing his trumpet as I danced round and it was the beady eyes over the trumpet that caught me. It still turns my heart today, whenever I hear him. I don't go very often but when I do it still has that magic. I was dancing round, I remember distinctly, for weeks and weeks, and then suddenly some passes were there at the door for the following Saturday night, so that I had to turn up, and he knew I was going to turn up, so he must have noticed me. But we never spoke. I always made sure he was there and make sure I danced past.

That was our highlight, it was the fun, it was the sparkle. The Albany was lovely. Mirrors all round, and the floor was sprung. And as you danced round you just felt a million dollars because you could see the reflection. And finally he asked me to dance, and we spent most of the time talking about batteries. I thought it was car batteries, but it wasn't, it was hen batteries.

It was romantic and you didn't have a lot of romance in your life. And it was just magic, it lit you up inside and you went with it, and the music of the time was exciting. It was all happening, and I was of an age where I appreciated it.

I remember going to the pavilion in Flaxman Avenue, it was a hut and they'd hold lots of dances for the invalids that came out of the forces and they would ask you to dance. They'd be tall, and I'd be stretched up to reach them. I remember if my dad got a tin of paint in his hand, that tin had to be finished and he got this bright blue paint, and everything in the house was painted bright blue, and he had a little bit left. I hadn't any posh dance shoes, and my friend hadn't, so he said, 'Leave it to me', and he painted our shoes this bright blue. We went to this dance, and I remember a gentleman asking me to dance. I think he took pity on us because we were so young, and we got up to dance, and he had a black suit on, and the bottoms of his trousers got all the blue paint off my shoes. I can remember blushing to this day, that blue paint on that lovely suit. But they were good days, Glenn Miller and the oldies.

But music has always been there. It's been the lighter side for us. Because you worked so hard in the daytime that that was your relief. It kept you sane. My mum was a wonderful singer. I was a child in the war and things were very difficult. They were drab days, but mum used to go to Woolworths, and buy the sixpenny sheet of music, and it would be all the words of all the songs of the time. She had to work in this factory and there was Music While You Work, and they learnt them from the radio. And she'd sing them to us. We'd go to bed about eight o'clock, and we'd say 'Sing another, mum'. And there was a girl next door, she'd knock on the wall and say 'Tell your mum to sing another one'.

Brenda wanted to perform from being a child:

I remember the Empire, when the circus came to town, I just wanted to fly. I even dream sometimes that I can swing through the air. But that is because it was so important to get on that stage. But I never could. So that's why Derek got all the encouragement that I could give him. It was very hard when he was playing, and I was left behind to do all these jobs, like calving that went wrong, and things like that.

After years of working on the farm and bringing up a family, Brenda in recent years has started a trio to entertain at residential and elderly person's homes. She finds this very fulfilling, because music more than anything else, is therapeutic:

Today we're doing Music Hall. The people are very old but they love it, they come alive. When we start singing, they're probably not even listening but you start on something they can reminisce with, and it wakes them up, and they sing. And it's amazing. Some people never talk, but they sing. You might see

The Embassy Players at the Co-op Hall in 1952. L to R - Taffy Jones, trumpet, Doug Green, drums, Brian Mullinger, sax, Sid Watson, standing, Len Cundall, clarinet, Denis Goodwin, piano, George Turner, tenor. *(Courtesy Denis Goodwin)*

somebody that hasn't spoken for maybe two years, then start to sing. That part of your brain must stay as it was.

I don't read music. But I bet I have over a thousand tunes in my head. I come to life when I get on stage. I'm a different person, it brings the magic back.

Everything in your life is centred round music. If you haven't got music, you just haven't anything. It brings the best out in people, it's there to uplift you. I've never known it not succeed. You'll go maybe some places, and someone's sitting there and, 'Right, go on, entertain me', and you know if you make them join in, really work on them, they all sing. I've done lots of things through music I would never had done, never had dreamed of. You can cope with anything, when you've something like music to look forward to at the end of the day. And I feel it's the same with Derek. He can work very, very hard, he never wastes a minute, I don't know if that's part of it, the energy you get from music. It was good that we chose each other, because the music's been our mainstay right through our lives. It's been the shine.

Brian Parker also loves music:

My father's father was village blacksmith and church organist at Healaugh, near Tadcaster. Strange combination, big meaty hands for a blacksmith,

161

playing the organ at church on a Sunday. My father loved music and my mother could sit and play hymns at the keyboard, a harmonium in the front room, which was later exchanged for an American organ, pedalled to supply the wind, single manual, 14 stops.

My brother Derek met a guy at Cooke Troughton and Simms who played in a brass band, and Derek got interested and he started in the York City Brass Band on the E flat soprano cornet. Hell of an instrument to start on, but he brought this little soprano cornet home and I was fascinated by it, and about a fortnight after Derek started, I went down.

I was given this battered old baritone horn, must have been about 100 years old, no case, and battered. George McEwan said, 'Take that home, get a Levi's tutor from Banks and when you can play one octave with a scale of C major, you're in the band'. I got this tutor, struggled away, and couldn't crack this one, it wouldn't work. It got to about three weeks and George was seeing Derek at work and saying, 'I don't think your kid's going to make it, he's not doing very well at all'. It was on the third occasion I went down, still struggling to play this scale when George said, 'Just a minute Brian, let me have a look at that instrument'. And he took the valves out of the cylinders, and number three valve was in number one cylinder, and one was in two, and of course he apologised, put them all in the right cylinders and said, 'Now try', and I rattled off the scale of C major. I was in the band! It was a case of, 'Now you're a baritone player, sit there between those two gentlemen, do as you're told and behave yourself, and play what bits you can'. And that was it, just thrown in at the deep end.

I was working for Shoukesmith's in Micklegate, I was an office lad, and I got a phone call there. 'Johnny Sutton here, I've heard about you my boy, I want you in my band'. I said, 'Oh no Mr. Sutton, I couldn't play in your band, I don't even read bass clef'. In the brass band, you just read in the treble or tenor clef on trombone, and all danceband copies were in bass clef which means your notation on the stave is in different positions so you've got to re-learn. He said 'Oh, you will when I've finished with you'. And that was it, I was sort of ordered to go and join the Modernaires. And I was fired with enthusiasm from the start when I was booked, because it was a pretty good band. I took the place of Alf Thomson, Henry's brother, who was leaving the area.

It must have been 1948. I used to shut myself in our front room every evening by myself and I said to the brass band, 'I shan't be seeing you, I'm not coming to rehearsals for a week or a fortnight, or however, long it takes'. Told them why and they were up in arms. Brass band people in those days were so blinkered.

162

There was no other music but brass band to a lot of them. Mention danceband, military band or orchestral playing, all rubbish. 'You don't want to be doing that, stay with the brass band'. But I stuck to me guns, and after about ten days I was feeling confident, after a fortnight I was in the Modernaires and playing pretty well.

It was well known if you had a brass band player having a go at dance band, he'd be as corny as hell, and no doubt I was when I started. But gradually, sitting amongst these fellas, dyed in the wool dance band players, some of them had never done anything else, especially the sax players, started off with that idea, they wanted to be dance band players, and so they had the style. Every now and then, maybe Ron or Johnny himself said, 'You're playing that phrase a bit corny Brian'. And you gradually learnt from your colleagues in the band, and from the overall sound and from the bit of listening you did to records you gradually acquired the right style. But it was quite tricky, and to this day, I may be considered a little bit on the straight side for playing dance band stuff, because my first love's always been classical music.

I did some gigs with the Assembly Players. It was in my early days of playing, because I'd borrowed this trombone from the old City Band I think, it was an old, what we called a 'pea shooter' trombone, because of its very small bore, and small bell. I could play that with dancebands although it was the wrong bore size really, but luckily it was the right pitch. And the plating was coming off and it was a bit dilapidated and because I'd got it on sort of permanent loan, I had a word with mum and said, 'Can we afford to have this trombone done up?' We enquired of Hughie Robertson how much it was gonna cost and we got a shock but he said, 'Let me get it done at this price and you can borrow my Con while it's being done'. Now an American Con, if you had one of those you were somebody. There was a ban on American imports in those days, the only way you could get American instruments was if you knew somebody working the boats, Atlantic crossings, so there were very few around, and Hughie had a Con, in very nice condition, and he bribed me with that.

It just about played itself. It was a joy to play. And then this instrument came back, and he'd made a lovely job of it, silver plated, and gold plated inside the bell. Although it was an old pea shooter trombone, I loved it, especially when it came back all gleaming, and newly plated.

Then came National Service:

I was in Ceylon and I got fed up of being without my trombone. They had a store of instruments and I even took up the alto sax just to have an instrument.

Brian Parker in Ceylon 1951, outside RAF
billet with trombone.
(Courtesy Brian Parker)

*There was a music shop in
Columbo. I went down and got a
sax tutor and some reeds, and
started having a go, I was missing
me trombone so much. I wrote to me
mum, 'Please take my trombone
down to Hughie Robertson and ask
him to pack it properly for a sea
voyage'. And it arrived, an
enormous parcel, well packed, but I
had to get a note from the adjutant
to get it through the customs shed. And it was damaged, a slight dint in the
side, and the slide run jammed solid. And I sat on the edge of my bed hour
after hour, pouring in the old fashioned abrasive metal polish, Brasso.*

*Wherever you went, if you were a musician, like sportsmen, you were excused
all sorts of duties, and you were one of the favoured. But I still had my signals
job to do. Coming back we boarded late at night, and I had full wadding on,
kit bag on the shoulder, trombone in me right hand, and there's two fellas
standing at the top of the gangway, in the jungle green outfit, band marks on
the sleeves, and I heard one of 'em say, 'There's a trombone player'. I said, 'So
there's a band?' 'Yeah, First Battalion Cameronians. You might get a blow with
the band, we had to leave our bass trombonist in the dock in Hong Kong, he's
too ill to travel.*

*We'll be having a band practice in the morning, come and see our boss'. He
looked me up and down, 'Are you any good on trombone?' 'Well I can't say I've
had military band experience, but I've done dance bands and orchestral
playing, started off in a brass band'. He was very cagey and ummed and
aahed and said, 'Come to my band practice at ten', and he put out Elgar's
Pomp And Circumstance March No. 1, which has a hell of a bass trombone
part. I was playing a tenor trombone and he put me with this bass trombone,
a really nasty bit, even for tenor trombone, but doing the bass trombone part,
like an octave down, it was well nigh an impossibility, and he knew it. But I
flannelled my way around it, and, 'Hmm, just do that bit again', and I
flannelled a bit better. 'Very good. Corporal Gow, fit our RAF friend up with a
uniform'.*

*He wouldn't let me play in RAF kit and he got me fixed up with a corporal's
outfit and I was just a senior aircraftsman. And you can imagine, every night,*

getting into the gear. Concert every night, rehearsal every morning. Wonderful trip home but I did go through it, getting into the Cameronian's outfit and all the RAF guys round me, 'What do you look like?' when I put me Glen Gary on, little tassels, ribbons down the back, pompom on the top.

Brian played with the breakaway Modernaires after August 1953, but even though there had been trouble, it was later forgotten:

Denis gave me a call and he says, 'I'm packing up and I've had a word with Johnny and if you'd like to come back, he would be only too pleased to see you', although I was one of the 'enemy', you know. I went down, a little embarrassed because I'd never spoken to Johnny since the big bust-up, and I said, 'Johnny this is a turn up for the books, I'm surprised you've asked me back'. He said, 'Forget about the old troubles, it's all in the past now, welcome back'.

Johnny rehearsed that band, getting all the details correct, the light and shade, the dynamics. He was great for that, so that when we played a number it was well rehearsed, and it was musical. It wasn't a big blow. And that was part of the joy of it. If you were playing a modern waltz, it's supposed to be nice and quiet and smoochy, and we used to play that way, but nowadays they always seem to want to blow their heads off. And when we'd get the top name bands coming to York, through Jack Prendergast, I used to get as much joy listening to those fellas as I did from listening to the Hallé Orchestra or the London Symphony Orchestra. It was so musical, beautiful.

Standards have improved tremendously over the years. Especially in the classical field, and I put that down to the advent of the University in the 1960s, and a thriving music department at St. John's. You get good young musicians, good players that are accepted on the course, and they are perhaps even better musicians by the time they've finished the course. But I think those days were better, in the danceband business. It was better from a musical point of view.

I'm a flautist as well. It's been a very serious study, I took it up in 1963. One of the best things I ever did, so teaching it, it's always been 50/50 brass and flute. I'm doing flute for a New Earswick company next month. I always look forward to those. A complete change, and a bit of ribbing as well, and in the brass section I talk about these namby-pamby woodwind players, and if I'm on flute I talk about these roughnecks in the brass section. It's nice to be on either side of the fence.

Music has been my life. From day one, when I first got that battered old baritone, even with the valves in the wrong place, I was still keen. I was determined to succeed and get that scale of C major off, and I made a start in the band, and my little bit of education you did get up to 14 years old, it deteriorated, because during a geography lesson I'd be thinking, 'Band practice tonight, I wonder what we'll be doing'. It was on my mind most of the time, and it became a big part of my life from then on. It's just sheer elation, making music with others. It's the great thing playing a monophonic instrument, you need to be with others, although private practice in the kitchen can be enjoyable. I always enjoy being amongst a crowd of friends and making music. Whether you're paid a nice fee for it or whether you're doing it for love like we do at the Guildhall Orchestra. I used to get a shiver down the spine every now and then especially when it was a nice trombone feature, three or four of us on our feet, doing a three or four part harmony. The thrill was there.

I think a person's nature comes out in his or her playing. The instrument becomes part of yourself. Every now and then I've fancied a change of instrument, not because the old one's done for, but just for a change. I just get another top quality instrument and the comment, when you're showing off a bit with your brand new instrument, is usually, 'I'm sorry Brian but it doesn't sound any different to your other one'. Well no, I'm producing my sound, my own particular sound, 'cos no two musicians produce the same sound, but only I know the ease with which I produce my sound on this instrument compared to me previous one.

Colin Baines, like many others of his generation, had piano lessons as a child, but instead of the classical pieces he was given to play, he yearned to play something more modern. Then he went to a youth club run by the YWCA in Cumberland Street:

And there was one or two of us who were interested in bands. The Parker brothers, Derek and Brian. Brian, a very fine trombone player. And another laddie, Alf Cross, a self-taught sax player. So we formed a band, and we had a girl pianist called Betty Perkins. Then I got calledup when I was 18. Came back out of the air force [in 1949] and met up with Gordon Cottom, a splendid pianist. Gordon and I worked together and he said, 'There's a shortage of bass players in York'. So I got a bass and the first job I ever played was with Gordon's band, the Modernaires. I wasn't very good. In fact I was pretty grim if I remember rightly. Another bass player came in who was also out on a gig that night, a man called Reg Peel.

You looked up at these people when you were kids with open mouths. They were the musicians of York. Reg Peel said to me, 'Is this your first job? Well you want those fingers taping,' and he went back to his car and he brought some

*tape and taped my fingers. And that saw me through the first night of playing.
I would have been blistered to hell. I mean I used to get blistered to blazes after
that, but all these chaps were interested in you when you were young. They
helped you. Another fine man was Len Cundall. That fellow's done more for
York musicians, young lads, than anybody. Len Cundall was a gem of a chap.
Nearly all the lads of my age have played with Len at some time or another,
because he took an interest in you. Jack Carr, Eddie Lamb, Billy Steel, they were
a bit above us. But all these people were our idols.*

*I used to play with one band, and as you know a lot of musicians like to drink.
So they would start as soon as it was starting time to play. And during the
intervals they had a pint. I'd laugh at this because with me being stood at the
back with the drummer, upright with a string bass, you could look down on
the front line and the thing you saw most of all was their necks. As the evening
went on, the more they had to drink, the redder the necks got. And when they
were blowing, they were bulging out. It must have been a strain. The only thing
I got was blisters on my finger ends. To have been blowing all night long,
particularly with a small combination, if there's only five of you in the band
you're all on your metal you see. But with a big band you can hide a bit. You
don't have to blow so hard. If you've got five brass you don't have to blow as
hard as if you were the only brass player. And all the smoke was whirling
around.*

*One of the finest characters was Dickie Bailey. He was a one-off. He liked a
drink and when the interval came at the Albany, he was straight down to the
Angler's Arms like a terrier after a rat. He got a pint of Old Peculiar and cider
and he would see that off within the space of minutes. And we were back down
Goodramgate, back to the Albany on the stand pretty quickly. He went to play
with Freddie Randall's jazz band. Rumour had it, that he was better than any
of the rest of them so they got rid of him. He was rather scruffy was Dickie and
in those days we played in evening dress, looking like penguins. Poor old
Dickie would come with snuff all down the front of his shirt, his black evening
dress would be green. But a great character. And what a jazz man.*

*Saturday night in particular you had to be there on the stand for eight o'clock
sharp in evening dress. And Charles Atkinson would make an appearance
about five to eight, with his watch, and he was absolutely immaculate. Eight
o'clock, 'Right chaps off we go' and there would be no one in, only the band. I
hadn't been playing there above two or three weeks and I was playing away
one night and all of a sudden there's a hell of an explosion. There's an awful
amount of pressure on the bridge [of a bass] because the strings are quite thick.
Next thing you know my bridge had whipped off. Just missed Dickie Bailey's*

head and scattered across the floor. A string had gone and it had pulled it out of skew. That was in the days when they used cat gut. As time went on you got more sophisticated. You used nylon strings, and then you got the ultimate, the wound spring coil which never snapped. And you got far more resonance. You didn't have to pull so hard. I mean, bass playing, until you really got used to it, used to knock you out, your finger ends blistered and so forth.

And then of course there was the Grand era in Clarence Street. Ted Rowell, he was one of the nicest fellas you could come across. And Derek Parker, Wal Walsh and Ronnie Walsh, and Gerry Allen, a marvellous tenor player. It was a lovely place to play. One of the nicest nights there was with a 'scratch' band. There was a very fine pianist called Clarry Clay and another, equally fine, was Valerie Mountain. They run two pianos this particular night, a one-off job. And it was first class.

In the old days when John Barry Seven was on the go, just prior to his era, there used to be Melody Maker competitions of course at the Rialto. Ray Phillips played with the Leithhart Quartet who were a super-smoothy Nat King Cole-type quartet. The pianist was Bobby Hirst. Ray was an absolute precision drummer, I would say without any question about the finest drummer that York's ever produced. I went down to the Black Swan one night, it was Bill Eadie got me dragged in, a jam session. Well you rarely get somebody that's a jolly good reader and a good busker. You've either got leanings one way or the other. I was all right busking, I could busk within limitations, providing people let me know which key it was in. We got in and there was this hooded figure in the corner, all muffled up. I said to Bill Eadie, 'Who's that?' 'Bobby Hirst'. We started playing all the standards, Lady Is A Tramp and all that, then Take Five, now that was very popular. If you get across the rhythm in Take Five you've had it. You've got an awful job to get back in, anyway Bobby started playing and of course during that time he'd sunk a few whiskies. He seemed to play better! Bobby Hirst was a very fine jazz pianist. He was in the strata of Derek Dunning. They were one peg above the normal dance band musician. They did the specialist stuff. They were the ones that could keep pace with Ronnie Scott if it came to it.

Music was important to Colin:

Some nights everything would go perfectly but you knew when you were not playing well. You knew when the band wasn't gelling together. But if you had a good night 'blowing' you were well away. When you used to dep, someone would ring you up out of the blue and you'd no idea really who they were or anything. I've walked into places they've asked me to play with a strange band, and you've walked through the door, seen a group of musicians at one end of the room on the bandstand setting up, they never spoke to you. You walk in with your bass which is rather a comedian-sort of situation in any event. Little fella, my size, pulling a big bass in. They would look at you and nobody would say a word. And probably the only conversation you'd get was when they gave you the numbers out of your pad to read.

Some of these arrangements for double bass, the person that arranges it's got to know what they're doing. Jimmy Lally. Some of his bass parts were really nice. They lifted the piano and the rhythm section. Take the bass away and it was flat. I got as much enjoyment out of playing a non-melody instrument as what they would do on the front playing melody. But, if you get three saxes lined-up there's probably only one playing the melody unless they swap around. The pianist very rarely plays a melody but he plays from what they call a piano conductor, he knows what's going on with everybody else. Music's the only interest I've got really, I still love it.

Johnny Bell also learnt piano as a child:

I got polio, and I was in hospital for about a year, and when I came out it had affected me hands and me legs and me chest, and though I could still play bits on the piano I couldn't play as well. I went to the doctors one day to talk about something entirely different, and he was quite a jazz fan and he said, 'Why don't you take up a wind instrument? It would help your chest muscles to develop'. And that's how I came to start playing a saxophone. In about 1942.

I was influenced a lot by a cousin, an extremely good pianist. He had a fabulous record collection, mostly modern jazz and swing, I got right into it, I liked playing eight to a bar stuff on piano, boogie-woogie! And I bought an alto. I did buy a Selmer mark 7 later on, which was one of the better ones, and I went to Derek Dunning for lessons. He was supposed to be the best sax player around in York at the time. One of the first in York to try out bebop.

I had an older brother who played drums. And he had some friends who were quite good musicians, Ron and Stan Drabwell. They'd trained with the Salvation Army Band, and another lad played clarinet, Derek Waterworth, he'd come round and have a session and eventually said, 'Let's form a band'. I wasn't a particularly good pianist, especially after I'd had polio, and our first gig was at Kelfield village hall and when we got there half the piano notes didn't work, but we had a bit of fun and it was quite good. We played once or twice and then only a trio, my brother and I and Ray Izatt, at Cookes's Club on Bishophill, most Saturday nights. They called us the Rhythm Aces. But the trouble was nobody could spell 'rhythm', notices for these dances, they could

The Bluettes with John Bell on alto sax, early 1950s. Probably Copmanthorpe village hall. *(Courtesy John Bell)*

never spell it, so we ditched that name and just became the Aces. This was a bit after the war.

Some of these village halls were fairly lofty and having a trio was hard work. So we added a trumpet player, I think the first one was Len White. We had a few over the years, and towards the end we had one in who played with the army band and was a brilliant musician. In fact we once played a ball at a camp at Strensall on Yorkshire Day, and there were about one and a half thousand people there. It's the biggest venue we've ever played. It was only because the lad who played trumpet was in the army there, and he got the job for us, and a very successful job it was. We got Bob Halford in that time to play tenor. Bob was a nice player, and we blended in, to say we'd never played together until that night, it worked very well indeed. We were the Bluettes. I left the band in 1961. The last dance we played was at Catterick village hall.

Dances were all the rage, it's amazing the number of people who'd go, no matter what the weather was like. We once played at Stockton-on-the-Forest about New Year time, and it snowed heavens high, and when we came out there was about a foot of snow outside, and yet the place was full.

Ray Cooper probably played more instruments than most other local musicians. He started in 1949 at the age of eight:

I was a violinist as a little boy. My father played with the Eric Gill dance band, which was a seven or eight-piece band. My dad was on violin, rather unusual. I think the reason that evolved just after the war, when Eric Gill was trying to form a band, typically for York he was having difficulty finding musicians, he wanted someone who was quite knowledgeable about music. So that's how my dad came to be with that band. The other players, some of them were quite inexperienced really, but they obviously evolved, and got better. And I distinctly remember being taken one night when the Eric Gill Band were in Great

170

Ouseburn, of all places, and they went on a coach, and I was helping the drummer to lift all his gear into the village hall. I must have been about ten or 11. The jackets that the band were wearing, were bright red but the feature of them is the collar, a rolled-type collar, which was something brand new. Mum had just bought me this new suit as a little boy, and it had one of these collars on, and we went one Sunday to the band call at the Joseph Rowntree Theatre, and the band were in the pit, and Eric Gill sat at the piano. Apparently they'd been talking about getting new band jackets, and Eric saw me with this thing, and said, 'By, that's smart', and they took a sketch of me and had these band jackets made in bright red with this new-style collar.

You had to find out things the hard way. Trial and error. I learnt violin exclusively until I was 16, so a good eight solid years on violin and then was smitten by the skiffle bug (see volume two).

Ray and his friend Greg Wadman became very keen on traditional jazz and wanted to form a band:

In the meantime our tastes were widening, I acquired a saxophone which took it away from the traditional area of jazz, into a more mainstream area. We were looking at our idols of the time, the Gerry Mulligan quartet, it didn't need a piano, and the only front-lines were a trumpet and a baritone sax and we needed a bass player. Mulligan played a baritone saxophone and I was playing alto at the time, and so we went to Shearer's music shop in Leeds, and we knew the man that ran the shop, Alec Swales was his name, and I said, 'I'm looking for a baritone sax'. So I acquired the baritone saxophone, which we lugged back to York on the train.

We were looking for a combination of different instruments to form a band and my musical tastes in jazz were opening up, and so being a raw traditionalist as I was known as, my taste in music was moving more towards mainstream music. My uncle had been a military band musician, clarinet and saxophone player, and I mentioned that I was getting interested in jazz, and I rather liked the sound of the clarinet part, and he said 'I've got a clarinet, if you'd like to have a go on it'. So that's how I got started playing wind instruments.

I worked at Rowntree's then, in the engineering department, with Geoff Towse, I just happened to say I'd bought myself a baritone sax, and Geoff being the kind of person he was, he says, 'Brilliant, come and sit in next Saturday, we're at the Assembly Rooms, I'll bring you the music so you can have a look at it during the week'.

So I got this library of baritone saxophone parts, and up to that point I'd only played in small group jazz, and classical music, so I got on the bus, again, with the baritone sax, and staggered to the Assembly Rooms in Blake Street, and there was a 12-piece dance-band, and there were some of the top players in York area, brilliant players. And I'd never played anything like this in my life, and I was amongst the sax section. When the band started it was so loud and powerful, and if you play baritone saxophone, being a big instrument, you've really got to blow pretty hard to make yourself heard, so I was blowing my head off, and of course in those days dances used to go from eight o'clock 'till 12 o'clock at night and by midnight I was flaked out. I had a headache, but highly elated, and wonder of wonders Geoff Towse says, 'Great that, would you like to come again next week?', so he gave me 10/-, and I thought this is it. Got ten bob, and a replay. 1961.

So I became a member of the Geoff Towse band, [the Modernaires], a 12-piece big band, and all the members were obviously much older than me, and very experienced, but that works wonders for your ability, you're swept along by playing with experienced players. If you're the baby in the band, you're carried forward. Then about the end of 1963, things were starting to wane a little bit in that area, the main rival big band was the Johnny Sutton Orchestra. A lot of the players played for both, there was a lot of interchanging of musicians.

We didn't even have a telephone in those days, I lived in New Earswick and I'd been out one evening playing at Rowntree's Youth Club, they had a little band down there, for a show, and at the end of the street there's this car, the door opened and this person got out and he said 'My name's Johnny Sutton'. I'd obviously heard the name, but I'd never actually met him, and he says 'You've been recommended to me, would you come and join my band?'. So I thought 'Blimey, this is magic'. And as one band faded away, or reduced its work, I stepped into the other band, and it was an absolutely miraculous piece of timing, but it was pure fate.

There was a chap called Brian Eden who happened to mention to Johnny Sutton that he'd like to play the saxophone, and Johnny had found this old saxophone for him to play, he taught him rudiments of music, and it was getting to that stage when he needed someone to play with, so Johnny said 'Will you come along Sunday morning and help Brian with a few tips on saxophone playing?' So I rounded up all the friends I knew, to come down Sunday morning, and from that we formed a new band, under Johnny Sutton's direction, a 12-piece band. We finished up with three trumpets, trombone and four saxophones, and a rhythm section, four-piece rhythm section and a girl vocalist. We became known as the 'JR Big Sound'. I used to write a lot of the music for that band, and Johnny Sutton approached the people at the old Spa Ballroom at Bridlington, and we got a summer season there. At that time hospital broadcasts were just a new thing coming along, and Johnny was approached about making a recording of his band to be played on hospital broadcasts. It was actually recorded in a Community Centre in Front Street, Acomb. So it's been a happy success of one thing ending, another thing starting without any gaps, just a constant evolution of music.

I was fortunate, I wrote for different bands who I played with, and could hear what I'd written played back pretty soon, it was mostly arranging of popular present settings. If you wrote an original composition, it's played to an audience once, and the chances of them picking it up are very slight. For dances and social functions people want to hear tunes they already know, so the requirement is for it to be arranged to suit a particular band, in a certain style, but people at least know the tune. So the bulk of everyone's library was stock arrangements, but Johnny had one or two specials, written specifically for the band, and when the JR Big Sound started, we were using stock arrangements. But when we started to include the vocalists, 1965-66, we were trying to play, apart from the usual big band swing things, something a bit more modern. Tom Jones and Sandie Shaw were the current flavour of the month. And Petula Clark, people who were singers who were going through a popular phase at the time, so we did cover versions of all those.

But it was fading fast to be realistic, It didn't have the adulation it had, in the early days, I was 20 years old, it was just at the end of that glorious era, so I regard myself as being extremely fortunate to have caught the tail-end of it.

There was a bit of apathy I think on the part of the danceband musicians who'd had it good during the war, and up to round about that time, things had been going swimmingly. Every dance hall in York was full on a Saturday, and in the outlying areas all the smaller villages had functions on, almost weekly, and the work was there for the taking. But as things started changing, which was the start of the decline for the traditional big band, it slowly ate away at it. The existing dance band players were getting on a bit in years, so to speak, or had no desire to make the change and adapt to that style of music.

With the evolution of skiffle and that type of music, and then into rock 'n' roll, the guitar really started to take over. If there were to be any wind instruments they were just used in ones and two, whereas in big bands the whole idea is a section of saxophones, a section of trumpets and a section of trombones. But this idea of a smaller band, basically guitar-orientated, with the occasional odd trumpet or saxophone added to it, the dance band players of the day, couldn't, or wouldn't, adapt to that.

In those early days I was still mad keen on playing wind instruments, and more interested in the jazz area of music, rather than rock 'n' roll. You go in one direction or you go another. Perhaps because so many other people were going towards rock 'n' roll, we just reacted the opposite way. My first recollection of anything which you could call a jazz club was just under Bootham Bar, it was called Pete Madden's restaurant, on a Sunday night, traditional jazz there, this would be 1958.

The famous Ted Pratt, he was a wonderful trumpet player, and Ted Akers, one of the other trumpet players who was a bit of a jazz player himself, a wonderful trombone player, Brian Parker and Bob Scott, another fine trombone player. In the saxophone department I suppose the main influence, and help to me, and still inspiration to me in some respects is John Greenwell, words of encouragement he gave you. And Gerry Allen playing tenor sax. All these people by encouragement helped me an awful lot. But when I sat next to John Greenwell in Johnny Sutton's band I can remember he played something and I said, 'That just sounds like Johnny Hodges', (Duke Ellington's famous alto-sax player) and John said 'Fat chance'. But he was and still is a fine player, so that's the first time I can recall sitting next to someone who had a distinctive style and sound and played with conviction.

I used to play with the big band on the Saturday night, but Towse had a separate gig out of town on the previous Friday night, and the drummer at the time was Leo Burrows, a wonderful drummer. Leo had this clapped out old car, long before MOTs were the requirement, and it was literally a rust bucket, dropping to bits, and they'd gone in Leo's car to this job and put the library, all the music in the back of the car. And coming back into York from somewhere up north, along Foss Island Road, the bottom of the boot of the car dropped out and half the library finished up in the river. And the wind blew half the library, and apparently there were people wading around retrieving bits of music. That was the early hours of Saturday morning, and they had the gig on Saturday night. I was fortunate, I kept my own music with the baritone, but I remember on Saturday night somebody saying 'We might have a bit of a job tonight, half the library's missing'. And the pianist at the time was a very fine pianist, Clary Clay, he was playing with these muddy pieces of music. Clary knew the parts anyway, he was such an experienced player, but I can remember seeing these muddy piano parts which they'd fished out of the River Foss. Fortunately with a piano you can 'comp' that is accompanying, comping along, and all it is, is a basic chord line, a good experienced pianist can do that. And if he plays a tune he's playing just for the rhythm section, he's not going to get into the way of anybody else, but a front line player has got to play off the copy, the bigger the band, the more important that becomes.

If you're playing in a dance band, we enjoy it, but it's a job of work. There are times when I'm playing with a traditional jazz band I've nearly got a lump in my throat. Nearly wound up at times. Jazz is a never-to-be-repeated experience, if you're actually involved in playing it, and it's going right, for whatever reason, it is an incredible experience. there's an awful lot of emotional feeling.

And I've played with musicians I don't even know, you shake hands, and 'Right we're going to play so and so', and things start to happen, and you can feel your empathy with him, 'cos you know he's thinking the same, a kind of connection we all have together, and you don't get that in any other kind of music.

But with traditional jazz, and other forms of jazz, we are playing for each other. It's nice to have an audience out there, it makes you pay attention a bit more, but you're still playing for each other. Whereas in a band, you are playing together, but you're being lead by the dots, but when you're out playing off the top of your head, you're inspired, if it's going to work, by the people you're playing with. I've got recordings of me playing with a band in Leeds, and it nearly brings tears to the eyes to hear some of the things they play. Incredible.

With a big band, that's another relationship, of a different type. That's elation, but not emotion. I've played with some wonderful big bands, but it's a different kind of elation. When you're playing in a big deal like the Ocean Room at Scarborough or somewhere like that, and you've got 500 people out there, having a tremendous evening, the whole place is leaping, and it's because of you, it's elation. And at the end of the evening you think, 'The place is cooking and we helped, we got that along. That was good'. So I get different kinds of stimulation that way from music.

Noel Porter started playing in dance bands in the 1950s:

When I was 15 I started in the music world and it was all music, all me life. All the surplus energy came out in me through the drums! Radio Luxemburg we used to listen to, about 1954. I bought a toy drum kit, nearly drove everybody barmy with it, and then I started going to Leeds for lessons, when I was 16 by a Leeds drummer, Geoff Myers, who came back into my life very unexpectedly. I was working in a cabaret band in Cayton Park Holiday Camp, in 1978, and the Sid Lawrence Orchestra was the cabaret for the night. We took all our gear off the stage, when who walked in with the drum kit but Geoff Myers. I hadn't seen him for 20 years. He was still going on. Geoff taught me all the intricate stuff about drummin', and how to read music. I was 17 when I got the job at the De Grey Rooms. That was Johnny Sutton And His Music.When you saw him you thought he was the bee's knees, he was always smart.

My first professional engagement was, at the Knavesmire Hotel, in the lounge, with a pianist, maybe 1955. Saturdays nights in there. I don't know how many weeks I did there but, I was the odd one out because they were students, they were right nice lads, and they played trad jazz, and they got this band going and said, 'Do you want a job with us?' [This was possibly the Hot Diamonds Jazz Band].

One night we got this job at Rowntree's Theatre, and somebody at the interval said to me, 'Johnny Sutton's in here and he's watching you',. And he came up and said, 'I'm looking for a drummer, and you are very good, but you have a lot to learn. Would you be interested in a so many months trial?   He came down to our house one night and he said to me mam and dad, 'You do realise he will be the highest paid drummer in York, can he handle the money?' Anyway the wage was £3.17/6d a week, but at that time I wasn't even getting that at British Gas, We did Wednesday nights, Friday nights, Saturday nights for nearly four years. We were on one night and Ron Backhouse, trombone player, was that keen on playing. He was in hospital with appendicitis, and he got

The Knavesmire Hotel was a hot spot for musical entertainment in the 1950s. The Cavaliers Dance Band - Dickie Wade, Charlie Abel, Derek Arness and Ken Vipas played there c1954.

out, got a taxi in his pyjamas, and he blew all his stitches out, he was in a right state, and we had to get an ambulance to get him back to the hospital again. Johnny Sutton went bananas! He was sat on t'stage playing trombone with his pyjamas on! And he'd just had his appendix out!

There was just something about the era, it will never be repeated. It was just at the time when the groups were coming in, and people started to wane from dancing, and we tried a rock 'n' roll night, but it never ever seemed to get going. Then I went to work for Derek Dunning who was another top band in York, but dance banding was coming to an end and we worked a small dance band after that, Harold Midgeley from Stamford Bridge, he was a bit of a character, and we did a lot of Young Farmers dances in the countryside, in the village halls - that was good fun. I did Katherine Worsley's wedding, when she married the Duke of Kent. Hovingham Hall, we did the big night there. That was with the Derek Dunning Band. Came out of there at four in the morning, full of champagne.

Dance banding was the best training you could get. I was lucky, I was trained in that type of work. You wouldn't get a rock drummer that could play in a dance band.

Denis Wright started out in dance bands but also favoured jazz:

We all used to go to the Rialto on a Sunday night. John Barry used to play a lot of jazz records before they started, it was over a good sound system. And John

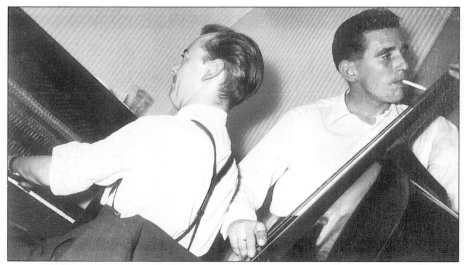

Denis Goodwin, left, and Denis Wright play jazz above Cairns in Colliergate c1956.
(Courtesy Denis Wright)

Johnny Sutton Band at De Grey Rooms, Boxing Day dance 1954. (12pm to 4am). L to R - singer Nancy ?, Leo Burrows, drums, Ron Backhouse, Gil Fox, Gerry Allen, Denis Wright, bass. *(Courtesy Denis Wright)*

Sax section of Johnny Sutton Band in De Grey Rooms, late 1950s. L to R - Ronnie Walsh, John Greenwell, George Turner, unknown. *(Courtesy Brian Parker)*

Barry taught me to read music. I was about 24, quite late, but I practised, and practised.

Denis remembers playing at jazz nights in a room above Cairns Hairdressers in Colliergate. Denis joined Johnny Sutton's band in August 1953 on Saturday nights until 1959:

Sometimes there was scrapping on the dance floor, there was a nasty piece of work that'd come in, always fighting. If there was any trouble, Bert Keech would come up behind them, he'd get hold of their ear and give it two turns right round. Straight out: they were absolutely paralysed. And that was it. But we had this lad, he was always fighting. He took on this young Scotsman and they flew through under my feet and they wedged under the piano. And poor Geoff couldn't work the pedals, he was kicking them off. And Johnny Sutton pulled em' both off, and they were both banned.

All the girls wore high heels then. Even when they were jiving and dancing. They were always in the corner near the piano where Geoff Knaggs was, and myself. I was stood at the front. Always jiving in this corner where there was a big radio gramophone. Much bigger than a telly they were. And they used to put that on, and records on in the interval.

In the early days, they were queuing to get in right back to the Theatre Royal. If you were late he says, 'Come on this is a paid job, it isn't a hobby.' On the

Denis Wright and Ted Pratt, May 1959, with bubble car in alleyway behind De Grey Rooms.   *(Courtesy Denis Wright)*

stand you had to be there at eight o'clock. And it was hard work actually. We used to ask could we take our bow ties off. 'After nine o'clock.' I'd be wet through, it was hard work.

There was one excellent musician called Gil Fox. He could take an arrangement down in his head. He was so clever. He says, 'I'll get that arrangement of Hawaiian War Chant, off Ted Heath's record.' I said, 'How you gonna do that?' He said, 'I'll do it at work.' He was on night shifts and he used to have a little flute. And he transcribed from the notes on the flute on to paper. Every 18 musicians' instruments. And he was dead correct. Every note down to the bass. Couldn't believe it! He was brilliant was Gil Fox. A real jazz man, there.

I had a bubble car. I could get my bass in, it had a folding sun roof. I used to get the neck stuck out, hoped it wasn't raining! One time, this policeman who was a good dancer, invited all the band to his wedding, a big wedding party down Marygate. And Leo was there, and all of them were putting whiskies and brandies into his pint of beer and Johnny said, 'Look Denis, he ain't gonna be playing tonight, can you take him home? Use his car'. And he had this old Vauxhall and we got him in and I remember going down past the Regal Cinema, and it had that much play on the steering you turned the wheel once before it moved half an inch on the road. And there was a cinema queue all watching me, and I was going from one side of road to the other!

To me they were great days. I enjoyed every minute of it. I never even thought of holidays, never had a Saturday off, or a Wednesday, or a Friday, for seven or eight years.

Brian Sutcliffe started out singing in a choir:

At St Margaret's, Walmgate. I enjoyed singing, I had a powerful voice. And then I sang in the choir at Nunthorpe. When I was about 13, my sister joined a division of ENSA with a concert party. We had a bus, and we'd go round entertaining the troops. Some army bases. The searchlights and the anti-aircraft zone where they had canteens.

And then my voice broke, and I had to pack in singing with the choir but I started again when I was doing National Service, in the air force. And when I came out, I met Gordon Cottom, and I joined the Modernaires.

In the 1950s Brian went on to sing at the Chase Hotel, now the Swallow:

with Bobby Hirst, quartet. They played dance music and myself and a girl singer called Nancy, and a foursome, piano, bass, drums and guitar. And it was the best jazz quartet you ever heard in your life, they were magnificent. I

The Bryan Kenny Four c1966. L to R - June Sutcliffe, Brian Sutcliffe, Geoff Oakland and Peter Williams. *(Courtesy Brian Sutcliffe)*

was there for a couple of years, very happy there. And then Bobby decided he wanted to have a sound like the George Shearing quintet and Gordon Cottom joined them as a vibraphone player.

Brian also recalls another York singer, Brian King, who appeared at the Chase:

And one night there was Harold Fielding in, and he liked him, so he signed him up and called him Johnny De Little, this is a year after I was there, so I wonder what would have happened if I'd have been there. He changed his name and got him a job with the Northern Radio Dance Orchestra, he cut a record Lover. Then Sandie Shaw's manager got hold of him, tried to promote him, and changed his name to Heathcliffe.

Eventually big bands folded because in came beat music, and you get four or five guys going out with guitars, for £50, you couldn't afford to pay a band any more. So I did the same thing. In 1964 I got married and then I formed a group, the Bryan Kenny Four. Two vocalists, my wife June and myself, a guitar player and bass player, Pete Williams, one of the finest bass players in the North of England. It was like the Seekers set-up and we played and sung tunes that I wrote myself.

We actually went to London, we had a manager, Don Robinson. We had a recording test and he tried to sign us up with a 20 per cent cut of everything and we baulked at this.

If you go to a ball, where you've got a big band, a 20-piece orchestra, they're not playing pop music all the time, they're playing mostly standards. They're still going, and they'll always be there, they will never ever die.

Radio was important in people's lives in the war, radio and music was important for entertainment. Music was very big anyway, because it was, it was entertainment. And in the 1950s, the dancing was a way for youngsters to get together and meet each other.

That's why people write lyrics to songs. It's a way to express yourself. And people react to it. It's a human thing, escapism to a point. You escape into a different world. You're writing your feelings down, like somebody writing a book. And watching a modern jazz quartet, it's like watching Picasso painting, you're hearing the same thing happening in the music, and it can never be the same again. It expresses how the person feels at that particular time, what he's thinking, his moods.

There's a danger that when youngsters go and be trained, if they're not very careful, they don't have any feeling for it. They are trained technically, and they have nothing else but the technical ability. I know pianists, who can sit down and play piano concertos wonderfully, put them in front of a piano and ask them to play something, they haven't got a clue without music in front of them. I honestly believe, the great pianists, the great jazz, and I use the word jazz deliberately, because jazz is an essence of composing music as it's happening invariably find, they sit down with a piano or a saxophone or trumpet, and it is a wonderful, wonderful, gift that they have. These trained music teachers haven't got that.

I think the great players can express the emotion but they've got to have the ability through their instrument to express that. Music is not necessarily a technical thing. Instead of playing ten chords, you only need to play three chords, four chords. You get too bound to the technicalities of the thing. A good musician plays the least number of chords possible, to express himself. Not the most. If you listen to George Shearing and people like that, when he's backing people, you can hardly hear him, the person is left to sing the song. The singer is the lead instrument and the piano and everything else is there to fill in behind, to make it sound good behind.

The Bryan Kenny Four were excellent musicians. They could play their instruments, and they could sight read. We actually had four-part harmony, that was a top notch group with a natural four-part harmony.

I was still young enough to adapt, I was only like 30s. I wasn't terribly enamoured by the Beatles, quite frankly I thought they were absolute junk, with one or two exceptions. Yesterday was beautiful. But I didn't think much to rock 'n' roll either, and I can't stand Elvis Presley, but I was fortunate because at that particular time there were some great singers coming in. Nat King Cole was a great singer, he made When I Fall In Love in the 1950s. And Sinatra was just coming through into the films. Songs For Swinging Lovers came out in the 1950s.

I took part in a competition in Manchester when I was across there one day, when I was on a selling course in the 1960s. I won second prize, I think I sang You Make Me Feel So Young. It's a fantastic buzz, probably the greatest buzz you ever get in your life, but any professional actor, who goes on to a stage and does it for a living, when you go on stage you're always nervous.

In essence I'm not a musician because I don't play an instrument. I'm still a musician, the voice is my music, like Sinatra. The interesting thing is a lot of jazz musicians don't rate vocalists. But they forget vocalists are the people who make the money. The jazz musicians don't make a penny, good vocalists are very difficult to find.

183

The most recorded artiste in the world is Frank Sinatra, probably more albums than anybody else ever will. Most of his albums are standards, songs that have been around for years and years. Songs that go back to the 1920s, and 1930s and they are being played today, people are listening to them, but these songs are also being played by jazz musicians and big bands all over the world. These are the songs that musicians choose, because they have a natural sequence of chords. You've got an idea where it's going to go to next.

But jazz music is like painting on a canvas, it's never been done before, this is what jazz music is. Music being played as it is then, and it's never played the same again. If a jazz pianist plays 32 bars of a song, the next 32 bars won't be the same.

It depends how you feel, your mood. And they choose these songs because they could find literally scores of different chords round the root chord that the composer wrote. And there are so many different ways to play it. Stardust is another favourite song. It's the second most recorded song in the world, after Yesterday. They are melodic, whereas a lot of songs written now are not melodic. And they disappear from the scene, overnight sensations.

Dancing was very important in York and in 1953 there were a number of dance schools. The Petina School Of Dancing at the Co-op Hall in Carr Lane offered modern classes and old time. The Albany called itself 'York's progressive ballroom' with dancing every Wednesday, Friday and Saturday, and instruction classes each Monday. The Misses Cowper had moved to Glenholme on the Mount and offered private lessons in ballroom dancing. Clark's shoeshop advertised ladies silver plastic dancing shoes for 17/1d and silver brocade dancing shoes for 23/6d.

In November 1919 the Grand Picture House, Café and Ballroom had opened in Clarence Street built by Reginald Pulleyn. He was well known in the city and became Sheriff and then Lord Mayor during the Second World War. In 1940 he announced that his personal contribution to the city's Spitfire Fund (which hoped to raise £5,000 to be able to present a fighter aircraft to the nation) would be a week's takings at the Grand cinema. Christies of Selby became lessees of the ballroom in September 1958 and it became a popular venue for dances. Unfortunately Christies Ballroom was gutted by fire in November 1959. The musical instruments which had been left on the stage by the band were destroyed. Wal Walsh was a member of that band:

That was another sax and clarinet that went up in smoke. We had a big band then, about 14 piece. We played three nights a week, Friday, Saturdays and one during the week. And being Friday night we never bothered taking the kit down, we just left the saxes on the stand. Next morning we found the place had been burnt, all the kit on the stage had gone.

And then they started disputing about the band instruments, 'each individual fella should have had his own insurance'. We never bothered, because we were given to understand that Christie's paid our insurance. We got it in the finish, but we had to go on doing gigs for Christie's all round the countryside.

And Eric Dawson was the original band there, the Terry Yorke Orchestra, but he left and got a job in Huddersfield, and the band was just Christie's band.

I remember Eric Dawson, he'd sometimes do a bit of conducting instead of playing, like Henry Hall. He used to wear tails. You were expected to turn out respectable you know. 'Cos he used to have the old army expressions as well, did Eric. When we were doing a gig like, and it started at eight, 'DD Eric?' [Dinner dress] 'No, mufti'. An ordinary lounge suit, he used to call it mufti!

Derek Dunning and his orchestra competed in the North Britain regional final of the National Band Championships in Huddersfield in 1955. Their three test pieces were a slow foxtrot, waltz and quickstep, and the songs were Out Of Nowhere, So This Is Love and Deep Night. The members were Derek on sax and alto clarinet, Tye Bruce on trumpet, Roy Bang on trumpet, Bob Scott on trombone, Ted Gee on alto, Gordon Knight on tenor, Henry Thomson on baritone sax, Peter Shorter on piano, Reg Peel on bass, Tony Whitehead on drums, Fred Mills on tenor sax and Gloria Lydon on vocals.

Gloria Lydon, now King, sang with both the Derek Dunning Band and Johnny Sutton. She remembers:

I loved to sing. Even as a small child I had a little rocking chair. I'd sit in that and sing to myself. The first time with the Johnny Sutton Band was in 1953 in the De Grey Rooms. I was with Johnny until 1954 then I was away from York and when I came back things had gone a bit down at the De Grey Rooms. I met up with Derek and sang with him, The Nearness Of You and Embraceable You.

And when you've been on stage you're up on a high. You don't come down for a while. I would hate to think that one could live without music. It gives us such an awful lot of pleasure, whether you're listening to it or actually performing it. I suppose you tend to take it for granted if you are able to sing. My singing teacher told me how to breathe from the diaphragm which I hadn't known before. Some people had raw eggs or a glass of sherry to relax your throat.

Bob Scott recalled playing at the Empire:

The Terry Yorke Orchestra at Christie's Ballroom. Back L to R - Don Claxton, bass, Ted Rowell, piano, Dougie Hayes, drums, Ted Lawty, Ted Akers, unknown, trumpets, Dickie Bailey, Alf Field, trombones. Front L to R - Eric Dawson, baritone, Wal Walsh, Arthur Jones, Derek Parker, Len Cundall.

(Courtesy Wal Walsh)

That was a bit of a farce! We played for roller skating. Unfortunately, the first night it opened the stage had been taken out and there was a big area where they danced, but all the old curtaining for the stage was left up, and there was years of dust on it. The Christie Brothers from Selby, they ran the Grand Ballroom, but Shepherd of the Empire, a bit of competition, they wanted to get open before the other one. And Shepherd was rushing, trying to get it open, and on the Saturday night he was still painting, and they were opening for dancing and somebody rattled these curtains, well the dust that came off it. And it covered all these seats that were laid out for people to sit at the side of the hall, the women in their nice dresses sat down and were covered in muck. But that night he must have got 900 people in. The next one, there was 500, the next one 300, and it just went down like that. This was ordinary ballroom dancing, there was obviously a demand for it. If the thing had been done right, and there was no muck about, he would have held them, but he didn't and it was cold metal seats they were, so he lost them! Then somebody said, 'I know, we'll do roller skating'. But the noise that roller skates make on the dance floor, it was a good floor he'd put in, bird's eye maple or something like that. There must have been about a couple of hundred people skating round on this floor, and the band set up here, and there's a master of ceremony, with a whistle, and we're playing and trying to play with this, and then they start skating and going round and round, and the noise is horrendous! And then as they start going round, they start the air circulating, and it's like a whirlwind! And all the music's blowing all over the stands! It was just absolutely hilarious! And him blowing the whistle, but all you could hear is the roar of wheels on the dance floor. So that fizzled out as well, and then I think he decided to have wrestling - and you don't need a band for that!

When I was playing with Geoff Laycock, there was this John Owen, who founded the Lowenbrau Beer Kellers. We were playing at his party. There was a top American singing group doing the cabaret, and he'd built this marquee in the garden, one part of it, just a section out from the main marquee, roasting a whole beast on a spit. And he'd built it over the swimming pool, with champagne floating and everything. We'd done a set and I was stood by this pool, and they were all in fancy dress, and they started to eat. And the rest of the band were all down by the patio. Anyway this bloke in fancy dress had come down from where they were eating, off this verandah, sneaked up behind and pushed me in the pool! So I had to dry out, I had no clothes and our roadie took me clothes away and he lost my underclothes. My trousers weren't dry and one of the bouncers, (they were all round the gate and everywhere, and they all had radio connection to each other), he lent me his trousers, but they didn't fit, so I declined to play - I wasn't going to stand there. So I had a few drinks, 'cos everything was free. I'd come with Peter, but Peter was playing, the small band finished it off, the big band finished about two, and I had to wait for Peter till four o'clock. I had no underclothes, and my trousers were wet and he said, 'Put my overcoat on'. So I came back completely starkers with this overcoat, if the police had stopped us I don't know how the hell I would have explained it. He lost my shoes as well, the roadie, I don't know what the heck he did! Because I couldn't follow him, could I?

Music can run in families and often two or even three generations of musicians can be found in one family. But identical twins who share a love of music and a talent for it, are rather unusual. Trevor and Brian Bousfield came to York during the Second World War as very young children. Their father had run dance bands in his native Hull and continued to do so on a smaller scale in York. The twins were also influenced by other musicians from the brass band world. Trevor recalls two brothers:

Arthur and Les Lambeth. Arthur worked at Rowntree's who gave permission for him to come to our school. He was probably the first brass peripatetic in York and that's how we started, when we were 11. Arthur conducted York Military Band and Les conducted the Cocoa Works Rowntrees Band. One got paid for it, the other didn't.

We had training in brass bands and we'd been doing little bits of solo work but it seemed the natural thing, to form our own dance band. Father formed a band again in York to try and get us started. The first dance was when Charlie Bousfield and his Criterions played at the Grand Dance at Sutton-on-the-Forest Cricket Club in April 1952, with prizes for the personality girl and the gent with the loudest tie.

But the band we formed was the Scarlets Dance Band, and our first engagement was at St Chad's but later we went all around the areas of York, Selby and Malton, with a drummer, Gareth Lloyd on piano, Morris Willey on accordion.

Their father continued to play:

There were still always pianos in pubs and he was always in demand. I can remember when we were in the choir at Haxby, I would delay coming home from Evensong, to walk down the back lanes, so I could listen to him for a while in the working men's club.

His ability, his eventual talent, is amazing because he didn't have a piano. He could afford a banjo and he managed to pick the notes out from the banjo, write them down and had a paper keyboard that he constructed with all the black and white notes. He would practise for hours on the silent keyboard, to his notations and then knock on a neighbour's door, to ask permission to play the piano. I think it's this simple desire to do something, there must have been some talent there.

We had a burning ambition to play and I can recall when it was our 21st birthday, some people would say you went out to work, because it was Saturday night, those that didn't understand, didn't realise I was doing what I wanted to do, what I've always wanted to do, which was to play. It wasn't work, it was fun. If I wasn't engaged somewhere, I'd go and sit in with somebody. At that time I was playing with the Modernaires, they were a split from the band at the De Grey Rooms and were playing every Saturday night in Malton, the Milton Rooms, - probably the worst place I ever saw for fighting. Dance halls were usually a very happy jovial place but for some reason, little jockeys love a scrap.

When I was in the forces, we played at Middleham, where there is a stables. And this little jockey came up and sat on my knee while I was playing and I was wise to these little fellas by then so I never said anything. He was very pleasant, he stuffed cigarettes in every aperture he could find and I must have looked a pure fool, sat there, playing away with him on me knee, and I never said boo to a goose. When he got down, the chaps I was playing with, said, "Didn't you know who that was?' and it was some famous jockey from Middleham. The one aperture he didn't find was covered with a mouthpiece.

In the towns you have the wide boys, the teddy boys, that would start something, but it wasn't too bad, even though Clifton Ballroom packed in because of that. The dances were beginning to attract a certain clientele, there was fighting to the point where I think the police had closed it down. And after a cooling-off period, they wanted to start dancing in there again and approached us to see if we would play. He says, 'Oh we'll make sure you're all right'. In one corner of the room they'd built the bandstand and built the front up like a big wave barrier that came over in a curve. 'That'll protect you'. So I said, 'How on earth's that gonna stop them getting at us?' and he said, 'To get at you, they've got to lean over, and then you've got the advantage, you can get the punch in first'!

It was suggested we ought to have some vocals. Ted Rowell must have been one of the influences in persuading me I could sing Old Man Mose, one of these old catchy things. So every Saturday night I would stand up there and make these horrible noises. On one particular night, we were closing down, it was pitch black, everybody had gone home, and there was a young man hanging over the fence like a washing line. He turned out to be absolutely drunk. So we marched him down the street to the telephone box, my overcoat on him to keep warm, and we were phoning the police to come and take him home. This chap says, 'Did you go to the dance'? 'Yes' I says. 'I come every week', he says, 'and there's a bloke up there, he tries to bloody sing every week and he's shocking', and I thought, he's stood there, he's in my overcoat, I've done my best to get him back home, probably an hour out of my own bed and he's stood there slagging me off!

We would play anything, anywhere, any chance to play, doesn't matter what it was, we would be there. In a sense it created a problem because eventually when we concentrated on dance band music, you offended the brass band world.

Once we'd started the Scarlets, Fridays would be the first nights to fill up, occasionally Wednesdays, but Saturday nights tended to be regular. I remember leaving the Assembly Rooms at midnight and going to the American base for the next four hours just for somewhere to play, and I'd played for four hours before that, but that's what you wanted to do. We were playing each week at Huby, and then this problem occurred. Somebody says, 'You're no longer required, we're going to run our own band and you're not in it', so we had to do something quick. We had two weeks to get a library, the standard library of saxophones, brass and rhythm sections, get the players, get them rehearsed and go in there.

We started then as the Imperial Dance Orchestra and we got Ted Rowell out of retirement and he continued to play from then on until he died. We poached

Imperial Dance Band. L to R - Derek Parker, Arthur Jones, Brian and Trevor Bousfield. c1953   *(Courtesy Trevor Bousfield)*

The Trumpet Twins. Trevor Bousfield, Violet Pretty (who became actress Anne Heywood), Brian Bousfield. Empire c1953. *(Courtesy Trevor Bousfield)*

Arthur Jones and Derek Parker for the saxes. Later on we changed the drummer for Dougie Cartwright, and they then remained the core that saw us through until we were approaching National Service.

It changed to the Trumpet Twins, not really of our choosing. It was the Press that did that. Carroll Levis used to visit towns to 'discover' people. So we said we'd better go and have a look at this. Apart from the fact we could play a bit, you can never escape this commercial aspect of two identical bodies, the circus act if you like. When we were in the forces, we fitted their bill perfectly, because we were the same height, the same looks, the same width, the same sound, we did the same thing. We were exploited commercially in the sense that we were sent off as a pair all over the place. So the Press said, 'Osbaldwick twins even made Carroll Levis rub his eyes'. So that was the start and there were other events that were results from that.

We were wanting to enhance the rhythm section and there was a strong argument, 'We must have a string bass'. If you listen outside a dance hall you can hear the string bass, feel this pulse. We persuaded them at Huby to increase the band size 'cos we wanted a string bass player. And at the end of the evening, we went along to get our money, and, 'Don't ever pull that trick again. That fella up there. (the bass player). We've been listening, and not one of us has heard him play a tune all night'!

People didn't have cars to the same extent as they have today. When we were at Huby, lots of people wanted to go so we started to run buses on a Saturday night and they would leave Exhibition Square. We booked the bus and charged some nominal fee, simply a case of how many's on a bus, divide that into whatever the fee was and that's how it would work. On one particular evening, we came out, got on to the bus, and there's a young man. He made some explanation, his pals had brought him, and left him adrift, and can he have a lift home. I sat next to him, 'Yes it would be all right', and he tried to persuade me that I ought to take something for my generosity and I agreed to take half of what I'd taken off other people, only pennies. But little did I know that he was the 'stool pigeon' from the Reliant Bus Company. Once I'd taken money from him, I had infringed the licence for public travel between York and Huby which was held by their company so I had to go to court and was fined 40/-.

The solution was to form a club, threepence subscription, so everybody on the bus was charged this penny, given a card and became members. The bus company, having got us into court once, thought they were on a field day and set traps for us. Bumper Castle, that's where invariably they'd put somebody to hail the bus down. We'd ignore them until it became a regular event. Hey, wait a minute, we recognise that person. Stopped the bus, you come out of the bus and behind you there's half a bus load of strong strapping lads that want to help you so it becomes a chase You chase these people and a few hundred yards down the road, it turns over the old railway line, and that's where the car was strategically placed. They'd jump into the car and hurl off before this load of strapping young men could pounce.

The thing about music is, if you don't make them listen, you've lost. And the thing that makes somebody listen is style and sound. Freddie Gardner on alto, you listen to him, what he did was nothing wonderful but the sound, sheer beauty. And this is what the likes of Eddie Calvert had. Wonderful sound.

We thought we could play. Never short of confidence. We were 21 in 1957 and we went to London then to Brighton to try to join Sid Dean's Band and be professional, but before that materialized, mam and dad came on holiday with a letter from Her Majesty,'Report to Catterick Camp'. National Service! It was Ted Pratt who told us, 'It's a major staff band, you can demand the right for an audition'.

So it was Richmond by train, one-way ticket. It was a bit like a death sentence at that time was Catterick Camp. You were brayed something awful, to bray every sense out of you, to put you in a mode of fear. We were both by then qualified engineers but we said, 'No, I want an audition for the band'. There was a reluctant audition and we went into a major staff band, Royal Corps of

Signals, and you practised everywhere. I was practising in the toilets, and I heard this noise coming from one of the other pews, it was another trumpet player and he was fantastic. He was 18, and he turned out to be Nigel Carter, later principal trumpeter of BBC Big Band.

It was very difficult when you'd lived the life that we had, which was extremely full and free. You just practised, you didn't have free time. Once you got into the band, things were different, a lot better, more privileged in the band.

I even spent two weeks in York pit orchestra when I was in the forces, and it was simply because somebody said, 'Could you play in the pit orchestra?' and we had a mad major in charge of us, we went and knocked on his door. 'We've been offered a job in the Empire Theatre, wondered if I could go'. 'My musicians play all over the country, of course you can go. How much are you going to get?' 'Union rates'. 'Right come and see me' after a certain date, 'I want x pounds', and it was a substantial sum.

On one occasion he said, 'Send for my Cocoa musicians', he used to call us, something to do with Rowntree's. 'Get your best reds on' so it meant you had to get the best epaulettes, best busbies, best tight wellies and you'd go there and he'd say the brigadier was to hear us play. 'Play him a fanfare' and you'd see this fat fella waddling down the corridor. He would say, 'A fanfare you fools, a fanfare'. You'd play the fanfare, put your instrument down, he'd slam the door, then open it and say, 'Go home for a few days'.

We used the trumpet like a lethal weapon and being of a rebellious nature, anybody that was within a short distance of that bell, suffered if they were deemed to suffer. In other words if they were regular soldiers, because remember, we were National Services infiltrating regulars. If you've got a sergeant that's been giving you a rough time, and you can just get your bell over his shoulder, he won't hear anything for the next 24 hours. You'd play things an octave up. It got to the point, there's a piece called The Mad Major, a march. You used to go up progressively, up to top C, and come down and finish off up to E and F. Well we never used to stop, we'd keep going up and up and up. A lot of these people out of brass bands, they'd never heard notes like that, and they used to wait for it and stop. So they'd stop playing and listen to this, and in the end the march seemed to stop and there's just this scream used to go up. So in the end they banned them from playing the The Mad Major.

Instead of playing strictly to the music we would add 'liptrills' or a few 'screamers' or even slightly modify the style here and there, giving a different approach to the music. This meant living dangerously, for if we were caught, it would mean a spell in the guardhouse with immediate dismissal from the band and demotion to general duties (a fate worse than death). One area for attack was the corps march which received special treatment, which wasn't favourably received by the army, who sought to solve the problem by altering the march, which involved replacing a long sustained note (ideal for liptrilling) with moving quavers at the point receiving most treatment. The problem of playing 'an octave above the score' was never solved, though the offending party was eventually tracked down to one of two people, and became known as the 'phantom screamer'.

I think we were foolish, we blew harder than we had to, because what used to happen was, if we got into trouble, they would say, 'You need slow march practice. 8 o'clock in that room'. And we'd deliberately not blow and there might be some brigadier or general they wanted to impress, and you'd say, 'Sorry it's slow march'. So every opportunity was taken to take the mickey or be rebellious, but, I think we probably paid the price for that.

While they were in the forces, the twins took on a new challenge:

We were called into the office one day and the major says, 'You're going to play some ancient instruments. You've to go to so and so and I've written some music for you and there's some music coming off the archives out of the museums'. There was a hotel at Catterick Bridge and we had to stay there until these people arrived. They had to get special police escort through. And they brought us home and we sat on the floor in the bedroom at home, with the back against the bed, to learn to play these things. It was typical of him! The Danish Embassy had got in contact with Musicians' Union. 'No! We don't have any lur players'. Got in contact with Nellar Hall, 'No, we don't have any lur players'. Some reason contacted the major, and he says, 'I've got two'!

We had to play in London and we'd gone into some studios and the major had written these pieces and the studios didn't like them. 'Go and get yourselves some rehearsal halls'. Well in the music rehearsal halls, there's signs up, 'No Brass Instruments'. You go in, buy your space, and go to your room, and they say, 'Are they brass?' 'No, they're bronze'. So off we went, we bought an hour and by the time we came out, there wasn't a soul in the building, we'd cleared the building out, but we'd had our rehearsal time.

Another occasion in London we were travelling by Tube with these priceless instruments, the Danish lurs, with no case, just corrugated brown paper. There was a film The Vikings and we were invited to play at the premiere, Leicester Square Theatre. We had to stand on either side of the stage in Viking uniform and lurs, and given a signal, herald the fanfare for the start of the film. There's an enormous cheer, whether that was because we were finishing or the film was starting. We were taken to a big hotel for the reception and our role was to stand on either side of the banqueting hall doorway and herald fanfares as they came from the premiere into the banqueting hall. We were given instructions. When Burt Lancaster comes through, we have to sound a fanfare. And you've probably guessed by now we didn't have a lot of time for films, even though Mr. Prendergast gave us an open ticket to go to the Rialto. We didn't bother going unless there was a band concert. So, 'Who's Burt Lancaster?' 'You don't know? Well, when Kirk Douglas comes in, play a fanfare'. 'Who's Kirk Douglas?' 'Don't you lads ever go to the films?' 'We went to see Bambi'. 'Well look, I suppose you'll recognise Sabrina when Sabrina comes in. Play a fanfare. Better still, just keep playing the fanfare every few minutes as they're coming in'. Well I suppose because drinks were free, people were constantly pouring in, I can remember seeing Clement Atlee coming through, and they would stop and talk to you and say, 'Young man you haven't got a drink. Waiter, he needs a drink'. So they would give you a drink, I think it was mostly gin and you'd put it on your seat and soon there was nowhere to sit, the seats were full of all these glasses of gin.

In December 1958 the Yorkshire Evening Press reported that the trumpet twins would be seen on BBC Television in a programme featuring a fanfare at the beginning of a Festival of Carols and Hymns at Beverley Minster. The programme was also to be relayed to The Netherlands by Eurovision. The Bousfield twins had appeared on television earlier that year dressed in Viking costume and demonstrating the lur horns. Trevor recalls what happened after their National Service.

Queen's Hotel, Leeds, 1958. Left - Brian, right - Trevor Bousfield, playing lurs.

1957-59 was the forces, and it didn't take a lot of time to re-establish, we began to start forming other bands and begin from scratch to get work again, but by then the signs were there. The dance halls were not being filled, the clubs were taking over. In our case being trumpet players, it's nice to play things like Cherry Blossom & Apple White. That was just a bit of icing on the cake.

Brian explains something of the extraordinary nature of the pair's abilities:

I think twins have this affinity, they know, even if you put them in different rooms, what is happening, it's because you've been together, you've done everything the same from being in your mother's womb to, even in the forces we were in the next bed. It gives you great anticipation when you're playing. You know exactly the style of phrasing, you don't have to put massive clues out, it's just instantly there.

When we went on doing concert work, dad was our pianist, and we never ever rehearsed with him. We'd walk out on to a stage with a packed audience, and we'd just tell him, 'We're playing this, this is the key', and he'd have to bring us in, in the right key, and he never rehearsed it.

Clifton Ballroom closed down, but it opened as an experiment on Thursdays, and the bands were being auditioned, and this young man, just a couple of years older than us, came to audition us. And we got the job. We didn't realise that the man auditioning us was John Barry, and he insisted the name be changed from the Imperial Dance Orchestra, to York's Trumpet Twins Dance Orchestra. Although John Barry himself wasn't the best trumpet player, he was still a very skilled arranger, and he had the knowledge and the ability to hear good music, to hear music played well, to be able to pick the best.

Trevor and I were playing with Johnny Sutton in the De Grey Rooms one New Year's Eve, and we'd arrived early, 'cos we had to hide our bikes at the back of the De Grey Rooms in the snow. It was too far to walk. And here was John Barry, and he was going to be playing with us. But instead of practising his trumpet he was just sat by the piano, playing different notes, and different chords. He wasn't playing as a pianist would play, he was experimenting with sounds. And that was my first experience of what an incredible man, the ability to take three notes, four notes, and turn a sound into something that's totally different to any sound you'd heard before. If you listen to his arrangements, they're very simple, they use octaves a lot, rather than throw an army of chords at something. And yet if you listen to some of his music that does give a massive sound, it's not because he's thrown an army at it, it's because he knows exactly how to orientate the notes and the sounds and the instruments to get these things. If you listen to music that John Barry's written, it's got his signature on it, that's an incredible ability, he'll be remembered in history.

So even though I didn't have the ability to compose all those different sounds, I would know when the sound was right and when it wasn't. Just as conductors walk in front of the orchestra and completely transform it. They're playing exactly the same notes. If you and I went in front of the Hallé with a baton, and if you think all you have to do is to beat in time, you'd find they'll play terrible, and it's the same notes, and then somebody else will come up, and he will know what he wants, he'll know what he wants to suppress, he'll know the rhythm. It's because the man at the front brings a totally new dimension.

Music can make you happy, it can make you sad, until you've had hate, until you've had joy, until you've been married, until you've lost a battle, until you've done all these things in life, you're hardly in a position to express them, because you don't know them. Music expresses all life's feelings, and if you have the ability to understand those, it can take you through all those emotions. And if you can hear a string pouring it out, and then instantly hear him get angry, all in just a piece of music, that's wonderful. Jacqueline Dupré, if you listen to her, the way she could pour emotion, and then somebody else plays the same notes but it's not good.

When Trevor and Brian were only in their twenties, they both suffered serious lung problems which meant that they both had to stop playing the trumpet. Brian went on to playing bass guitar for a while and Trevor took up guitar and later conducted the Rowntree Brass Band. Brian explains:

If we'd just played in the very simple ordinary quiet way we'd have perhaps still been playing now. I've no doubt we just blew our brains out. Just gave. In those days if you were a principal trumpet player in a big band you really had to come out on top no matter who else was playing there. That sound had to come out on top, and it could be very hard.

If I'd have been a pianist I would have done exactly the same. If I'd have been a drummer I would have done exactly the same, probably got thrown out of every job for putting too much into it. That's just part of the enjoyment, that's what makes it a pleasure. So, do I regret it? No, life has probably taught me an important lesson and that's to get up and move on. Was it easy? Of course it isn't easy, but, you know the successful people in life are those who made their success out of a tragedy.

When we were in the forces we used to practise about six hours a day, and the instrument would blow itself. When we'd get home on leave, we would still practise six hours a day, even though we might be playing at a dance. We would even play for nothing. There were many times we played for Johnny Sutton for nothing.

Just to go into the Milton Rooms in Malton and expect to get hundreds of people takes a lot of doing, so all sorts of gimmicks were tried to encourage more people, and one of the players played at Rowntree's and could get lots of chewing gum. So one night, as the dancers are dancing round, this man's throwing handfuls of chewing gum to people and they were catching it, and picking it off the floor, and everyone's dancing and chewing. But it only lasted about a minute, and then tasted horrible, so they'd spit it out. Now eventually the dancers, instead of sliding on the floor, they're foot to foot with a piece of chewing gum. So that was banned. No more throwing of free chewing gum.

We once played a nine-to-one job in Huby. And when the dancers finished, we didn't have to take everything off the stage because we were playing there the next night. When we got the car, two tyres had been let down. What a mess, and it was pouring with rain, and muddy.

We had to spend the night there, and by then all the heat's gone, and we took the curtains off the windows, and laid on coconut matting with curtains on top, in our full evening dress, shivering, until daylight. The drummer sat on this chair, creases perfect in his evening dress.

When it got to the early hours, we got some help and eventually got somebody to jack the car up. And about seven o'clock there was this bus passing, and all the dancers who worked at Rowntree's, who looked so beautiful the night before, are in their curlers, going to do overtime at Rowntree's, and they're waving at us. We're in a mess and one man is trying to wash the mud off the tyres and the hubs of the car, and this drummer says, 'Look, I wasn't in the navy for nothing, stand back'. And he got a bucket, and he threw this water at the hubcap, it hit perfectly central, turned round and covered him full of mud.

In the army, you get this thing, the soldier marching by, quick march, and off you go. Now, this is the bass drummer hitting the first big bang, and so we marched, that's going all the time. Now we as trumpet players would stand behind the bass player if we could, and four or five of us, would turn our bells, including Carter, this brilliant trumpet player, and we would blow as hard as we could, but we would be very slowly pulling the beat down.

We were doing a parade where there was a cannon, and we marched up to the cannon and come back on yourself, making sure you missed the cannon. And we did lots of different manoeuvres. But we just moved the band a bit to the left or to the right, which meant that the bass drummer can't see a thing, first thing he hit was the cannon.

Oh if we had a man at the front who wasn't terribly experienced, we'd look for an opportunity, and the man at the front said The Banner Of St George. But what he meant to stay was The Standard Of St. George. And there is a march called The Banner Of... something else, and, since we could blow louder than the rest of the band put together, at the front they slowly joined in and we totally changed the tune.

Before dinner you had to do mess calls. The bloke with me, he didn't know, but we played a horrible mess. As soon as we got out of the place I rang the musical director and said, 'Look, we're in trouble here, because the fanfare we've just blown at the mess call was terrible'. 'Why's that, my famous star?' 'Well they stood us next to a radiator, the thing was totally out of tune, I couldn't believe what was coming out of the bell'. They told me he said they'd had some complaints but he put them right. You lived on the seat of your pants, because you couldn't memorise everything.

Playing 'screamers' was a dangerous practice because the remainder of the band quickly learned at what point in the music these additions were being made and on arrival at this point in the music would stop 'blowing' to listen for the 'screamers', this emphasised the effect but also pin pointed the offender, thus necessitating a tactical change in attack to avoid detection. After each successful mission, the returning band would enter the foyer of the band block to be met by the announcement boldly displayed on the notice board - The Phantom Screamer Strikes Again.

Trevor went back to the brass band, teaching and conducting. Both Trevor's and Brian's children got involved in music. Trevor's son Ian Bousfield, got a scholarship to the Guildhall, and after six months got the job as principal trombone of the Hallé Orchestra when he was only 19. After six years he got a job at the London Symphony:

That was his dream really. And now he's won that job at Vienna Phil and State Opera now. He's the first Britain to ever play in the Vienna Phil. He said to me, 'Do you know when we played Mahler Three, the audience wept? I thought it was just Vienna, but when we were in Carnegie Hall, a few days later, you could see tears in the audience'.

Now the very first time he did that, was the most moving. Ian said, 'That was a special occasion for me, one of those moments in my life'. And they said, 'That was one of the moments in the life of the Vienna Phil'.

CHAPTER SEVEN. I'LL TAKE ROMANCE
Dance Bands in the 1960s

With the advent of rock 'n' roll in the mid 1950s, and the beat group scene in the 1960s (the subject of volume two of this publication), the music scene in York became very diverse. Dance band music was waning but it never actually died and some bands who managed to stay with it, were as popular as ever. Some people say that music changed overnight, others that it was more gradual, depending on where they fitted into the scene. A few bands stopped playing but others adapted and included more modern music in their repertoire to attract younger audiences. There were still openings for dance bands in village halls and private functions, but many of the musicians went into working men's clubs. Of course by the time the 1960s came, the dance band musicians were getting older, and had less energy to play and hold down a day job as well. Wal Walsh recalls:

You think you can blow for ever, it was really hard work playing three or four nights a week, four or five hours a night. When you get older, you get weaker. I played at Tramways for quite a few years, down Piccadilly. But there was resentment really 'cos it took a long time to learn the basics, to read music and these groups didn't need it, it was all busk with them. I still don't like it really. It's just noise.

Charlie Druggitt played for a time at Tang Hall Club with Trevor Wheeler, and was later resident at Burnholme Club with Eric Betts. Harry Warrington played solo at the Promenade Club, and on Sunday nights would open with a classical piece. His daughter Liz remembers watching him receive standing ovations there. He found another niche playing for old time and sequence dancing, drawing on his 'vast musical knowledge and great library of music. Gordon Cottom played piano for several years with the drummer Ken Kenyon at the Crescent Club. Bob Halford was resident at Severus Club, Percy Hick at Lawrence Street Club, and Charles Hutchinson played with Doug Green and Albert Appleyard on Thursday nights at the Crescent for ballroom dancing, which Charles really enjoyed:

It went down like a bomb. Albert was a beautiful tenor sax player, miked up to a Copykat. And of course it's a big Steinway grand in there. I had the time of me life because it was a beautiful instrument. And Doug was the best drummer in York at that time.

Val Mountain was taken by surprise:

The Doug Green Band at an earlier time. L to R - Bob Halford, Arthur Burcombe, Doug Green, Albert Jackson, Henry Warrington. *(Courtesy Jean Halford)*

It was a real culture shock when all these twanging guitars came in. It didn't do it gradually, it was all of a sudden. It was a shock, because they were so bad. You think back, 'That was the best time of my life', but at the time you don't think anything about it, it's just happening. You'd think that sanity would prevail one day, and I think it's coming back, 'cos you can't beat the big band sound.

Tiddy Mead had always said that he would not play in clubs, but he was in demand and the money was useful:

I did do some Sundays at Clarence Street, I depped for a couple of years, and came back with a band at Bishopthorpe Club but I'll be quite honest, I formed my own groups after that and just ploughed my own way. The twangers were beginning to come on the scene, Bill Haley with the rock 'n' roll, and when the Beatles came, every kid in creation wanted a guitar, and you're fighting this sort of battle. I can't remember the band I was playing with, but we did a job in the Technical College in Clifford Street for the students, end of term. But the kids didn't want us, oh no, when the twangers came on they went berserk, and not one of 'em could play or read a note of music, it was just twang, twang, bang, bang, crash bang. That's not music, I've always termed it 'tribal warfare', I still do, and we knew then we were up against it, the whole scene changed.

Gerry Allen found that bands in clubs were getting smaller, but he could play alto sax with piano and drums backing, and got a lot of work. He played at Poppleton Road Club, was resident in Fulfordgate Club, and found that a seven-piece band was possible at Bishopthorpe Club, using three rhythm players, three saxes and a trumpet. Arthur Jones had a different tactic. He moved on to playing the organ:

I bought a cheap one, just a single manual with foot pedals, and Stan Seeds, a dance band organist, took me on for a year and I came back into the business as an organist. It's a different world now, you can buy these keyboards and they just do everything. Just sit there and press a button, and you've got your strings, your rhythm and your bass, you put the chords in, and out come the bass parts, and everything.

The transition was not always easy as Colin Baines observes:

You could play at working men's clubs for £2 a night, they were getting cheap entertainment, and then comes the organ and drums era which was the demise of dance bands. There was trouble at Poppleton Road Club when the band had gone and they got an organ and an automatic drum machine. The Musicians' Union came down on them like a ton of bricks. One man with about five keyboards around him and an automatic drummer! At that time, mid 1960s, the union was quite observant and there was hell on.

We used to have two libraries, modern dance music, and then old time referred to as the Noddy book. When the pianist said, 'Right lads, in your Noddy book', everybody would go uhhh! Nobody really liked the old time waltzes but you've got these sticklers, particularly in working men's clubs, who were ardent fans of old time dancing. Ray Phillips was a brilliant drummer but like the rest of us, old time music wasn't his scene. One night at Poppleton Road Club, there was a man and a woman who were absolutely paranoid about old time dancing. And if you varied your timing a little bit they knew and this fellow started gesticulating at the band. Ray Phillips was the drummer, playing away, and this fella was ranting on about timing. Next thing I know, this bloke and Ray were having a row over this timing.

Colin's band, like some others, began to include pop numbers in their repertoire but there was another problem:

Take for example the Beatles, Love Me Do. Played by them it is acceptable. If somebody takes that and transcribes it and puts it into a piece of dance band music it sounds terribly corny because you're not producing the sound which goes with it. And the other one, [From Me To You], stands out in my mind because I thought when we were playing this stuff it didn't sound right. It was about that time when everybody shouted, 'Give us Telstar', and you're struggling with a five-piece band, all mature gentlemen, doing our best! Just didn't sound right.

Bill Haley's lot, it was unthinkable. You never dreamt of standing on your double bass to play it. Half this stuff now I just don't understand, it's garbage to me. But that's the era isn't it? You had to play a total cross-section. They liked their shaking, rattling and rolling. We had the music to cope with that. But it was more quicksteps, foxtrots and waltzes and old time than anything else. We were very lucky at Poppleton Road Club because in its heyday they were queuing to get in at six o'clock on Saturday night.

Colin also played at Leeman Road Club and recalls:

Playing at Leeman Road you might as well have been playing in the middle of a field because you were banging away and the sound just bounced back at you. The committee were all lined up with their big pints on the table, like Wheeltappers And Shunters it was.

Lew Skords believes:

There were two significant things sounding the death knell for music in York. The first was the change in licensing hours. The pubs opened half an hour later to 11. If a pub shut at half ten you would be allowed to drink up and the men would go to a dance hall and pay, even if it was for the last hour, but not for half an hour. The second thing was the arrival of Bill Haley and rock 'n' roll, and that, so far as public dancing was concerned, killed it stone dead, virtually overnight. It was incredible.

I used to like going into the Shoulder of Mutton in the early 1970s. Keith Laycock's dad ran it in the old days. Nice people, no arguments, and then I happened to go in, and I was the only one in and there was this bloody loud row. I said, 'Can't you turn that down?' 'Well the public like it'. I said, 'I'm the public, I'm the only one here. It's incessant, I can't stand it'. I don't think she knew where the knob was to turn it off or down. Never been in since. It's impersonal, this kind of music. It's inflicted, that's the only word, it's inflicted on you.

There was still work to be had for those who were keen. In the first three months of 1966, Bob Halford played at Helmsley, Rillington, Cottingwith, Yearsley Hospital, the Chase Hotel, the INL club, and a dance for the Knights Templars, as well as two nights a week at Haxby Working Men's Club. His band (comprised of Harold Arthur, Harry Warrington, Fred Mills, Clary Clay, Bob Carter and Jack Potter, who would alternate for some of the gigs) got a lot of work at the Station Hotel, with dances for the Agricola Lodge, the Motor Traders, the Master Plumbers and the Master Butchers. Later that year he worked with a trio run by the pianist Betty Brooks, with Harold Arthur on drums and in the following year he worked with Leo Burrows, Derek Mackfall, Gordon Cottom, Ray Izaat, Eric Gill and Denis Bunce at various times, as well as 18 gigs with Charles Hutchinson. Betty Brooks was described by Arthur Burcombe as 'one of the nicest pianists you ever saw, a lot of pianists learn how to dodge music, not play it'.

In November 1960 there was the grand opening of the Hazelbush Café and Restaurant on Malton Road, with its own ballroom which had a maple dance floor. The ballroom was advertised as being 'one of the most modern in the district'. The first dance was to be held on November 5 with the Dougie Hayes Quintet and afterwards there was dancing each Friday and Saturday.

Some bands, like Johnny Sutton's, started to involve younger musicians in their ensembles. Two members of the JR Big Sound were John and Carol Addy. Music played a huge part in their lives as Carol recalls:

It was after we first went out together and we were waiting for a taxi and started to sing No Two People Have Ever Been So In Love. One sang the song and the other sang the harmony and that was the beginning. We were and still are soulmates. I think music's very good for your health, music brought us together. A lot of musicians are reticent about putting it into words and they put it all into their music. It's an outlet. There's something in you, it's your romantic spirit that comes out.

John had been involved much earlier:

I was in a brass band in Norfolk when I was eight, 'cos I had asthma and my father thought it would be good for expanding my lungs. When I came to York, I joined the TA band at Lumley Barracks and we went on camps for a fortnight every year. We never did any drill at all, we just played, and then I started playing in pubs.

John started with the Sutton Band in 1963 and Carol would go along to watch them rehearse:

My father liked music very much, he didn't play anything, but he was the person who gave me a love of music. We used to sit in the twilight and listen

The JR Big Sound at Ocean Room, Scarborough December 1965. Full line-up is - Mick Brown, piano, Brian Eden, baritone sax, Len Rawding, second alto, Mick Pickard, first alto, Ray Cooper, tenor sax. Back - Derek Miles, bass, Alan Birkin, drums, Chris Boyes, guitar, Carol Butterfield, vocals, Johnny Sutton, third trumpet, Greg Wadman, first trumpet, John Addy, second trumpet and vocals in this picture, Clive Marshall, trombone (not all in picture). *(Courtesy John and Carol Addy)*

to all the bands on the radio. And I loved Doris Day, Frank Sinatra, Peggy Lee and Ella Fitzgerald.

I used to hum when I was with John, and I'd sing if I knew the words. And one day Johnny Sutton came up and said, 'Do you sing?' and I said, 'Well I'd like to, but I haven't actually done any.' 'Well, what do you know?', 'Blue Moon', Well come on then, get up and have a go'. And the pianist found me the key, and I got up, and they all ended up joining in and that was the start to being in music.

We played all over, mainly on the coast, Scarborough Spa and then at Brid Spa. Johnny seemed to think that although they played a lot of the standards, it would be good, because we were in the 1960s, and the Beatles were very much on the go and Sandie Shaw, if we had a little pop group within the band, and I was actually the person who did the Diana Ross's and Pet Clark's and that sort of thing. John and Ray would sing behind me and we did things like Down Town, Always Something There To Remind Me. He said it would be nice to have a girl in the band, because it just lifted it.

The first night I sang I was absolutely terrified, and he said, 'Come on glamour', and he took me to the bar and bought me a double whisky. So there's this 17 year old walking out on to the stage and all these heads bobbing on the floor beneath you. It was a great feeling but I was very frightened for a while, and then I got more used to it. Johnny was very dapper, and he'd wear a camel haired coat and brown trilby, he smoked cigars, and he looked very much like Ted Heath. He had big blue eyes, and he always drove a Rover. He actually gave me away when we got married in 1966 and the band played at our wedding. Poor Johnny, he used to have a real time with us, 'cos we were young and daft, and he used to have to be quite strict. We'd go round and rehearse with Ray and him, 'cos Johnny gave me singing lessons as well so that was quite fun, and his wife would prepare chips for us all. She was great.

Ray Cooper was the arranger within the band, and if there were any numbers that weren't in the right key for me, he could transpose everything, and write all the band parts. It was one heck of a job.

We'd go on a bus to the venue, and all the girlfriends would come and I'd pass them off as people who were helping me to get dressed, so they didn't have to pay to get in. We had a great time, really good camaraderie. We'd rehearse at the Winning Post and people would come in and have a drink so it ended up more like a performance. Johnny was a real showman, and if there was anybody with ears in there he'd give them a show. We were very flattered that he bothered with us 'cos we were only young. He did a good job to encourage younger people and we were his last band really. He'd lose his temper with us sometimes but he was a smashing guy.

They all wore blue jackets and grey trousers and each section had a different coloured tie, and I'd always have a new dress every time we sang and my mother would say, 'You're not buying another dress are you?'. The girls in the audience could be a bit, 'Who does she think she is?' But it made it more interesting.

Johnny Sutton wouldn't let me go out front before the band came on, because I'd change in between and he'd say, 'You have to keep yourself separate from the people'. The boys would go into the bar but John would bring me a drink. I sat on the stage and played maracas, or marimbas, or tambourines, and Johnny showed me how to do all that. I like percussion very much and it was still the time when the female singer was meant to look glamorous, smile at the audience and talk to them.

There'd be this little pop group within the band, to keep the young people at the dances happy. We did Make It Easy On Yourself. John would sing the main song and Ray and I would do the descant. You'd get older people who'd want to hear the more standard tunes like Moon River. I loved getting dressed up in the long dresses, I was a bit of a show-off and it was a more glamorous way to do it being a weekend singer, than it was to be a full-time one, where it just becomes a job.

John and Carol actually met when Carol worked at Mackenzie's Record Browserie. John was a regular customer, and said, 'they had the best jazz library in York'. Carol remembers:

All the musos of York would come into Mackenzies and Brian King was the manager. We had a girl there called Jean and she was going out with a teddy boy. He had a great big motorbike, but he was an enigma 'cos he liked all the most wonderful classical music. It was strange, you'd expect him to say, 'Can you put Jerry Lee Lewis or Elvis on?'

Jean was brilliant, she'd sell the records every day, we had them in lines, row and rows of different records, and they'd come in and say, 'Have you got so and so?' and she could just put her hand on it like that. The charts were very important, we had to do those every week, all on 45s. Now people get promoted on television, and it's all pre-arranged, whereas in those days, people had to promote themselves, and the music had to be good, and it had to appeal.

Then young Mr Mackenzie, Roderick, said to me, 'Has John Addy been in yet?' and I'd say, 'Who's he?' 'Oh, you'll know him when you see him, he wears a Frank Sinatra hat with a white, light coloured band round'. One day I was serving and there was this tall slim chap, with this Frank Sinatra hat, staring at me. I went really red, and I had to go underneath the counter. I said to Jean, 'Who's that?', 'Oh that's John Addy', and Mac said, 'If you go out with him, be careful, because the first thing he'll do, he'll take you down one of these little alleys. Watch him, he's a right ladykiller'.

And the first night I went out with him he said, 'We'll just take this short cut', and I thought, 'Oh, no, here we go'. Mac used to tease me unmercifully. His dad owned it then. George Mackenzie. And he was a character as well. They had these booths, like a telephone box, and you went in, and put the record on the turntable. John bought the trumpet off me, we had a room at the back, and we had drums, and guitars and trumpets, but they could order things and he ordered this Besson.

John feels that playing music is so worthwhile because:

Sometimes you can have this magical time, you create something. If you're a musician, everybody knows the look, you've shared that look.

A major exception to other dance band leaders was Charles Hutchinson, who was still playing in the 1960s and 1970s. He tended to specialise in hunt balls and events for the county set:

I started piano lessons with a lady who lived opposite when I was 11. All the other lads were off out, playing football and cricket, and I was stuck having piano practice, so for two years, or more, I didn't look at the piano. They could have chopped it up if they'd wanted to.

Then one day I was in Mr. Noyes' music shop, where Bettys Café is, and he had quite a few pianos for sale. I went in there to buy a record, and there was a man playing a new piano. It was beautiful, it was how I wanted to be able to play, it was syncopation in a word. And on the spur of the moment, I was only 15, I asked Mr Noyes who it was playing the piano, because it was professional, really good, and he said, 'Eric Betts. He does give lessons'. I came home and told me father and mother and they were very pleased that I was going to go back and they arranged my first lesson. By that time, war was on, I went to him for over two years, where he concentrated purely on the left hand, it was the method of lefthand rhythmic playing. I got that off and he was about to put me on to some tuition for me right hand, filling in and syncopation when he got his calling-up papers, but then two or three months after that, I got mine.

I'd actually started, with a three piece, at the Grey Village Hall at Sutton-on-Forest, every Saturday night, for a dance. It was a favourite of the Canadians who were stationed at Eastmoor. I'd bike down from Stillington, play at the dance, eight 'till 12. That was in 1942 and I'd asked some of the girls that were dancing at that time, whether I was playing it fast enough, or too fast, and they were very helpful. They didn't know anything about music, but they knew whether they could get the steps in or not. It was basically me on piano and a drummer but I used to pick a third one up if there was one available. That's how I started, and of course that got knocked off when I was called up at the end of 1943.

When I came back I wanted to get into this dance band business. There was only one local band here in Stillington, Hudson Smith And His Band. His wife was the pianist but he wanted me in the band as well and he offered to teach me the sax. We had an alto, which had belonged to me brother. So I went to him twice a week on the bike, to Easingwold and he taught me to play and eventually brought me into his band.

Before Hudson Smith formed his own band, he was part of the BSK Dance Orchestra which was founded in 1925 as a trio, Baines, Smith and Knowlson. Madge Baines later married Hudson Smith and he formed a bigger band.

BSK Dance Orchestra. 1st April 1932. Back row L to R - Madge Smith, neé Baines, piano, George Mason, ukulele, Herbert 'Jazzy' Knowlson, drums. Front row L to R - Frank Buckle (Bukaveskas, a Hungarian), violin, Hudson Smith, sax, Eddie Smith, trumpet. *(Courtesy Charles Hutchinson)*

That would be the winter of 1948, and I started to play dance music again, on sax rather than piano. He used orchestrations, and so I had to learn to read orchestrations, different things from piano copies. When you're playing alto sax you've only got one line of music, when you're playing piano you're reading three lines all the time. But nevertheless, it's a skilled job is playing the sax. You had the problems of finding a suitable reed, as it wore out you had to find another that suited you, or if somebody caught it with their jacket when they got up, and ruined it, you were in trouble. I used to keep two or three that I could play all the time, and then if one got damaged you had something to fall back on. New music was coming out all the time, a few of the old tunes that you used for old time we called evergreens, but the new stuff, you included that in your library too.

The instrumentation provides you with the sweet sound, the orthodox line up of a big band then was piano, bass and drums, four or five saxes, and perhaps two or three trumpets. When the guitar group era came along, that's when the decline of the bigger sweet sound started to happen. The organisers of dances couldn't afford to pay, so they began cutting the size of the band down. Now that altered the sound. You got down to two saxes, or three, first and second alto and a tenor. The baritone went by the board, it could be done without, you could cut the bass player out and manage with piano and drums. You got down to one trumpet, and trombones were a rarity, so it gradually resolved down to your key instruments, which you could not do without if you were going to provide any music for dancing, and that was piano and drums, and probably a lead alto. The orchestrations are written in such a way, that the melody is being played by first alto or trumpet, and then if you could afford any more, you added on your luxuries, like a string bass, or a trombone.

I must have been about 11 years on saxes, alto five or six years, and went on to tenor, then in 1959 Hudson Smith died and I took his band over. I took his engagements, and continued them and hoped that my band would be as popular as his had been, and it turned out to be. I didn't have any trouble in finding engagements, and we operated all the way through the pop era. I did actually lead and operate a dance band longer than Hudson Smith had done, about 36 years. I was listening to Charlie Kunz and Billy Mayerl, solo pianists, but then I was interested in vocalists. It was a comprehensive interest I had in all kinds of music, brass bands as well. Harry James playing Flight Of The Bumble Bee, that sort of thing.

You bought sixpenny copies of music to start with, you didn't use orchestrations then, and you listened to the wireless, and there were plenty of programmes of dance music, and you found out by trial and error. Obviously you knew if it was a waltz it had to be in three-four time and military two-steps had to be six eight. But quicksteps and foxtrots, you learnt from the wireless. There was nothing written down. You couldn't get it from books what to play for what dance. It had to be your own intuition. But you learnt as you went on. I had a piano copy of the St. Bernard's Waltz, and I played it, but I didn't know for a long time, that it was 32 bars, the chorus, and the steps that they were taking were in multiples of 16. I just played the piano, until very much later, when I learnt all this when I went into sequence dancing with me own band.

The engagements were all over the North Riding, Easingwold, Thirsk, Northallerton, Bedale, Stokesley, Redcar, Malton and all the villages in between. The key thing in our favour, which sustained my career as a dance band leader was the fact that although guitar groups had come about, and it was a different kind of music, we held on to a large number of jobs, because the organisers were people of my age, who wanted my kind of music. A lot of bands fell by the wayside, I'm afraid, during the pop era, they weren't in the right kind of engagements, and we were fortunate that we were. Masonic ladies' nights, for example, the Masons wouldn't tolerate a guitar group, they wanted smoother quiet music.

Hudson Smith Band at Assembly Rooms 1953. L to R - Eddie Smith, Charles Hutchinson, Eddie Delaney, Hudson Smith, Madge Smith on piano, Joe Gill.

(Courtesy Charles Hutchinson)

We never lost a job once we got it, which was a source of pride for me. We must have been doing something right. Our choice of music must have been right. Our choice of dances must have been right. Our appearance must have been right and our prices must have been right. Rillington Hunt Ball was the longest, 18 successive years we played for them.

Red jackets, that was Hudson Smith's uniform before ours, so I would start wearing it in 1948, and I carried on with me own band. Replacement jackets got a bit expensive, £100 or more but I wore them right until I retired. Hudson Smith had the same stands, same shape and everything but when I took his band over I had them repainted and CH put on the front.

I had a basic five piece, which I supplemented if the occasion warranted it. Myself on piano, my brother on tenor sax, Arthur Burcombe lead alto for many years, and then Tiddy Mead. But I used others as well, and David Smith, Hudson Smith's son, was lead alto player for years. The drummer was John Burton, followed by Doug Green, who had given his own band up at that time. Clive Marshall played trombone a number of times, Bob Halford did many jobs on alto, and George Turner did five or six years on alto. I had a pool of musicians that I drew from. York bands weren't getting the work, so they were willing to come.

I had about 900 pieces of music in me library. There were special numbers that you featured at hunt balls, which you wouldn't use at a Masonic do. Do Ye Ken John Peel, and the Hunting medley. Our library was geared, through experience over the years, to providing what we knew each function would be expecting. The country was always more subdued, they required a more modern programme in the town. Vanbrugh College, when we played functions there, it would be a town programme, quicksteps, foxtrots, modern waltzes, perhaps valeta, Gay Gordons, and two pop sessions, one in the first half and one in the second, stuff like Beatles selections, which we wouldn't dream of playing in these wayside village halls, because they didn't want that kind of thing.

One night we were playing at our annual function at Carlton in Cleveland, a hunt ball. It had been snowing hard all day, and we said we'd be lucky if we got back home on the A19, it was likely to be blocked. A farmer and his wife were there, and they said, 'I don't think you'll get out on the top road. Well you know where our farmhouse is, come back here'. I had a van carrying all the gear, and it had town and country tyres so we thought we'd be all right. We got packed up and off, and I could get out with the van, but the drummer had his car there, and it was just a private car and he got stuck fast. So we had no

Charles Hutchinson Band late 1970s at Fulford School. (They played every fortnight for old time and sequence dancing). L to R - Mick Reeder, Arthur Burcombe, John Burton, Charles Hutchinson.   *(Courtesy Charles Hutchinson)*

alternative, we piled everybody in the van with the gear and back to the village and the farmer's wife was waiting for us. 'I've made all the beds, bottles in them'. So six of us stayed the night. You should have seen the farmhouse table next morning, it was absolutely loaded with breakfast for us. That's the only time that I remember never getting home from an engagement.

We must have worked for five or six or more different hunts, we were the only band specialising in hunt balls. I got a lot of satisfaction out of booking the jobs, attending to the details, the length of the supper interval, all these preparations. I'd stipulate that we would not play after two o'clock. But all the details were done beforehand. I'd sit with the whole set of six libraries on the floor, and arrange the programme before every function. I would have it in my mind what tunes we were going to play. But I didn't stick rigidly to that. When you get on stage, and you've got the crowd there, you can judge who was there, and I knew what they would want, so I made sure that those particular dances would be included. I got a kick out of it, more so on piano, I think piano was the daddy of them all, because when you're playing piano, from orchestrations, you are reading what the front line lads are doing as well, so that you can cover for them if they don't come in at the right time, you can pick it up straight away. It was extending, it was stimulating, but I had good men, they were all good musicians. But nevertheless as band leader I had to keep me eye on what was going on all night in the band and that's where I got me satisfaction from. The drummer, he can suggest to you how to fill in certain things on the piano. Doug Green in particular encouraged me, by his drumming, to do things on the piano which I perhaps wouldn't have thought of. One of the other chaps that played with me a long time, Bryan Pearson, he left me after three or four years, to go on the boats. He was a good lad, he could play piano if I wanted a number off but he played string bass, and Hawaiian guitar, and he was a good player. He really gave the band a lift, he was brilliant.

Bryan Pearson played bass guitar with Charles from 1968 to 1971 before he left York to become a professional musician. He was one of the few musicians to play in dance bands and later in beat groups (see volume two). His first dance band work was:

with my piano teacher, Herbert Macintosh. He was a great influence in my musical development as well as running a dance band Mac And His Music. Mr Mac came from Wighill and he'd tell me about when he was a child and he had to pump the organ for the organist at the church. To amuse himself he would let the pressure in the bellows get very low, and when the organist called out to complain, he would pump the bellows so hard that he could hear the organ groan.

213

Mac And His Music at Riley Smith Hall, Tadcaster. Far left Fred Richardson, far right Herbert Macintosh, second right Mary Macintosh. 1940s *(Courtesy Adrian Macintosh)*

Adrian Macintosh, (see volume two) now drummer with the legendary Humphrey Lyttelton, is the son of Herbert and Mary Macintosh who ran their own dance band, with Mary playing the drums. Herbert also taught piano and tuned pianos, and Mary ran her own dancing school.

David Horner was a dance band musician who made the transition to pop music and was very popular. His band had the first electronic piano in York and he had two females in the band:

I had the idea of starting the Dave-a-Tones in the early 1960s along with a pal of mine, Dave Atkinson, who played trumpet in the band. This was the time when the Beatles were on the up. I can remember them doing their first performance at the Rialto in York, and we had a dance at the Gimcrack Rooms the same night. I'd just applied for a guitarist, which I couldn't get. After interviewing eight I found that none of them could read music, and so I stuck to our idea of having an electronic piano to do the bass. I got the idea from the organ at the Minster, you have every instrument on the organ, and it worked exceedingly well, because the bass is the most important part of a dance band for me, which was rhythm. My music career started at the Minster School, and then I got roped into the York Railway Band, and then I did a bit of drumming with Stan Brough, playing for old time dancing. I went into the RAF, came out and played with Harold Midgeley at Stamford Bridge, who was a wonderful

Herbert and Mary Macintosh in York, late 1940s. *(Courtesy Adrian Macintosh)*

performer. I learned all my tricks of the trade from him. But after a few years with him, we started the Dave-a-Tones. We never imagined it would take off like it did, we were very popular with the young farmers, cricket clubs, village halls, any organisation. We did places all over Yorkshire.

We went right through the beat group era, even through the disco era, the type of music we played and the sound we gave off, people were happy with it. All your Jimmy Lally's, and dance tunes. From the 1930s to the present day, all the Beatle stuff that came out, and we had a vocalist as well to push this out. Not many dance bands had a vocalist that put out modern tunes, and that's where we scored as well, because they could go to a beat group and hear these tunes, possibly sung by a male, but in my case I had a female as well.

Beat groups hadn't a lot of material to play but we could go on all night. I had an electronic organ, lead trumpet was David Atkinson, alto was Freddy Mills and a tenor saxophone. But if we got bigger dances, in a big barn or something, we played with 14-piece. We had one control unit and each individual section, saxes, trumpet, vocals and probably piano, were all amplified, so that they could bring the sound in when we wanted it, at that time. That's how it developed, very much like the beat groups did in their own little way of developing their guitar playing. It was the same thing, but in dance bands. And so the amplification grew and we had huge speakers on either side of the stage, and a control unit in the middle.

We were playing at a place called Marr which had a resident organist, like a dance club with food and a bar. The organist played from eight o'clock until about nine and in the interval. When we came to the interval he said to me, 'I'll carry on and keep the dancing going so nobody has a break'. So I told him the piece we were going to play before the interval and he came in and operated and all the lads walked off the stage ready for the refreshments. When we looked back, there's this organ playing on its own! This chap had taped all the music that we'd been playing and just put it on tape and walked off himself! So he got easy money for the night. We played mostly rural areas, but I played a lot in the city, big company dances in York, big organisations. And Easingwold Young Farmers, they had their place at the town hall, and they thought it was marvellous when you got a band coming from York and playing all the modern tunes. They put on beautiful things for the suppers, we all got well fed, with plenty of booze about, in the days before the breathalyser. You didn't get drunk because you were playing, but we've seen many a person leave the dance absolutely blotto and get into his car!

David remembers playing at one farmers' dance, and the dancers were exhausted by the end. One of the young farmers came up:

Dave-a-Tones at Marr near Doncaster 1966. L to R - Cindy Mottram (ex lead alto with Ivy Benson), Dave Atkinson and singer Wendy Floyd. *(Courtesy David Horner)*

Completely beat. We'd get them in a lather, and he said, ' I get more knackered here than I do on me 'orse!'

Music's been my life. My father sang in the male voice choir, my grandfather was head bell ringer at York Minster, so we've all had a connection with music. We had a theme tune, Zing Went The Strings Of My Heart, and we always ended with I'll See You Again for the last waltz.

It is not easy to explain why music has the effect it has, both on those playing it and on the listener, why it leads to such passion and commitment, as Trevor Bousfield says:

If you need it describing, you never will understand. If you could put this thing down, and measure it and define it, some people are born musicians, there are some people who can take you to pieces and they're playing exactly the same notes as somebody else. But it's this different emotional content that they're able to generate, and this is the difference between a born or a manufactured musician. You come across a lot of musicians who are probably professional, who are no magicians. They can produce the notes but they never make you stop and listen. And you can listen to somebody else, they only play a simple tune and they'll take you to pieces. I wouldn't like to think I could analyse it because it would make it of a worldly nature, and I don't believe it is. I listen to some music and I think God must be speaking through that composer. I cannot find any other explanation. There is some music, it's just out of this world, some superior being communicates through that composer. The Mozart Requiem, now if that played properly doesn't take you apart, you don't have a soul. Now how did it get there in the first place? It's communicated, I think. They're born with that ability, you couldn't measure it, or everybody'd be a Mozart. And it's not always the notes, it still takes the musician to produce that with the notes.

There isn't a definition that says the order or the sequence of these notes makes it a type of music. Music is the grouping of notes, certain intervals apart, certain rhythms, certain beats, certain frequencies. My old man used to say, 'Give me three notes from a pianist and I can tell you whether they've got a sense of touch', and this is part of the conveying of emotions, simply through your fingers and he's dead right! You can see some people who use a keyboard as though they're blacksmiths. You listen to others, you're probably not conscious of what it is. It can come off any instrument, this conveying of human emotions. But if music doesn't convey anything to you, it isn't doing its job, and that's got nothing to do with whether it's country and western, popular, ballad, classical, dance band, brass band, military.

When I was in the forces, the first time I went into the gym and the last one in is on jankers. So you've got your clothing all over the place, they're braying hell out of you in the gym and I was as low as I could get, and the corps band came past and my soul lifted. I'm talking about a march now. If you listen to a band playing a march and you can't march behind it, there's either something wrong with you or the music. If you're in Vienna and they play Viennese waltzes and they don't get up and waltz, there's something wrong. You listen to a slow movement on Mahler Five. If that doesn't take you apart, you don't have a soul.

The music from the dance band era, the songs which have stood the test of time, will never die. The big bands may have largely finished but individuals have adapted to changing times. Talking to the musicians from this period, it is clear that they have wonderful memories of a very special era, filled with excitement and emotion. We are very privileged to share with them some of the 'magic moments' when everything was going well, when 'rhythm and romance' came together.

DANCE BANDS PLAYING IN YORK & SURROUNDING AREA

The following is a list of York dance bands appearing in advertisements in York newspapers, listed in the decade in which they first appeared. Some bands continued for more than one decade but are only shown once.

1920s
The Albany Dance Orchestra. Ankers Ebor Dance Band. Hal Arthur's Band. Miss F Barker's Orchestra. Mr. Bartley's Orchestra. Reg Bennet's Bijou Dance Band. Blakey's Orchestra. British Legion Dance Orchestra. Eddie Brown & his Orchestra. The Californians. Chillian Quartet. T H Cooper's Orchestra. Dunnington Dance Orchestra. Len Edward's Band. Paul Edwards & His Music. Follies Orchestra. Mr Geilern's Orpheus Dance Orchestra. The Golden Serenaders Dance Band. Emlyn Harries Band. Hawaiian Revels Band. The Jazz Orchestra. Bert Keech Band. Mr. Littlefair's Band. Lyricals Dance Band. P Medcalf's Band. Metronome Orchestra. Neal's Band. Night Hawks Variety Troupe. Pogson's Band. Premier Jazz Band. Billy Pritchard's Roadio Band. The Radiance Dance Band. Rialto Revels. The Spartans Dance Band Alex Sylvester's Band. Symphonic Quintette. Mr Gallon's Synco Orchestra. Mr J.P. Thompson's Famous Jazz Band. Mr R.M Thompson's Orchestra. Tramways Employees Orchestra. Treasurer's House Quartet. Eddie Worthington's Band.

1930s
Almonian Quintette Orchestra. The Ambassadors Dance Band. Miss Andrew's Orchestra. Ankers Dance Band. Arcadians Band. Ray Archer's Modernists. Astorians. Jack Baines Band. Billy Barnes's Band. Jack Bartley & His Royal Crescent Orchestra. The Blue Aces. Blue Birds Dance Band. The Blues Dance Orchestra. Bobby's Rhythm Monarchs. Broadway Revels Band. Stan Brough's Band. Ted Brown & His Eight Maniacs. BSK Band. Kathleen Butler & Her Millionaires. Billy Carton & His Band. The Clarions Dance Orchestra. Benny Connell's Prize Band. The Embassy Players. Faulkner's Top Hatters Band. Georgians. Reg Goodrick's Band. Grand Kit Kat Orchestra. Doug Green Band. Jack Greenwood & His Band. Grosvenor Dance Band. Ceres Harper Band. Harmony Boys Dance Band. Norman Holmes Orchestra. Percy Hutchinson & Company. The Imps Dance Band. Hugh Lockheart's Band. Ed Long's Band. Lyrians Band. Bob Mason & His Piccadilly Music Weavers. Edgar Matthews Trio. Mayfair Band. Melody Boys Orchestra. Mr. H. Midgeleys. Ray Moorhouse & His Players. Nightbirds Band. Nursery Orchestra. Orpheus Band. Paramount Orchestra. The Pom Poms. Postonians Dance Orchestra. Alf Powell's New Follies. Premier Dance Band. Rhythm Four Orchestra. Rialtonians. Roadhouse Revellers Band. The Robo's Dance Orchestra. Ted Rowell & His Kit Kat Band. Lew Sadler's Band. Reg Skinner's Rhythm Boys. Lew Symon's Revels Eight

Dance Band. Conri Tait's Band. Tutill's Modern Melody Dance Band. Bobby Ward's Dance Band. Whitehurst's Orchestra. The Windsor Quartette. Winter's Band. The York Dance Band. York Instrumentalists.

1940s

The Ambassadors. Assembly Players. Jos. Q. Atkinson & His Band. Reg Blenkarn's Band. The Blue Quavers. Buckaveskas & His Band. The Carlton Players. Jack Carr's Melody Aces. Charles Trio. G Coulson's Band. Len Cundall's Embassy Players. Billy Davies & His Orchestra. DD's Band. Dixie's Band. The Ebor Dance Trio. Graham Foster's Band. Walter Garrard's Orchestra. Tommy Henderson's Band. Jimmie Honeyman & His Orchestra. Charles Hutchinson's Band. K.O.Y.L.I. Army Band. The Melody Makers. The Metronomes Dance Band. Johnny Sutton's Modernaires. NFS Band. The New Kit Kat Dance Band. The New Windsor Orchestra. The Nightflyers. Old Priory Youth Club Band. Gordon Reed & His Latin American Music (Albany). Gordon Reed Quartet (Chase Hotel). Harry Warrington & His Revels. Ron Astan's Rhythm Aces. Rhythmic Dance Band. Bill Serby's Band. Starliners Band. Charlie Steele & His Orchestra. West Yorks Band (Army). White Rose Band. Yorkists.

1950-1955

Blue Rhythm Band. The Bluettes. The Castonians. Gordon Chapman & His Band. Garry Christian & His Band. The County Players. Charlie Bousfield's Criterion Dance Band. The Downbeats Dance Band. Derek Dunning & His Orchestra. The Flamingoes Dance Band. The Harmony Boys. Don Hattee's Hawaiian Swingtette. Albert Honeyman & His Band. Mr Huffington's Dance Orchestra. The Imperial Dance Orchestra. Eddie Lamb & His Music. Mac & His Music. The Melodians. The Modern Tones. The Modernaires. The New Rhythmists. The Premier Dance Band. The Ramblers' Orchestra. The Rangers Dance Band. The Rhythm Aces. The Scarlets. Hudson Smith & His Band. Johnny Sutton & His Music. Ralph Turner Band. The West Yorks TA Regt Band. Terry Yorke & His Orchestra. York's Trumpet Twins & Their Orchestra.

1956-1970

The Geoff Alan Orchestra. Betty's Babes Dance Orchestra. Don Carlton Swingtet. The Cavaliers Dance Band. Christie's Dance Band. Dave-A-Tones. Alan Dawson Orchestra. Roger Dean Quarter. Malcolm Dennis & His Trio. Alan Gordon Trio. Chas Gordon Trio. Dougie Hayes & His Music. Dave Jackson's Band. H Knowlson Band. Mike Lancaster's Dance Band. The Roddie McDonald Quintet. Dave Moore Trio. The Nightbirds. Trevor Norman & His Band. Fred Percival & His Band. Graham Peters Band. David Philips Trio. Regency Players. The Rhythmaires Dance Band. Syd Richardson & His Music. J Rooks & His Band. The Silver Chords Dance Band. The Mike Smith Band. Billy Thompson's Band. The Syd Watson Dance Orchestra. West Side Quintet.

Other titles by the same author

History Of A Community : Fulford Road
District Of York.   (College Of Ripon And York St John) 1984.
Reprinted 1985.

Alexina : A Woman In Wartime York. 1995

Rich In All But Money : Hungate 1900-1938.
(Archaeological Resource Centre) 1996

Beyond The Postern Gate : A History Of Fishergate And Fulford Road.
(Archaeological Resource Centre) 1996

Humour, Heartache And Hope : Life In Walmgate. (Archaeological Resource
Centre and York Oral History Society) 1996

Number 26 : The History Of 26 St Saviourgate, York.
(Voyager Publications) 1999

York Voices. (Tempus Publishing Ltd) 1999

Voices Of St Paul's. (edited) 2001

Something In The Air. An Oral History Of Popular Music Vol. 2.
(York Oral History Society) 2002

Other titles by the same publisher

York Memories. 1984

York Memories At Work. 1985

York Memories At Home. 1987

York Memories Of Stage And Screen. 1988

Open Minds. 1990

Through The Storm : York Memories Of The Second World War. 1992

Public Houses, Private Lives. (co-published with Voyager Publications) 1999